Quicknotes

L. 12

MPLIFIED BIBLE COMMENTARY SERIES

hebrews THRU revelation

WISDOM FOR TODAY—AND FOREVER

CONTRIBUTING EDITORS:

Robert Deffinbaugh, Th.M.
Dr. Hall Harris
Dr. Stephen Leston
Jeffrey Miller, Th.M.
Dr. Robert Rayburn

CONSULTING EDITOR:

Dr. Mark Strauss

D0167316

© 2008 by Barbour Publishing, Inc.

ISBN 978-1-59789-778-5

All rights reserved. No part of this publication may be reproduced or transmitted for commercial purposes, except for brief quotations in printed reviews, without written permission of the publisher.

Churches and other noncommercial interests may reproduce portions of this book without the express written permission of Barbour Publishing, provided that the text does not exceed 500 words and that the text is not material quoted from another publisher. When reproducing text from this book, include the following credit line: "From *The QuickNotes Simplified Bible Commentary Series, Vol. 12: Hebrews through Revelation*, published by Barbour Publishing, Inc. Used by permission."

Scripture quotations marked NIV are taken from the HOLY BIBLE, NEW INTERNATIONAL VERSION Copyright © 1973, 1978, 1984 by International Bible Society. Used by permission of Zondervan Publishing House. All rights reserved.

Scripture quotations marked NLT are taken from the HOLY BIBLE, NEW LIVING TRANSLATION copyright © 1996. Used by permission of Tyndale House Publishers, Inc., Wheaton, Illinois 60189. All rights reserved.

Scripture quotations marked TNIV are taken from the Holy Bible, Today's New International® Version, TNIV©. Copyright 2001, 2005 by International Bible Society®. Used by permission of International Bible Society®. All rights reserved worldwide. "TNIV" and "Today's New International Version" are trademarks registered in the United States Patent and Trademark Office by International Bible Society®.

Scripture quotations marked ESV are taken from THE HOLY BIBLE: ENGLISH STANDARD VERSION, copyright © 2001, Wheaton: Good News Publishers. Used by permission. All rights reserved.

Scripture quotations marked NASB are taken from the New American Standard Bible, © 1960, 1962, 1963, 1968, 1971, 1972, 1973, 1975, 1977, 1995 by The Lockman Foundation. Used by permission.

Quotations designated NET are from the NET Bible® copyright ©1996–2006 by Biblical Studies Press, L.L.C. www.bible.org. All rights reserved. Used by permission. The NET Bible is available in its entirety as a free download or online web use at www.nextbible.org/

Cover photograph: Walter Bibikow

Produced with the assistance of Christopher D. Hudson & Associates. Contributing writers include Libby Britt, Stan Campbell, Ben Clayton, Carol Smith.

Published by Barbour Publishing, Inc., P.O. Box 719, Uhrichsville, Ohio 44683, www.barbourbooks.com

Our mission is to publish and distribute inspirational products offering exceptional value and biblical encouragement to the masses.

Member of the
Evangelical
Publishers A

Printed in the United States of America.

TABLE OF CONTENTS

JUDE

REVELATION

HEBREWS

INTRODUCTION TO HEBREWS

The book of Hebrews is rightly identified as a letter (or "epistle") because it was written to a specific group of people to address problems and concerns of that community. Like a letter, it contains some personal comments and greetings (13:22–25). But in contrast to most other New Testament letters, Hebrews is fundamentally a sermon—a word of exhortation (13:22). It can be read aloud in less than an hour, and, like most sermons today, is structured around the citation, exposition, and application of scripture. It is not unlike a traditional contemporary sermon.

AUTHOR

No one can say with certainty who wrote Hebrews. Some attribute it to Paul, yet in every other Pauline letter, the apostle opens by identifying himself. In addition, the author's statement about hearing the gospel from others (2:3) does not jibe with Paul's other statements that emphasize his receiving the gospel directly from Christ (Galatians 1:11–12, for example). Furthermore, the language, style, and theological perspective are very different from Paul's elsewhere. Other educated guesses for authorship include Barnabas, Luke, and Apollos. Perhaps the best perspective comes from the insight of the early Christian theologian Origen. Concerning the author of Hebrews, he commented, "God alone knows."

PURPOSE

The original recipients of this letter, as the title indicates, were Jewish Christians. They had suffered persecution for their new faith and had stood firm. . .at first. But as time passed, they had begun to waver and were tempted to return to the comfort of their old, familiar ways. Some had apparently already made the decision to leave the Christian faith and return to Judaism, which placed added pressure on the ones who were still in the church.

OCCASION

No one is certain where the letter was written (perhaps Italy [13:24], although it is equally possible that the *recipients* were in Italy). Still, the occasion of the letter remains clear. The author was well informed about his readers and knew that, while they had once been faithful to Christ and active in the church, some had left to return to the familiarity of Judaism and others were preparing to join them. The writer makes an impassioned plea for them to reconsider, and he lays out a series of strong arguments to verify that Christ is superior to any of their other options. Indeed, Jesus is the *only* option that provides lasting salvation. To reject Him is not only foolish, but spiritually dangerous.

THEMES

Hebrews competes with Galatians for being the most single-minded book in the New Testament. The author makes numerous arguments around a single theme: the absolute necessity of persevering in the Christian faith. Any portion of the letter becomes more pertinent when the reader acknowledges this overriding theme.

HISTORICAL CONTEXT

It appears clear that Hebrews was written prior to the destruction of Jerusalem in AD 70. The author's comment in 2:3 indicates that he is addressing only the second generation of Christians, so a date in the 60s of the first century seems most likely.

CONTRIBUTION TO THE BIBLE

Hebrews presents a masterful explanation of the preeminence of Christ—His superiority to Moses, priests, angels, and everything else. The book also shows not a contrast between the "old" ways of the ancient Israelites with those of the "new" Christian era, but rather the similarity between Old Testament and New Testament believers: Both received the gospel, are saved by grace through faith, look forward to the promised rest of God, and so forth. Hebrews also provides some of the Bible's most direct warnings about the consequences of rejecting Christ and ignoring the work He has completed to provide salvation for humankind.

OUTLINE

HEBREWS 1:1–14
THE SUPREMACY OF CHRIST

Setting Up the Section

In response to hearing about a number of Jewish Christians beginning to leave the church in order to return to the familiarity of their traditional rites and rituals, the author sends this letter to show them exactly what they are abandoning. In the opening chapters, he describes the superiority of Jesus by making a number of contrasts. In this section he begins by comparing Jesus to angels.

📄 **1:1–4**

THE WRITER'S THESIS

The first sentence of the Hebrews sermon is an opening salvo. The author immediately begins to set Jesus Christ high above everything and everyone that people might otherwise trust for salvation and security. He does not say, however, that Jesus' message is any different from that of the prophets. The content of the *message* is never contrasted, as will become apparent with a close reading of the letter. But the dignity and authority of Jesus Christ is far greater than any other because He is no less than the Son of God, the heir of all things, and the Creator of heaven and earth (1:2). And the salvation He has accomplished brings to fulfillment all that came before.

The phrase "last days" (1:2) has its background in the Old Testament, referring to the time when God would bring about the restoration of fallen creation. The life, death, and resurrection of Jesus represent the climax of God's plan of salvation, beginning the period of the "last days." At the same time, the writer of Hebrews continues to turn his readers' eyes to the future as he writes about the eventual consummation of their salvation.

The full deity of Jesus Christ is made evident in that He is the Creator of all things, His nature is the same as that of God the Father, and He does what only God can do (1:2–3). After completing His great work of redemption, He is again in heaven at the place of highest honor and authority—God's right hand (alluding to Psalm 110:1–2). The observation that Christ sat down indicates that His work of offering the sacrifice is finished. That point will be reemphasized in 10:12–14, and the reasoning behind this emphasis is that any view of life, any system of salvation, and any approach to God that does not center around Jesus Christ is obviously false and stands self-condemned.

Demystifying Hebrews

"Majesty in heaven" (1:3; 8:1 NIV) is a typical Jewish *periphrasis* for God. In order not to break the third commandment of misusing the name of God, even unintentionally, the Jews began to use other terms to avoid speaking it at all. Some people became almost superstitious about pronouncing God's name.

The comment that Jesus inherited a better name (1:4) does not mean He did not have it by right all along. After all, the writer of Hebrews has just attributed to Christ the creation of the universe, among other things (1:2). But the rewards and inheritance that are due Christ because of His incarnation, death, and resurrection will be shared by those who place their faith in Him.

1:5–14

JESUS IS SUPERIOR TO THE ANGELS

The concept of Jesus being better than or superior to other things will be a recurring pattern in Hebrews, occurring in more than a dozen other phrases. The writer begins, however, by citing Jesus' better name and His superiority to the angels.

This would have been a particularly relevant and potentially sensitive subject to many Jewish believers. The Jews held angels in high esteem. Beyond a doubt, angels held important roles as messengers of God. Particularly significant to the Jews was the fact that angels had participated in the giving of the law to Moses on Mount Sinai (Deuteronomy 33 2). So the author uses no fewer than seven citations from Hebrew scripture to make his point.

The first and second citations (Hebrews 1:5), from Psalm 2:7 and 2 Samuel 7:14, respectively, show that Jesus is far more than just another one of God's heavenly messengers. The first quotation is from a psalm that looms large in the New Testament as a prophecy of the incarnation, the ministry, and especially the resurrection of Jesus Christ. The second was originally a covenant promise to David referring to Solomon that was later appropriately applied to Jesus. And by quoting these two passages, the author of Hebrews states boldly that the name of Jesus—the one that is superior to that of the angels—is that of *Son*. Jesus had been God's Son from the beginning, of course. But His incarnation and resurrection were demonstrative examples of that fact. That's why it is said here that Jesus inherited the name (1:4) and that "today" God has become His Father (1:5).

Angels are sometimes referred to as sons of God, just as believers are considered children of God. Yet the singular use of *Son* is a reference applicable to Jesus alone. No angel or person can claim to be *the* Son of God. Angels are only servants of God; Jesus stands high above them as God's Son.

The third Old Testament reference (1:6) is from Deuteronomy 32:43 but is based on the Septuagint—an ancient translation of the Hebrew scriptures into Greek. The Septuagint was translated in the third century before Jesus' birth and would have been the version of scripture familiar to many of the recipients of the letter to the Hebrews. (The text used by those translators had a clause that isn't found in other manuscripts, so the section quoted in Hebrews 1:6 is not found in Deuteronomy 32:43 in most modern Bibles.) The point the writer is making is that the angels, who were exalted by certain people, worshiped Jesus. Christ is not equal to angels; He is their object of worship. This point is made stronger by the writer's reminder that Jesus is the firstborn of God—a title less to do with birth order than to indicate position, authority, and preeminence.

The fourth reference (1:7), from Psalm 104:4, makes a similar point. Not only do angels worship Christ, but they are also His servants—God controls them as He does the winds and the flames. Angels could announce Jesus' birth in Bethlehem and attend to Him in the Garden of Gethsemane, but they couldn't take His place in living and dying for the salvation of humankind.

The fifth reference (1:8–9) is from Psalm 45:6–7, a wedding song for a triumphal king. But since the king is addressed as "O God" and has an eternal throne, the description certainly points to the messianic king. The author of Hebrews shows that Jesus is this king—one of the relatively few texts in the New Testament where Jesus Christ is directly said to be God.

The emphasis is also on this ruler's love of righteousness and hatred of wickedness. Since Christ is being contrasted to angels, it is important to remember that not all angels are good. The focus on righteousness might have been directed to the Jews who still believed that Jesus had been a false prophet who had misled their people.

The next Old Testament reference (1:10–12) is to Psalm 102:25–27. It is a continuation of the previous thought and suggests that while angels are created beings, Jesus is the Creator. To human beings, the life span of a universe appears eternal, but from God's perspective, worlds are created and eventually wear out like a suit of clothes. The reminder that God (Jesus) is eternal and unchanging must have been a welcome consolation to first-century believers during a turbulent time in human history.

Critical Observation

Just as there are numerous denominations and groups that comprise the Christian church today, so were there different sects that professed Judaism in the first century. The Pharisees and Sadducees are mentioned most frequently in scripture, but another group was known as the Essenes. They were nonconformists who tended to isolate themselves in various communities (one being Qumran, the site of the discovery of the Dead Sea Scrolls). Among their nontraditional beliefs were extravagant speculations regarding angels. For example, they believed the archangel Michael would play a decisive role in the coming kingdom. Some Bible scholars think that this section of Hebrews might have been a point-by-point refutation of arguments posed by Jewish Christians who had come out of Essene Judaism and were being tempted to return to it.

The seventh and final reference in this section (Hebrews 1:13) is from Psalm 110:1, and it reiterates the royal status, the divine rule, and the promised inheritance that belong to Jesus Christ. Then, linked with the quote, the author adds his own insight: that angels not only serve God and Christ, but also human beings—those who will inherit salvation (1 14). Some angels minister in the very presence of God, but only Jesus Christ sits at God's right hand.

In addition, here is found the first of many indications in Hebrews that "salvation" is more than the believer's initial commitment. The author will repeatedly speak of salvation as something believers are yet to inherit.

Take It Home

Modern culture has a fascination with angels that may or may not be grounded in biblical fact. From the bumbling Clarence in *It's a Wonderful Life* to the belief by some that we become angels when we die, there are a lot of twisted perspectives. What is your personal belief about angels and their status in comparison to Jesus and to human beings? What questions do you have about angels?

HEBREWS 2:1–18

SUCH A GREAT SALVATION

Setting Up the Section

After an emphatic opening showing that Jesus is far superior to any other prophet and even the angels, the author now applies that knowledge to personal faith. Throughout the letter he will repeatedly return to the importance of persevering in the Christian faith.

📄 2:1–4

NO BETTER OPTIONS

In some early translations of scripture, the word used for *drift away* (2:1) was *glide*. Sometimes a departure from faith is not as much a conscious decision as it is a careless sliding past the point where one ought to be (akin to losing a ring from one's finger without noticing). Either way, it is wise to heed the writer's admonition to pay more careful attention.

The author also begins an ongoing argument that the gospel of Christ is not a new teaching. The Jewish readers of this letter were steeped in the ancient scriptures and had no doubts whatsoever about the authority of those writings. They took the Law and Prophets seriously because they believed scripture had been mediated by angels (Acts 7:53; Galatians 3:19), and those who did not submit to it would be subject to severe punishments.

Therefore, after making it clear in Hebrews 1 that Jesus is superior to the angels in numerous ways, the logical question is how the Jewish Christians could ignore what He had taught. If they honored the presence and work of God's angels, how could they possibly overlook or reject the personal appearance and message of God's Son? And if breaking the commands of the old covenant brought severe punishments and discipline, how much greater was the danger of rejecting the much greater revelation given through the Son? In addition to hearing the message itself, the people had witnessed signs, various miracles, and gifts of the Holy Spirit (2:4). So the question begged to be asked: "How will we escape if we neglect so great a salvation?" (2:3 NASB).

What, exactly, should people hope to escape? Although not a popular topic in many churches today, the writer of Hebrews is making a reference to hell and God's judgment of nonbelievers. He will be more specific later (10:26–31).

📄 **2:5–9**

THE WORLD TO COME

After stating his clear warning, the author returns to the theme he had begun in Hebrews 1: the superiority of Jesus Christ to the angels. He wants his readers to consider the world to come (2:5), and he makes it clear that this is what he has been talking about all along. If indeed the Hebrew believers were being influenced by members of the Essene communities, they would be presented with teachings that included the exaltation of angels in the end times.

The Essenes had not missed the scriptural description of the influence of angels—both good and bad—throughout human history. For example, Michael (the archangel) had come to the aid of Daniel and Israel by opposing other evil angelic beings (Daniel 10:20–21; 12:1). The author of Hebrews does not bother to differentiate good angels from bad, but simply raises the issue and declares that God did *not* appoint the angels to rule in the world to come. Like so much of his argument throughout this sermon, he states the position of the opposition and disproves it biblically without stopping to reconfigure the doctrine from the ground up.

In this case he quotes a portion of Psalm 8 (verses 4–6) to make his point (Hebrews 2:6–8). The psalm can be read as simply a description of how human beings fit into God's creation. Yet the writer perceives the messianic implications of the psalm, acknowledging Jesus as the quintessential human being. Jesus frequently used "Son of man" as a reference to Himself, and in the author's interpretation of the psalm, that title has a double meaning, referring both to human beings generally, and then to Jesus as the fulfillment of humanity's destiny. *All* people have been created a little lower than the angels. Yet this high status is not seen today because of the fallen state of humanity. But through His perfect life, death, resurrection, and ascension, Jesus reversed the results of the fall and achieved this glorified status predicted in the psalm (see Philippians 2:6–11). In Christ the true dignity and destiny of humankind are fulfilled.

Critical Observation

Psalm 8 happens to be a psalm of David, but the author of Hebrews doesn't single him out. A current tendency is to highlight the individuality of biblical authors and analyze their personal outlooks, styles, and theologies. While certain benefits can come from such an approach, the downside is that people begin to look at scripture as just another human book. The Jewish perspective—and the one taken by the author of Hebrews—is to see scripture as God's authoritative Word. If something is included in scripture, it is valid no matter who said it. Throughout the author's writing can be seen his belief that human authorship is a matter of no great importance, but the Word of God certainly is.

The image portrayed by Psalm 8 and Hebrews 2:5–8 is far different from that of some people who see human beings as merely specks in the universe, lost amid the vast cosmos. The psalmist and the writer of Hebrews acknowledge that humans are not only created in the image of God, but are also given authority to oversee creation.

Hebrews 2:9 reprises the author's thought expressed in 1:3–4, which will be a repeated theme throughout this letter. Even though being a little lower than the angels sounds quite impressive to human ears, for Jesus it was a demotion. Yet He had to voluntarily submit to such a status in order to take on human form and sacrifice Himself for all other humans. Because Jesus is now sitting at the right hand of God, believers should acknowledge that setting aside one's own entitlements for the good of others will certainly result in receiving God's reward of glory and honor when it really matters.

📄 2:10–18

JESUS, HUMANS, AND ANGELS

Since the writer of Hebrews is making the point that Jesus is far superior to the angels, he explains why the Son of God had to become a man and suffer and die as a human being. The author is extolling a figure who incurred unprecedented suffering and ignominy in His death. Yet Christ's suffering was the only way God could redeem His people from their sins and deliver them from the wrath to come. Jesus' incarnation was not a pageant or a mere role play. A salvation that would meet the requirement of a just God and atone for the sin of guilty humans required suffering that only a divine-human Savior could endure.

The heavenly Father is referred to here (2:10), as often in the New Testament, simply as God. He is regarded as the source of salvation. The description of Jesus as *author* of salvation (2:10; 12:2) might better be translated as "pioneer" or "trailblazer" (6:20). As the perfect and obedient human being (Psalm 8), Jesus is the "pioneer" of our faith, who brings "many sons and daughters to glory" through His death and resurrection for them (Hebrews 2:10 TNIV).

At first it may appear odd to consider that God *made* Jesus perfect (2:10), since Jesus *was* God. The answer is that Jesus was made perfect or "complete" in His *humanity*. As a human being, He was conceived and born without sin. He lived without sin. And by His obedient suffering, He became the perfect sacrifice for sin and so achieved complete or "perfect" humanity—the position of glory that Adam and Eve failed to achieve because of their rebellion against God. Jesus reversed the results of Adam's fall and became the perfect mediator and High Priest for us. He is now able to save us, as well as to truly sympathize and help us in the midst of trials and temptations.

In Hebrews, sanctification, or being made holy (2:11), does not refer to the moral renewal of a person's life after he or she experiences salvation. Rather, it speaks of the person's reconciliation to God. So here the reader begins to see the great significance of Jesus' incarnation. The Son of God not only forged an identity with very unworthy people, but also was not ashamed to do so. It was an honor beyond anything human beings could ever imagine! And it was something that only Christ could do. No angel was capable of such a feat.

The proclamation of Jesus' solidarity with His people is followed by three citations from Old Testament scripture as proof (2:12–13). The first (2:12) is from Psalm 22:22. The second and third (2:13) are from Isaiah 8:17–18. The Old Testament prophet had expressed faith in the Lord and a willingness to oversee the children of God. Such commitments, when applied to Jesus, were even more powerful. During Jesus' incarnation, He shared the human need to live by faith and put His trust in God the Father.

Jesus was certainly an exemplary human being. Rarely are people both sympathetic and strong. Christ, however, could relate to the limitations of humanity even as He was overcoming the forces that imposed many of those limitations (2:14–15). Had Jesus not accepted the limitations of humanity, He never could have tasted death on behalf of all people (2:9, 14–15). Only Christ was a perfect human being. His humanity allowed Him to die. His perfection made Him an appropriate sacrifice to God. And His willingness to go through with such an awful sacrifice was the only way to break the hold of sin and the devil.

It was Jesus' mission to provide salvation for human beings (Abraham's descendants)—not angels (2:16). Jesus helps in a very real way by seeing His people through whatever they are facing. He relates to human suffering because of His incarnation. He had to take on human form in order to die, and by doing so, He also experienced the emotions, pains, and temptations common to all human beings. His experience perfectly qualifies Him to act as High Priest—an intercessor between sinful humankind and a perfect God (2:17–18). No one can rightly claim that God doesn't understand how he or she feels, because Jesus lived through everything any human being can face—and worse. The writer of Hebrews will have more to say on this topic later in the letter.

Take It Home

Jesus' humanity, and the suffering that went along with it, was what enabled Him to relate more personally and completely to the human experience. Can you think of a similar way in which your own sufferings have, in retrospect, provided you with greater empathy and insight into how someone else was feeling? As a result, have your own sufferings enabled you to be a better minister to someone else who is suffering?

HEBREWS 3:1–19

JESUS COMPARED TO MOSES

House Servant vs. Homeowner	3:1–6
The Consequences of Losing Faith: Then and Now	3:7–19

Setting Up the Section

Knowing of his readers' high regard for angels, the writer of Hebrews has just concluded a section of how Jesus is far superior to the angelic beings. In this section he turns his attention to another hero of the Jewish people—Moses. While his readers had good reason to admire Moses for his faithfulness and great accomplishments, his deeds pale when contrasted to the life of Jesus Christ.

📄 3:1–6

HOUSE SERVANT VS. HOMEOWNER

The writer of Hebrews has just summarized his argument that Jesus Christ is worthier of his readers' praise and admiration than any angel. He continues that thought with the 'Therefore" that opens Hebrews 3. The author isn't merely attempting to win a debate; he is attempting to show his Hebrew readers what benefits they could enjoy as a result of Jesus' preeminence. They were not only "brothers" with their Lord and all other believers, but "holy" brothers at that (3:1).

In addition, the writer attempts to clarify the Jews' perception of Jesus. They would have well understood the importance of the role of high priest. The high priest was the figure who stood between the sinful worshiper presenting an offering to God and the holy figure from whom forgiveness was being asked. To have a high priest who had such compassion and empathy and was not ashamed to call them brothers (2:11), was indeed a privilege.

The Jewish Christians were probably less familiar, as are many contemporary Christians, with the concept of Jesus as an apostle (3:1). But the word simply means "one who is sent," and Jesus was certainly sent from God to minister to and save a sinful world. He was God's personal representative and showed humankind in clear and tangible ways what God was like. He demonstrated in no uncertain terms the sometimes overlooked aspects of God's character: love, mercy, grace, forgiveness, and so on.

Since Jesus represents humankind to God as high priest and represents God to people as apostle, He is in a unique position to mediate. This is the great application of the letter of Hebrews. If believers do not stand fast in loyalty to Jesus, what other hope do they have for reconciliation with God?

Critical Observation

It is in this section that many interpretations of Hebrews begin to go seriously astray. Some commentators allege that these verses amount to a contrast between an inferior Mosaic order/administration and the superior administration introduced by Christ and the apostles, resulting in the belief that the Christian era is superior to the Mosaic one. But a close examination of this passage reveals that is *not* what the author is saying.

The author has already briefly contrasted Jesus with the Old Testament prophets (1:1–2) and more explicitly with the angels (1:3–2:18). Here he begins a contrast between Jesus and Moses. The Jews perceived Moses as a great man, great prophet, great leader, and great lawgiver. Yet Jesus fulfilled all those roles as well—to a greater degree than Moses. Both Moses and Jesus were called by God and sent to help His people; both ministered to people who were subject to powerful forces (whether the Egyptian empire or the power of sin) and were being called to freedom; and both brought a message from God to provide clear direction for living in this world while anticipating a better one to come.

But as the writer contrasts Moses with Jesus, his imagery makes his point (3:2–6). Moses was a faithful servant in God's house, but Christ was the builder. Moses was never anything more than a worker in the house over which Jesus ruled as the Son of God. Jesus is clearly superior to Moses.

There is but one house of God and one people of God. Moses himself pointed ahead to the Christ who was to come. Jesus had said that Moses spoke of Him (John 5:45–47), and Paul wrote that Moses' message was the same as his own: salvation through faith in Christ (Romans 9:14–16). So it is a fundamental assumption of the author of Hebrews that God's church has run continually throughout all ages of history. He refers repeatedly to the people of God but never once distinguishes eras or epochs or generations. In all ages, the people of God are those who are saved by persevering faith in Christ.

Demystifying Hebrews

The writer of Hebrews is beginning an argument that will become clearer as he goes on. By the end of the letter, he will state plainly that Jesus Christ is the same yesterday, today, and forever (Hebrews 13:8). Christ Himself was at work in building the church in the ancient epoch. Hebrews 12 clarifies that it was Christ who led the people of God out of Egypt and through the wilderness, who gave the law at Mount Sinai, who talked to Moses in the Tent of Meeting, and whose glory was reflected on the face of Moses. The author is already making that assumption in 3:2–6, although the reader might not yet be aware of such an assumption.

📖 3:7–19

THE CONSEQUENCES OF LOSING FAITH: THEN AND NOW

The writer of Hebrews makes it as clear as possible that any Jewish Christians who were considering abandoning their faith were making a serious mistake. Hebrews 3:7 begins a long hortatory section (where the author makes an urgent appeal by mixing exposition with application) that stretches to 4:13.

He begins by quoting a portion of Psalm 95, which would have accomplished a number of things. First, the passage was a call to worship frequently used in first-century synagogues. More importantly, it recounts the story of the Israelites in the wilderness. By the first century, Moses stood as one of the undisputed heroes of the faith. Yet the psalm is a poignant reminder that the people under Moses' leadership had rebelled. As a result, neither they nor he reached the Promised Land where they were headed. God prevented all the stubborn, complaining people from entering the land, and it was possessed instead by a more faithful generation. In addition, the psalm was more than historic; it was current. The promise and warning for "today" (Hebrews 3:7, 13) are just as relevant in the first and twenty-first centuries as they were in the wilderness.

The story cited by the psalm has obvious parallels to the point being made by the writer of Hebrews. God was trying to elevate His people from one set of circumstances to a much more joyous and rewarding one. Yet as soon as they got started, some of them wanted to turn around and return to their more familiar, though less fulfilling, way of life. The Jewish Christians tempted to return to the stringent adherence to the rites and laws of Judaism could not have missed the writer's point.

The psalm also refers to the ultimate goal of the people as God's rest (3:11). The writer would soon say that the promise of entering God's rest still stands (4:1), so it becomes apparent that the psalmist had something more than the land of Canaan in mind. The rest of God remains, as it has always been, as fellowship with the Lord in heaven.

Here again is the futuristic perspective of Hebrews. Failing to enter God's rest means nothing less than failure to obtain eternal life. Entrance into the Promised Land had been but a symbol of something much greater.

The Jewish Christians receiving this letter would have been more familiar with Psalm 95 than most modern readers. The section quoted by the writer of Hebrews was the latter half of the psalm (verses 7–11). What came before (Psalm 95:1–6) was a rousing call to worship God with joy, thanksgiving, and gratitude. The readers of Hebrews would have known what was expected of them; the writer was simply reminding them.

From the psalm, the writer moves right into a plea for ongoing faithfulness. He never questions the authenticity of their conversions, but addresses them as brothers (3:1, 12) and attempts to reason with them. They had the responsibility for monitoring their own thoughts and beliefs (3:12) as well as regularly (daily) encouraging one another (3:13).

The deceitfulness of sin is an ongoing concern, and believers need to be ever vigilant to prevent becoming apathetic or rebellious toward the things of God. Allowing improper thoughts or attitudes to linger can be disastrous, so the time to act is now (3:15). And again, the author reminds his readers of his main point: Believers need to persevere in their faith so they don't miss out on anything Christ makes available to them (3:14).

It was not enough to know God's plans and purposes. The Israelites who had crossed the Red Sea between walls of water could see beyond a doubt that God was with them. He was ever before them in a pillar of cloud or fire. Yet they had still rebelled against Moses and against God, and were subsequently forbidden from entering the land (3:16–19). The Hebrew Christians also knew God's plans and purposes, but some needed prompting to keep from departing from the truths they knew.

If indeed the recipients of this letter included Jews with an association to the Essenes at Qumran, this historical reference would have been especially pertinent. The Essenes regarded the wilderness generation of Israel as a pattern or paradigm for their lives. But the author of Hebrews is reminding them that the generation that had started out loyal to God had quickly become a tragic example of unfaithfulness and apostasy. Paul makes a similar point in 1 Corinthians 10:1–13.

Throughout Hebrews, the author does not dwell simply on the problem of unbelief, but rather on apostasy—the turning away from the faith by someone who once believed, or at least professed to believe. As indicated in 3:12 and 3:19, there will be an ongoing emphasis on the connections between disobedience and unbelief, and between faith and obedience. What was true for the Israelites in the wilderness remains just as applicable for believers today and in the ages to come.

Take It Home

Can you recall times in your spiritual journey when you went through a period of apathy, disbelief, or rebellion? What was the reason for those feelings? How did your life during those times compare to periods when you felt close to God? What do you think is the best course of action to avoid similar conditions in the future?

HEBREWS 4:1–13

REST FOR THE FAITHFUL

Setting Up the Section

The writer of Hebrews began a persuasive argument in 3:7 that continues in this section. He is reminding his hearers of the history of Israel in the wilderness and of the people's failure to enter the rest of God because of their unbelief. He is also warning them that if they turn away from God, they must expect the same consequences. In this section he continues his comparison of the first-century Hebrew Christians to the Israelites of the Exodus.

📄 **4:1–2**

THE SAME GOSPEL

The author has just noted that the Old Testament Israelites were poised on the brink of entering the *rest* of God. He uses that term (rather than *Promised Land*) because he will bring the same concept into the present and apply it to his readers as well. The Israelites, as well as the first-century Jewish believers who were tempted to abandon the clear teachings of Christianity, were apt to lose much more than a temporary earthly possession. Forsaking their faith could have eternal consequences as well.

Another word the author uses frequently is *promise*, and the first of its fourteen appearances in Hebrews is found in 4:1. He uses the word to encompass the world to come, eternal life, and the final consummation of salvation. This promise was made to God's people in the ancient epoch and is still being made to believers. The author of Hebrews clarifies that the promise will be fulfilled in the next world for those, and only those, who have followed the Lord Jesus with persevering faith all the way to the end of their lives. People in the church whose faith flags and who turn away from following the Lord forfeit that promise.

In another unusual word usage, the writer of Hebrews calls God's message to the Old Testament Israelites the gospel (4:2). That in itself was not unheard of at the time. Paul makes similar statements in his letters (Romans 10:15–16; Galatians 3:8). But the phrasing in Hebrews 4:2 is distinctive. The writer doesn't say that those in the Old Testament had the gospel preached to them, just as those in the first century had heard it. Rather, he says that the New Testament Christians had heard the same gospel as the ancient Israelites. The assumption he makes is that no one would doubt that Israel heard the gospel. Nothing could more profoundly demonstrate his point that the message of salvation in Christ, and the requirement of faith in Christ, has always been the same.

A SABBATH-REST FOR GOD'S PEOPLE

In light of his reasoning, the fact that the Israelites would blatantly ignore God's truth is even more appalling, and that's exactly what the first-century believers were beginning to do. Twice more the author quotes Psalm 95:11 (Hebrews 4:3, 5) as he had in 3:11. He makes it clear that entering God's rest is the issue, and the possibility of failing to enter it is very real.

The fact that the writer uses present tense in verse 3 creates potential problems with interpretation. Some people leap to the assumption that he is saying that the Old Testament saints couldn't enter God's rest because it hadn't yet been made available by Christ's death and resurrection, while believers after Christ can enter God's rest immediately. This view makes no sense, however, in light of the fact that the author had just stated that the promise forfeited by the Israelites was the same promise the current believers must be careful not to abandon. He says the gospel is the same, then and now. And he says, as he will repeat again and again, that the promise (the gospel, salvation, and all things related) ultimately refers to heaven, not just to the partial experience of salvation believers enjoy in this world.

A better interpretation of verse 3 is to read it as a futuristic present tense. For example, Paul and Barnabas had preached, "We must go through many hardships to enter the kingdom of God" (Acts 14:22 NIV). It is clearly a principle that applies to entering the kingdom of God in the future, and the thought remains the same if *rest* is substituted for *kingdom*. That's what the writer of Hebrews intended. It makes little sense to say that New Testament believers have already entered the rest of God when the writer's urgent admonition is that they continue to persevere in faith lest they fail to enter the rest! Hebrews 4:6 and 4:11 both make it clear that the author is looking to the future as he discusses God's rest. Another possibility is that the present tense carries a progressive sense. Believers are entering the rest through the process of salvation but must endure so as to fully enter that rest at the consummation of their salvation. Not to persevere means to fail to enter God's rest (salvation).

The concept of the rest of God was certainly nothing new. From the beginning, God had demonstrated a period of rest at the end of one's work (4:4). After the six days of creation, God rested on the seventh day. So at this point, the rest of God is identified as participation in God's own rest that began immediately after the creation of the world. This is the rest that the Israelites had failed to obtain—not because it wasn't available to them, but because they did not continue to put their faith in God.

Demystifying Hebrews

The writer of Hebrews makes it clear that some people will enter God's rest while others will not, even after hearing the gospel (4:6–7). The difference is a person's *response* to the message. And here he repeats himself about the need to respond while there is still time (3:15; 4:7). God has been making the offer for centuries, in an extended stretch of time called "today" (4:7). This "today" is the whole period of time in which the gospel message of salvation is being offered. It is a limited opportunity. The writer urges his readers to act while there is still time.

The first generation of Israelites missed the opportunity to enter the Promised Land because of their lack of faith. They missed out on God's rest. The author of Hebrews takes this idea of rest and applies it to God's ultimate "Promised Land," what he defines (in various places) as the better country, the enduring city, and the world to come.

The author uses a word that might literally be rendered *Sabbathment* but is usually translated *Sabbath-rest* (4:9). The word is found nowhere else in the Bible and has been detected in no earlier uses than this one. The writer may have invented the word to define what he was talking about. No doubt the term evoked in his mind a connection to the weekly Sabbath. Just as God rested from His work on the seventh day of Creation, so He now invites believers to enter into His rest, signifying both His presence and salvation. Just as the seventh day of Creation represented the completion of God's work and a time of rest, so the Sabbath-rest for believers symbolizes the consummation of their salvation and entrance into God's rest.

Some Christians use this passage to justify doing away with a weekly day of rest for Christians. This, however, is not the author's point (but see Romans 14:5–6; Colossians 2:16–17 for Paul's perspective on the Sabbath). He is simply drawing an analogy between the weekly Sabbath-rest and our salvation. Both involve entering God's rest, which the author uses as a metaphor for the presence of God and the salvation He provides.

Hebrews 4:12 is an often-quoted and frequently memorized verse. As such, it may seem that the writer suddenly shifts topics, from rest to the Word of God. Actually, he is emphasizing a point. He began his discussion of rest at 3:7 by quoting from scripture, attributing not a psalmist, but the Holy Spirit for the text. The psalm is a warning against hardening one's heart and rebelling against God.

So the point he makes in 4:12 is that God's Word is nothing to be taken lightly. It can never be ignored or dismissed with impunity. It is the living voice of God that gets right to the bottom of things. Someone may look fine in the eyes of other people, but God's Word exposes the true condition of the heart, the real character of one's faith, and reveals a genuine spirit.

Critical Observation

The phrase "soul and spirit, joints and marrow" (4:12) is simply a way to refer to the inner life of a human being in all of its aspects. Although some people use this verse as evidence that a person is composed of three parts (spirit, soul, and body), someone else could just as easily cite Mark 12:30 to speculate that people have four parts (heart, soul, mind, and body).

God sees every action. He knows every thought and attitude. No matter how hard people try to hide their sins, the truth will eventually come to light and they will be expected to give an account (4:13). How much better it is to respond to God and await His rest. According to the writer of Hebrews, "today" won't last forever.

Take It Home

The modern church can benefit by a renewed excitement over the celebration of a Sabbath—one day each week set aside for refreshing rest in anticipation of the eternal rest of God that awaits us in the world to come. With a focus on rest and worship, the principle of Sabbath can keep alive one's immediate sense of joy and expectation of even better things to come. Is this typical of your own experience? If not, what needs to change in order for you to make the most of your Sabbath days and preparation for the ultimate rest of God?

HEBREWS 4:14–5:10

JESUS COMPARED TO AARON

A Sympathetic High Priest   4:14–16
The Role of the High Priest   5:1–10

Setting Up the Section

So far in his letter, the author of Hebrews has demonstrated how Christ is superior to the Old Testament prophets, to the angels, and to Moses. In this section he continues his series of contrasts by comparing Jesus to Aaron and other well-respected high priests.

📄 **4:14–16**

A SYMPATHETIC HIGH PRIEST

Remember that the Jewish Christians who were receiving this letter had been in discussions with certain other Jewish advocates who were pressuring them to return to a more traditional Jewish perspective, which would require that they abandon many of the Christian teachings they had already professed to believe. One topic especially relevant to this dialog was the role of the high priest in regard to a person's salvation. The early Christians were coming to see the traditional rites as only a prefiguration of the final and ultimate provision for salvation made in the life, death, and resurrection of Jesus Christ. But the ongoing Jewish view was that the Levitical priesthood and its ceremonies were still, as had always been the case, God's definitive provision for the salvation of humankind.

The writer of Hebrews has a habit of mentioning a topic early in the letter that he examines later in more detail. He has already presented the image of Jesus in the role of high priest (2:17; 3:1), but in this section he goes into much more depth. He also changes his tone dramatically. After a section with a dire warning of what could happen to those who harden their hearts and give up on their faith, he begins a warm entreaty for them to realize exactly what Jesus had done on their behalf.

The Jews would have been familiar with the procedure of the high priest interceding with God on their behalf. It was a solemn and somber ceremony. One day a year, the high priest—and only the high priest—would enter the Most Holy Place of the temple to sprinkle blood from animal sacrifices on the ark of the covenant (Leviticus 16). The ark was symbolic of the presence of God. Anyone who violated the Most Holy Place or the ark would die (2 Samuel 6:6-7).

But Jesus didn't just step symbolically into God's presence in the temple; He went through the heavens to be literally in the presence of God (Hebrews 4:14). And His qualifications as High Priest were unsurpassed. Not only had He been the spotless, perfect sacrifice whose blood was shed, but He had also shared the human experience with those whom He was defending. He knew exactly the temptations they faced and the weaknesses they felt (4:15). He felt the full force of human difficulties and understands them better than people do, from God's perspective.

Demystifying Hebrews

In order to comprehend the importance of Jesus as High Priest, it is essential to understand the significance of His humanity. Although He displayed great power while on earth, He had to receive power from God as the other human prophets and apostles did. He was a true, authentic person who walked with God. He had the same temptations and troubles as any other person, yet chose to live by faith, trust His heavenly Father, and put on holiness as all believers are called to do. He had a sense of His purpose in life and how His life would end, yet—in His humanity—He was not omniscient or specifically aware of what the next day would bring. He does not make the ideal High Priest because He is God, but rather because He was fully human and lived out His life the way each person must live it.

The writer of Hebrews says that Jesus had been tempted in every way, just as other people are. Obviously that doesn't mean Jesus faced every single possible temptation. He never faced the problems that come with old age, for example. He didn't face the temptations involved in marriage, child rearing, or wealth. Yet the author's point is well taken. Jesus lived a human life that was beset with more stress, trauma, and pain than most people can even conceive. His temptations were many and varied, and He resisted every one of them. People fail to understand the significance of such devotion to God because they so easily give in to temptations. But Jesus never surrendered to temptation. He never sinned, even though His temptations were strong and His pain intense. He endured them all to the bitter end.

Many people memorize Hebrews 4:14–16 as a passage of beautiful sentiment and wonderful hope, which it is. Yet most tend to gloss over the fact that it takes real, sturdy faith to believe that Jesus truly understands how they feel. When life takes a turn for the worse, one of the first things people tend to do is blame God, or at least seek a logical explanation when none exists. It is a great privilege to stand before God with confidence, expecting mercy and grace (4:16).

5:1–10

THE ROLE OF THE HIGH PRIEST

Jewish religious purists might have ruled out Jesus as a likely high priest simply because of the fact that He was from the tribe of Judah, when the priests were required to be descendants of Levi. So in this section, the author takes care to establish that Jesus is in every way fitted to be the believer's great High Priest.

A significant level of maturity was needed in order to be an effective priest. The person needed an awareness of the power of sin and had to be capable of overcoming it in his own life. Yet the role also required a vulnerability borne out of the recognition of his personal weaknesses (5:2). Before priests could offer sacrifices for others, they had to make sacrifices on their own behalf (Leviticus 16:11, 15; Hebrews 5:3).

Additionally, a high priest had to be appointed. He could not take the office on his own (5:1). Originally, God had specified who would serve as high priest. By the first century, however, the role had become entangled with both Jewish and Roman politics and was more of a status symbol than a legitimate spiritual calling. Both Jesus and Paul had encounters with high priests who were lacking in both humanity and spiritual maturity.

With these expectations in mind, the author begins to demonstrate how Jesus met each requirement. Jesus had been called by God, just as Aaron had been. Two prophecies from scripture are quoted as evidence of His divine appointment. The author has already referred once to Psalm 2:7 to show that Jesus is the Son of God (Hebrews 1:5). But not only was He God's Son; He was also designated a priest by God the Father (Psalm 110:4).

In fact, Jesus had quoted from Psalm 110 while asserting His claim to be the Messiah (Matthew 22:41–46). Throughout the Gospels, Jesus makes the point over and over again that He had received His commission from God the Father. Although He willingly offered Himself as a sacrifice, He did not seek the mission for Himself. It was laid upon Him as a charge by God.

The Old Testament verses used by the writer of Hebrews to show how Jesus is a great high priest could be used to prove Christ's kingship as well. The two divinely appointed offices—priest and king—combine in the life and work of Jesus Christ.

Critical Observation

If indeed the letter to the Hebrews was intended to refute some of the teachings of the Essene sect of Judaism, this section would have been particularly appropriate. One of the reasons the Essenes had withdrawn from worship in the Jerusalem temple was their feeling that Israel's current priesthood, under control of the Sadducees, was corrupted beyond repair. In addition, the sect was looking for two messiahs—one to perform in a priestly role and the other as a victorious king. The writer of Hebrews demonstrates that Jesus fulfilled both roles, and was not tainted in any way by corruption.

Jesus had never offered sacrificial animals as the high priests before Him had done. There was no need, because His death would be the only sacrifice ever needed, as the writer of Hebrews will explain later (7:27; 10:10). Instead, Jesus' offerings to God were prayers and petitions, accompanied by loud cries and tears (5:7). The image evokes Jesus' intense prayers in Gethsemane or His cries to the Father from the cross. The tears and cries are reminders that Jesus was never immune to any of the sufferings of life. He succeeded in His life and work, not because He was spared anything other humans must experience, but because He prayed regularly, learned scripture, struggled against enormous temptations, and remained faithful until the very end of His human life.

The writer of Hebrews drops in a couple of references to Melchizedek, the king/priest who had associated with Abraham centuries before (5:6, 10). This is another example of how he tends to briefly introduce a topic before delving into it later. His full discussion about Melchizedek comes in Hebrews 7. At this point, however, where Jesus is being compared to Aaron as a high priest, it should be noted that Melchizedek served as priest long *before* the law was given—before Aaron was even born.

Jesus was God's Son, which held certain entitlements (5:8). Yet He willingly opted to obey through suffering, for the good of humankind. He, more than anyone else, is qualified to rule not only as Lord, but also as High Priest.

In closing this section, the writer of Hebrews connects salvation with *obedience* to God (5:9). It is more usual to associate trust or faith with salvation, but this is not the Bible's sole exception. It is appropriate to use such different terminology because true faith is always expressed through obedience. Not only that, but faith is itself an act of obedience. Everyone who hears the gospel is obliged to believe it as a summons, a command from God. Any response other than belief is a form of disobedience and rebellion. The gospel is more than an invitation to be saved by faith in Christ; it is a command to be obeyed.

Christ rules as king and serves as High Priest. To disobey His truth leaves no other option for salvation. So as the author of Hebrews continues, he will next address the problem of believers who fall away from the faith.

🏠

Take It Home

Consider how the knowledge of Jesus serving as your High Priest can help you in practical ways. What situations or emotions are you facing where you would find consolation to realize that Jesus fully understands your feelings? For example, consider the experience of loneliness. It is a crushing burden for many people and a catalyst for the temptation to sin. For many people, the experience has resulted in unbelief, despair, anger, and resentment. Jesus well knew the temptation and sorrow of human loneliness, yet His response was not to succumb to temptation, but rather to get up earlier to spend quality time with His Father (Mark 1:35). How can Jesus' humanity inspire you to overcome or endure a circumstance you are currently facing?

HEBREWS 5:11–6:20
STEADY GROWTH AND STRONGER HOPE

Setting Up the Section

In the author's alternations between exposition and application, this section brings us to another section of application. He is preparing to move on to another segment about the importance of Jesus Christ, but first he pauses to prepare his hearers. His preparation includes a scolding, yet what he has to say is a reminder, in no uncertain terms, of the basic theme of the letter.

TIME TO GROW UP

The author of Hebrews has been developing a deep spiritual thought about Jesus using various scriptures and common knowledge about the work of the high priest. Yet he pauses to concede that his readers might not be ready to hear what he is saying. He compares his teachings to a child's diet (5:13–14). When very young, a baby cannot handle solid food and needs only milk. Soon, however, milk is not enough, and he or she needs to move on to solid food.

The writer was distraught to realize that the Hebrew Christians were still in need of "milk." Yet their situation was not unlike that of many current believers. Their spiritual childishness was a result of their contentment with the status quo. Further progress in their Christian growth and devotion to Christ would only increase the distance between themselves and their Jewish family members, friends, and acquaintances. It was easier not to press the issue.

But as the writer goes on to explain, spiritual stagnation is dangerous. Genuine spiritual growth and vitality requires solid "food." The spiritual and ethical discernment necessary to keep from falling prey to falsehood and the temptations of the world demands a deepening knowledge and the constant exercise of faith. Sitting on the fence between their old Jewish ways and their new Christian commitment wasn't doing any good.

By this time, a number of believers should have been qualified to be teachers. Instead, an outside instructor was still required to teach them elemental truths (5:11–12). Theirs was not an ideal situation.

A PROPER APPRECIATION FOR SALVATION

Although the writer is direct and firm, he does not appear to be angry with his hearers. He is writing out of concern, not merely to criticize. He urges his readers to keep moving forward, beyond the elementary aspects of their faith, into a mature relationship with God.

It wasn't as if they were being asked to forsake everything familiar to them. In fact, the early church had incorporated many of the customs of Judaism into their worship ceremonies. Many of their beliefs were the same as well. The first-century Jewish faith and worldview included repentance from sin, professions of faith, baptism, the laying on of hands (although more in regard to sacrifices and ordination than the bestowal of the Holy Spirit), resurrection, and God's judgment. The Christian church began with Jewish believers who built on what they had already been taught about God.

Yet many of their rites and ceremonies had become hollow traditions. The life, death, and resurrection of Jesus Christ imparted to them the meaning that had been lost. Or more accurately, the awareness of Christ *should* have enlightened their thinking concerning the centuries-old practices they held to. They needed to open their spiritual eyes and begin moving forward into the "meatier" aspects of their faith.

Critical Observation

In this context, the mention of baptisms (6:2) seems to be a clear reference to Old Testament Jewish ceremonial washings rather than the more current application of the word. The author will soon (9:13) make reference to the ritual of the red heifer (Numbers 19) that required bathing and washing one's clothes.

This section is a source of debate among contemporary scholars. Numerous Bible passages affirm that a genuine believer is in no danger of ever losing his or her salvation—and that list includes the final verses of this section (6:16–20). The Hebrew Christians appear to have been genuine believers: They had been enlightened, had reveled in the Word of God, had shared in the Holy Spirit, and more (6:4–5). On the other hand, scripture also points to instances where people seemed to begin the Christian life, sometimes very impressively, yet were later revealed never to have been born again, never to have become genuine followers of Christ (Matthew 7:21–23; 1 John 2:19).

So were the Hebrew Christians true believers or just professing imposters? And if their faith was genuine, was the writer of Hebrews saying they could lose their salvation?

Yet another possibility is that the author is posing a what-if situation. His shift of pronouns (from *we*, *us*, and *you* to *those* and *they* [Hebrews 6:4–6]) might suggest a hypothetical circumstance. Theoretically, if someone were to place faith in Jesus for salvation and then decide to retract that decision, it would clearly be impossible to find any other alternative. Not only would such a change of heart be ineffective, but disgraceful as well—like crucifying Jesus all over again (6:6).

Whatever view the reader takes, the author clearly desires for his hearers to repent, turn back to God, and strive for maturity without further delay. The gift of God is not to be neglected or despised. To do so would be like a soaking rain on dry earth that produces only thorns and thistles, when the same rain should have instead provided nourishment and growth for a life-giving crop (6:7–8). No one would keep investing in worthless land. It is even more tragic when people refuse to produce after experiencing the numerous wonderful gifts of God.

The author's suggested response is practical and doable. Show diligence. Don't be lazy. Imitate those who set good examples (6:11–12). And through it all, remember that God will never be unjust (6:10). God would never condemn anyone unfairly. Therefore, the Hebrew Christians could be confident of improving and expecting good things in their future. The writer again refers to the promise of God that would be experienced only through faith and patience (6:12).

AN EXAMPLE FROM ABRAHAM

The Jews revered Abraham, and the writer has already referred to them as Abraham's descendants (2:16). So after exhorting his readers to incorporate more faith and patience in their lives by imitating those who had previously set good examples (6:12), he follows with a reference to Abraham (6:13). Characteristic of the writer, he drops in a quick example at this point, but later (in chapter 11) he will come back to more fully develop his thoughts about faith and perseverance.

Demystifying Hebrews

It would have been difficult to find a better example than Abraham to demonstrate perseverance in regard to the promise of God. He had left his homeland in Mesopotamia and traveled hundreds of miles to get to Canaan. God had promised that he and Sarah would have a son, yet it was twenty-five years before the promise was ultimately fulfilled—long past the time Sarah could be expected to still bear children. Then, after all that, Abraham was tested to see if he would still be obedient to God when the life of the child was at stake (Genesis 22:1–19). The writer of Hebrews is challenging his hearers to also demonstrate ongoing patience and faith as they await the promise of God.

The specific promise of God to Abraham was that he would have many descendants and become the father of a great nation. Abraham waited, and he eventually received what God had promised. . .to an extent. The birth of Isaac was the event that fulfilled one specific promise (a son), and it made possible the fulfillment of another (that Abraham would be the father of a great nation). So the promise, for Abraham, was not unlike the promise for first-century believers. God was faithfully seeing them through their present trials and challenges, but His ultimate promise was still in their future. Abraham received what was promised (6:15), yet God's promise to Abraham is still being realized.

All believers throughout the centuries have been heirs to God's promise to Abraham (6:17). And they have the same guarantee that the promise will be honored. God cannot lie (6:18), and He has no need to take an oath to ensure His trustworthiness. Yet He did so (Genesis 22:15–18), perhaps as a concession to the human tendency toward disbelief. And since there is nothing greater in the universe, God swore by Himself. There is no stronger assurance available.

The symbol of this assurance is an anchor (Hebrews 6:19)—strong and secure. So when scripture speaks of the hope believers have in God, the concept is a far cry from the fingers-crossed, against-all-odds "hope" of which many people speak. Biblical hope in God refers to the certainty that God's promises will all be fully fulfilled. It is a source of ongoing encouragement (6:18).

The writer will have much more to say about the work of the priests and how Jesus' ministry compares. But at this point he makes one very important observation. He says that Jesus entered the "inner place behind the curtain" in the temple—the Most Holy Place (6:19–20 ESV). The privilege of doing so was given only to the high priest. In Jesus' earthly life, He never went into the Most Holy Place in the temple. So this passage is a clear reminder that the temple in Jerusalem was only a copy—a replica of a greater, heavenly version. Jesus didn't need to sprinkle blood on the ark of the covenant once a year. His sacrifice was offered to God directly, in heaven. It is there where the perfect High Priest still offers intercession for people.

The writer is most assuredly not telling his readers that if they hold fast to Christ they will get something in this world for their pains. Instead, he is saying that if they hold fast to Christ, they will inherit in the world to come. That is why he has already urged them to press on to the end (6:11). He will continue to emphasize this point throughout the letter.

He also makes another reference to Melchizedek (5:10; 6:20), which he will explain in great detail in the following section.

Take It Home

Consider the emphasis in this section about how God honored the promise He made to Abraham. The birth of Isaac occurred as promised yet was against all reason, logic, and expectation. Believers today have the New Testament and teachings of Jesus that reveal a great many more of God's promises. What are some that are most meaningful to you? How might your life change if you believe with greater assurance that God will surely do all He has said He will do?

HEBREWS 7:1–28

JESUS COMPARED TO MELCHIZEDEK

Setting Up the Section

Continuing his explanation of how Jesus Christ is superior to the Levitical priests in regard to providing salvation, in this section the author focuses on Melchizedek. He has already mentioned the Old Testament character a few times (5:6, 10; 6:20) but will now explain the significance of *when* he appears in scripture and *how* his ministry prefigured that of Jesus.

📄 7:1–3

THE STORY OF MELCHIZEDEK

The writer assumes his readers would know the account of Melchizedek, and most first-century Jews certainly would have. However, the story is foreign to many twenty-first-century believers. The character shows up only briefly in Genesis and is mentioned one other time in Psalms. Yet as the author is about to explain, those brief mentions are more important than they may first appear.

The first mention of Melchizedek is tucked into the story of Abraham. After Abraham and Lot had separated and settled in different places, Lot was among a group of people kidnapped by a coalition of foreign kings (Genesis 14:11–12). When Abraham heard the news, he quickly assembled a rescue party, safely retrieved Lot, and recovered a great many valuables that had been stolen.

Afterward, as Abraham met with the king of Sodom, Melchizedek appeared. He brought a meal and blessed Abraham. In return, Abraham gave him a tenth of all the plunder he had taken from the kings he had defeated (Genesis 14:18–20).

The name *Melchizedek* means "king of righteousness," and he was identified as both king of Salem (the place that would later be called Jerusalem) and priest of God Most High. As the writer of Hebrews points out, the Genesis account says nothing of Melchizedek's lineage, neither his birth and ancestry nor his death and posterity. In this sense, he was without father, mother, genealogy, birth, or death (Hebrews 7:3).

Critical Observation

The brief mention of Melchizedek, the comments that there was no beginning or end to his life (7:3), and the mystery that surrounds him, have led some people to theorize that he was a supernatural figure—perhaps even a preincarnate appearance of Christ to Abraham. One line of thought supposes that the occasional presence of supernatural beings during the early stage of human history spawned the mythology of superhuman figures found in various cultural mythologies. But the fact that the author of Hebrews compares Melchizedek to the Son of God would seem to suggest that they were not the same being.

As strange (and as short) as the description of Melchizedek is, there is still ample information to provide a comparison to Jesus. Melchizedek's home, Salem, was a variation of the word *shalom*, meaning "peace." Both "king of righteousness" and "king of peace" are apt titles for both figures. Melchizedek was both king and priest—exactly the point that the writer of Hebrews had recently made about Jesus (4:14). Some people emphasize that Melchizedek served bread and wine (Genesis 14:18), although the phrase simply refers to a regular meal. And although the New Testament sacraments for the Lord's Supper are meant to be reflective of a normal meal, to say Melchizedek's bread and wine were symbols of Communion stretches the imagery too far.

Clearly, the author is treating Melchizedek as a "type"—an enacted prophecy of the Lord Jesus. The Old Testament is replete with types that served to prepare God's people for the coming of the Messiah. Such types could include people (Moses, David), institutions (the priesthood, royalty, prophecy), events (the Exodus, entry into the Promised Land), or ritual actions (sacrifices, the Passover). These symbolic people and events all embody in a special way the ultimate truths of salvation and the ministry of the Messiah as it would unfold once He appeared in the world. Believers would have found it even more challenging to understand Jesus Christ and His work if they hadn't had all the historical prefigurements.

📄 7:4–10

MELCHIZEDEK COMPARED TO LEVITICAL PRIESTS

The significance of the account of Melchizedek as retold at this point in Hebrews is a matter of historical timing. People were attempting to lure the Jewish Christians back into their traditional rites and ceremonies, including the dependence on their priests for atonement. So the author of Hebrews uses Melchizedek to clarify God's perspective on the importance of priests.

Melchizedek is proof that there were other priests of God besides the Levitical priests (who wouldn't exist for a number of centuries). Those priests would proudly trace their ancestry back to Aaron to justify their authority, yet Melchizedek did not depend on a genealogical right to be a priest. His is the example that foreshadows the ministry of Jesus.

The author then makes an interesting argument. He was writing to people so dependent on the priests to intercede with God on their behalf that many were considering forsaking the gospel and their relationship with Christ to return to that system. So he points out that people acknowledge the authority of their priests by bringing a tithe (7:5). At the same time, they took great pride in being descendants of Abraham. Yet, as the author notes, Abraham offered a tithe to Melchizedek. Symbolically, then, the Levitical priests (through Abraham) deferred to the priesthood of Melchizedek. Jesus was not a high priest in the tradition of Levi/Aaron, but rather in the order of Melchizedek, which was clearly greater.

The fact that no genealogy was provided for Melchizedek, or any record of his birth or death, gave him the perception of ongoing life and ministry. Christ *is* eternal, which is why the comparison to Melchizedek is so appropriate. In contrast, the Levitical priests ministered, died, and were replaced by someone else with the right genetic qualifications (7:8). The priesthood of Melchizedek was exemplary of the priesthood of Jesus that would eventually arrive and never expire.

📄 **7:11–28**

A PERMANENT PRIESTHOOD

As the author continues his argument, he wants to know, if the Levitical priesthood was intended to be God's definitive, final, sufficient provision for the salvation of His people, then why would scripture so clearly point to someone who would not only be David's lord, but who would also be a priest in the order of Melchizedek (non-Levitical)?

This seemingly simple argument is actually quite masterful. Scripture teaches people to expect one like Jesus and look for a priesthood higher than that of Aaron and the sons of Levi. If Aaron's priesthood alone was enough, then why does scripture prophesy the appearance of a priest in the order of Melchizedek (Psalm 110:4; Hebrews 7:17)?

Demystifying Hebrews

Evidence found at Qumran (one community of the Essenes, who were thought to be influencing the Hebrew Christians) suggests that they believed Melchizedek to be more than human—even angelic. The author of Hebrews seems to be aware of such a train of thought. Even if Melchizedek were an angel—which there is no good reason to assume in the first place—he has shown that Jesus is superior to the angels. And if Melchizedek were a highly regarded human priest, Jesus is of the same order, but a high priest. Either way, the author shows Christ's superior authority.

And as the quote from Psalm 110:4 is introduced, the author reminds his readers that for Christ, the priesthood is forever (7:21). The Law of Moses had made no provision for any such priesthood. This reference by the psalmist is obviously not the Levitical priesthood of the law.

The author is subtly leading up to another very important point. The real issue wasn't just *how* one type of priesthood would replace another; the root of the matter was *why*.

It is here (7:18–19) where the author plainly introduces the great interpretative problem of Hebrews. How could he describe the grand rites and ceremonies of the Mosaic ritual as useless? A reading of Exodus and Deuteronomy would certainly never leave one with that impression.

And this is the crucial point. The author legitimately condemns the old practices because they could not make the worshiper perfect. Their purpose was to point out the sinfulness of human beings and so direct them to God's mercy and grace. Yet the people kept gravitating to a religion based on ritual performance and outward conformity rather than a living faith in God. Numerous Old Testament prophets had attempted to correct such a mentality (Isaiah 1; Jeremiah 7; Amos 5; et al.), but the faulty thinking repeatedly established a foothold in Jewish traditions.

At the time when Hebrews was written, Jewish Christians were still participating (and rightly so) in sacrificial worship in the Jerusalem temple, yet most still had an incorrect or incomplete perception of the significance of such rites. Many Jews of the first century looked at the Mosaic arrangements as a complete way of salvation. They were comfortable with the system, so they felt no need for a redeemer who would die for their sins. Because they perceived their sacrifices as salvation itself, they didn't see that the sacrifices actually symbolized something (or someone) else.

While the author of Hebrews isn't against sacrificial worship, per se, he wants his readers to see the shortsightedness of their hope for peace with God based solely on religious rites and ceremonies. He will build this argument as he continues, but he begins here by showing that scripture clearly reveals another priesthood beyond the Levitical one. And if the Levitical priesthood was all that was necessary, why the need for a future priesthood?

As he identifies Jesus as the king/priest who had come (7:22), his argument begins to make sense. Although from the tribe of Judah rather than Levi, Jesus still qualifies as a priest in the same way Melchizedek did. He is the one who lives forever and continues to intercede before God on behalf of human beings (7:23–25).

In addition, He is superior to the Levitical priests in that He does not need to offer sacrifices on His own behalf (7:26–27). Jesus Christ is a high priest who is holy, blameless, and pure. And He only needed to offer a single sacrifice to God. The sacrifice of Himself was once for all. Its effectiveness covered past, present, and future. The Levitical priesthood was not the last word in salvation; Jesus is.

Take It Home

It may not be easy for today's believers to relate to high priests, sacrificial worship, and unusual figures like Melchizedek. But can you think of any practices in the modern church that might be compared to the offering of sacrifices—something that people tend to cling to, yet in which the genuine meaning may become lost in the ritual?

HEBREWS 8:1–13

THE WORK OF A HIGH PRIEST

Setting Up the Section

The author of Hebrews continues his ongoing discussion of comparisons and contrasts between the role of Jesus as High Priest and the priests who came before Him—Aaron and Melchizedek among them. In this section he shifts his perspective a bit, focusing not only on *what* Jesus does in His role of High Priest, but also *where*. And he makes some significant observations pertaining to the new covenant contrasted to the old covenant.

📄 **8:1–6**

WHERE CHRIST SERVES AS PRIEST

To this point in his current stream of thought, the author of Hebrews has been describing how Jesus compared to previous respected priests in terms of qualification and right to serve. Here he begins an examination of the work itself—yet another indication of the superiority of Jesus.

Remember that the readers were being tempted to believe that the Levitical priesthood was a completely adequate provision for one's salvation. They were missing the point that the Old Testament priesthood was only an instrument of God's grace in Christ—not the means of salvation itself. The tendency of humans to embrace external rites and ceremonies to convey the substance of God's love had been going on for centuries and would continue long after the writing of Hebrews. (The Protestant Reformation was a movement to correct the same fundamental confusion.) So the writer maintains the single theme of his letter—that an ongoing commitment to Jesus Christ, expressed with living faith, is the only way to get to heaven and receive the full promise of God.

The sphere of Jesus' ministry clearly sets Him apart from other priests. The Jewish temple contained no chairs because the work of the priests was ongoing. Yet the author provides an image of Jesus seated (8:1), indicating that His work has been completed. In addition, Christ sits on a throne at the right hand of God the Father. (*The Majesty* was a Jewish term to refer to God without invoking His name, thereby avoiding any unintentional breaking of the commandment to not misuse the name of God.)

Jesus' sacrifice—the offering of Himself to God—was complete (7:27). Yet His service continues (8:2). He didn't die for humankind and then just forget about them; He continues to work on their behalf. And His service is conducted in the very presence of God. It is not limited by time or location, as is the work of earthly priests, but is heavenly and eternal.

Despite all the emphasis many of his readers were placing on the Mosaic laws, the author clearly shows their limited vision (8:3–6). Jesus, he explains, is not just one more in a long line of priests. Jesus, in fact, is the original and true priest. His heavenly priesthood was the blueprint the earthly priests were expected to model. The Levitical system was a copy of the true priesthood; the work of the Old Testament priests was but a shadow of the real thing.

The Jewish people of the first century—especially the nonconformist Essenes—were inclined to regard the life, history, and experience of Israel as a paradigm of their own. They felt a strong association with the wilderness generation under Moses and stressed the Mosaic covenant. And they were inclined to feel that they need not do anything more than duplicate the pattern of life established by their forebears. So the writer of Hebrews begins to address the issue of the covenant.

📄 **8:7–13**

A NEW COVENANT

Although the first-century Jews felt such an affinity to the Mosaic covenant, they didn't understand the covenant to be the proclamation of the gospel that it was intended to be (4:1–2). The author of Hebrews has already pointed out that the wilderness generation of Israel was not to be emulated (chapters 3–4). After all, that generation perished and failed to obtain God's salvation. They had the rituals the Jews were still so fond of, but they didn't have the faith necessary to finish what they had begun (3:16–19).

He has also shown that the rest, spoken of in regard to the Israelites in the wilderness (Psalm 95:11), was not a reference to the Promised Land. Otherwise, why did God tell the generations of Israelites *after* those in the wilderness that they, too, needed to enter His rest (Hebrews 4:8)?

As the author moves to the topic of the covenant cherished by the first-century Jews, he uses a similar argument. They wanted to believe that the covenant between God and Moses was a lasting one, and they were continuing to try to live according to those rules and regulations. But if that were so, queried the author of Hebrews, why did God later promise a new and better covenant?

Demystifying Hebrews

Just as there was a new and better priesthood than the one established by Aaron, and a new and better rest than that offered by the Promised Land, there would be a new and better covenant than the one established with the unfaithful Israelites in the wilderness. The very fact that scripture promises another covenant to replace the one with the ancestors of the first-century Jews is evidence that the original covenant was inadequate. So clearly it should not be the model people choose to live by. They should have been looking for the new covenant rather than clinging so tightly to the one that had failed.

The crucial point that many of the first-century Jewish community were missing was that the previous covenant failed because God had found fault with the people (8:8). The problem with the Mosaic covenant was not in the covenant itself, but in the unfaithfulness of the people. They did not truly believe God, so they failed to combine the message with true faith (4:2). The same problem was creating problems in the first-century church.

What follows this statement is the longest single quotation of the Old Testament found in the New Testament (8:8-12). The quote from Jeremiah 31:31-34 says specifically that the new covenant would *not* be like the one God had made with Israel in the wilderness. God had been faithful, but Israel had broken their promise. The new covenant would be one where *all* the people would relate to God.

Critical Observation

One reason so many people misunderstand the difference in the old (Mosaic) covenant and the new covenant may be attributed to the adoption in the late second century of the terms *Old Testament* and *New Testament*. It was a way for them to separate scripture that preceded the incarnation of Jesus from that which followed. But in the centuries that followed, believers have instinctively begun to think that there were two theological, spiritual arrangements succeeding one another in time, with the latter significantly superior to the former. Scripture itself does not support such a dichotomy. There was nothing wrong with the old covenant. As the author of Hebrews is attempting to show, concepts such as God's grace, the gospel, and salvation by faith are found in the old covenant as well as the new. As Paul elsewhere points out, the old covenant (the law) was our guardian, or tutor, to lead us to Christ (Galatians 3:24–25). All along it was pointing forward to its fulfillment in Christ.

That the old covenant did not teach a different, inferior means of salvation is evident from various considerations:

1) The author has said it was the gospel that was preached to Israel in the wilderness (4:2). Their failure to obtain the rest of God was not due to any defect in the message, but rather to their failure to believe. They lacked the required faith. The same is true of those under the new covenant.

2) The assumption that modern believers have an easier pathway to God is not supported by Hebrews or anywhere in scripture. Christians have the same responsibility as God's people in the Old Testament. The gospel has been proclaimed, and they are under the obligation to believe it and obey it. The author of Hebrews asks believers in Christ to do what believers had always done to be saved. If they continue in their faith, they will reach God's heavenly country; if not, they could fail to obtain eternal life. Hebrews never contrasts Old Testament believers with New Testament Christians. Rather, it always identifies the spiritual situations of God's people from the beginning of history to its end.

According to the author of Hebrews, the first covenant was the system of ceremonies that included animal sacrifices, the priesthood, and the temple. That first covenant could never truly take away sins (10:4), but was only a shadow (10:1) of good things to come—the salvation available through Jesus Christ, the once-for-all sacrifice for sins.

The first covenant had been broken, and the people had attempted to replace a genuine relationship with God with adherence to a system of rites and ceremonies. The same problem was taking place among the first-century Christians—and continues with certain believers today. The author of Hebrews knew it wasn't enough to be an Israelite, just as it wasn't enough to create a ceremonial practice of Christianity. What is necessary for salvation is a true, living, persevering faith in Christ, the eternal Priest who offers an infinite sacrifice and is able to make perfect those who draw near to God through Him.

Take It Home

The work of a priest is to intercede between a holy God and sinful people. The high priest was the one who entered, to the extent that it was humanly possible, the presence of God. So as you consider that Jesus is a high priest serving in heaven before God Himself, having offered His own life on your behalf, how does that image affect your relationship with God? Does it inspire more confidence? Gratitude? A stronger desire to live a life pleasing to Him?

HEBREWS 9:1–28
SACRIFICE AND SALVATION

Setting Up the Section

In the previous section the author had begun a discussion of the superiority of Christ's priestly work to that of the Levitical priests, but had included a brief parenthetical section about the difference between the broken Mosaic covenant and the "better covenant" that had replaced it. In this section he will return to his original thought and describe how the sacrificial blood of Christ would at last provide genuine and lasting cleansing for sin.

📄 9:1–15

LIMITATIONS OF THE LEVITICAL PRIESTHOOD

After portraying an image of Jesus performing as High Priest in a heavenly temple (8:1–6), the author returns to a consideration of the work of an earthly priest. The system of sacrificial worship in the Old Testament was solemn and somber but had limitations. Many of his readers were seriously considering giving up on the freedom offered by Jesus and returning to the Levitical priesthood and its ceremonies. Their mistaken view of what was required for salvation was no small problem.

So the author begins a close-up examination of the earthly priesthood. His readers seemed to associate more closely with the wilderness period of Israel's history, so he chose to describe the tabernacle rather than the temple. The work of the priests was essentially the same. The priesthood of Aaron and his descendants had been established along with the portable tabernacle where the Israelites worshiped as they traveled from Egypt to the Promised Land.

Another reason for referring to the tabernacle was likely the fact that he had already pointed out—those Israelites had heard the gospel presented to them but lacked the faith to believe and apply it. Consequently, they had failed to enter God's rest (4:1–2). If the first-century Jewish Christians didn't renew their faith in Christ, they were in danger of making the same mistake and turning the gospel into a theory of salvation by ritual performance.

The author reviews the basic setup of the tabernacle (9:1–4). The furnishings in the Holy Place and Most Holy Place were described in great detail in Exodus (chapters 35–40). However, most people never got to see those items because only the priests were allowed within those enclosed portions of the tabernacle (and later the temple).

Demystifying Hebrews

The author appears to have made a glaring contradiction with what had been prescribed in the Old Testament. He writes that the Most Holy Place contained the golden altar of incense, when in fact it belonged in the Holy Place (Exodus 30:1–6; Leviticus 16:17–18). However, his intent was most likely to show the inseparable connection between this particular altar with the critical work of the high priest who entered the Most Holy Place only once a year on the Day of Atonement (Hebrews 9:6–10). The close association between the altar of incense and ark of the covenant was no mistake and is identified this way even in the Old Testament (1 Kings 6:22).

It is here (Hebrews 9:4) that we discover the contents of the ark of the covenant. The ark held a gold jar of manna to commemorate the provision of God during the Israelites' wilderness journeys (Exodus 16:33), the stone tablets bearing the Ten Commandments, and Aaron's staff that had budded to verify his authority after being challenged by others (Numbers 17). All were symbols of God's unwavering faithfulness during trying times. And yet the first-century believers were wavering in *their* faithfulness.

The author has hardly begun his review of the tabernacle furnishings when he opts not to go into a lot of detail (Hebrews 9:5). There was little need for him to do so, because his Jewish readers would have been well familiar with the tabernacle and its setup.

Instead, he recalls the events of the Day of Atonement (9:6–8)—the most solemn day of the Hebrew year. The letter to the Hebrews was almost certainly written prior to the destruction of the temple in AD 70, so the observance of the Day of Atonement would still have been an annual ritual. It would have been just as significant for the Jewish Christians as for any Jews—perhaps more so. Just because a Jewish person placed faith in Jesus during this time didn't mean giving up all Jewish practices. We even read of Paul celebrating Jewish rites to show his solidarity with other Christians who continued to observe their traditional Jewish customs (Acts 21:17–26). The problem was not that Jewish Christians continued to participate in their traditional rituals; the problem was with holding to those rites while falling away from their faith in Christ.

The author addresses his readers' faulty perspective as he describes the restricted access to the Most Holy Place and the inability of the sacrifices themselves to bring the worshiper to God (Hebrews 9:8-10). This is not to suggest that believers in the ancient epoch did not have direct access to God or full forgiveness of their sins. Paul makes a strong argument for justification by faith when he shows that Abraham and David received God's forgiveness and drew near to God by virtue of Christ's work—their faith was in anticipation of what Christ would do, while a modern believer can look back and see in retrospect what Christ has done. At this point, however, the author diminishes the importance of the sacrifices' power to take away sin because he is refuting his listeners' viewpoint that those sacrifices, in themselves, could bring the worshiper to God. Without the final and ultimate sacrifice of Christ, those previous sacrifices were worthless.

Translations vary for what the author writes in verse 11. Some Greek manuscripts say Christ came as High Priest of the good things that are already here. Others refer to "the good things that are coming," as the author will say in 10:1. Both affirmations are true from the perspective of the theology of Hebrews, since the salvation Christ has accomplished is both "already" and "not yet." It has arrived through the death and resurrection of Christ but has yet to be completed in the future. A decision on which is the original reading is very difficult. The author's frequent reference to salvation as a future inheritance would favor the second view. But it is also true that a later copyist would have been more likely to change a reference to present salvation into one pointing to the future, rather than vice versa (the "harder reading" is usually the more original one).

The author's next statement, however, is quite clear. Jesus' death was no random tragedy or act of circumstance. It was an intentional and spiritual sacrifice. Although He died on a cross outside the walls of Jerusalem, His sacrifice is represented as having been offered directly to God in heaven (9:11-12). And the author is intentional about acknowledging all three persons of the Triune God in the work of securing the salvation of humankind (9:13-14).

Here again, the term *mediator* is used as a synonym for *guarantor* (9:15), as in 8:6. The author continues to allude to the promised eternal inheritance that no one has yet received, but ongoing faith in Christ ensures believers that they will one day be given everything God has promised.

9:16-28

THE REQUIREMENT OF BLOOD

The Greek word for *covenant* could mean "last will and testament," and the prior reference to "eternal inheritance" (9:15) also brings to mind the concept of a will (9:16-17). A person draws up a will however he or she wishes, and it doesn't take effect until after the death of the person. Similarly, God initiated all the biblical covenants—with Abraham, Moses, David, and the new covenant being described by the writer of Hebrews. People have nothing to offer God, so He is the originator. People *are* expected to respond, however.

The matter of death is also important. In the Levitical system, it was the death of the sacrificial animal—the shedding of blood—that effected God's forgiveness (9:19-22). When the covenant with Moses was confirmed, blood was required to be sprinkled in various places (Exodus 24:1-8).

Critical Observation

Some of the spiritual history referred to in Hebrews is not recorded in the Old Testament (such as the sprinkling of blood on the tabernacle [Hebrews 9:21]). Yet the assumption seems to be that the readers would be familiar with it. It might therefore be assumed that they had other sources of such information that are no longer available.

And ultimately, it was the shed blood of Christ that finalized the new covenant that God established with humankind. It was His death that made possible the inheritance believers had been promised.

This is the contrast the writer has been making all along. Christ's sacrifice was not a copy of the real one, and it was not offered in a temple that was a copy of the real one. Quite the opposite: The earthly priestly system was a copy of the genuine one. Christ's sacrifice was the blood of the perfect, divine substitute, and it was offered in the heavenly sanctuary (9:23–24).

The earthly priests had to enter the tabernacle again and again, year after year, to reenact the ceremony and offer more blood. Not so with Christ. Here again the author uses "once for all" (9:26) to describe Jesus' sacrifice, and he will elaborate more on it in the following section. (This verse is also frequently cited by Protestants to dispute the Roman Catholic claim that in the Mass, Christ continues to be sacrificed again and again.)

Similarly, the following verse (9:27) is among those used to refute the teachings of reincarnation. Hebrews states clearly that people die once and then face judgment.

The statement that Christ's appearance on earth was at the end of time (9:26) suggests that His sacrifice was the pivotal point of human history. Clearly, history wasn't brought to an immediate conclusion, because two thousand years have passed since then. Yet everything needed to bring human history to its fulfillment has now taken place, and only the Lord's return remains.

Notice once again the future-oriented perspective of Hebrews and the definition of salvation as something to be fulfilled at some future point (9:27–28). Salvation as a present possession appears often in the New Testament. Jesus announced the kingdom of God was "at hand" (Mark 1:15) and spoke of salvation as coming "today" to the house of Zacchaeus (Luke 19:9). Paul wrote that with Christ's coming, the culmination of the ages had arrived (1 Corinthians 10:11), and announced that salvation had come to the Gentiles (Romans 11:11). In the Gospel of John, Jesus defines eternal life as knowing God here and now (John 17:3). Many other biblical examples of such usage can be found. But the author of Hebrews places greater emphasis on future salvation—what believers will obtain in the world to come. To him, faith is a matter of persevering and patiently waiting for that time to arrive (9:28).

🏠

Take It Home

Because the author of Hebrews places such emphasis on the importance of developing a persevering faith while awaiting the return of Christ, it can be beneficial to examine oneself as to the ability to wait for something. Modern society places great importance on instant gratification of one's desires, immediate access to information, and so forth. Circumstances where waiting is expected grow fewer and fewer. And those that continue (traffic tie-ups, bank lines, and so on) are stereotypical pictures of great frustration. So how do you do when it comes to waiting for something? If you sense a degree of impatience, do you think that such a mentality drifts into your spiritual disciplines as well? (For example, do you ever attempt to hurry God along, urging Him to act sooner?)

HEBREWS 10:1–39

THE ONLY MEANINGFUL SACRIFICE

Setting Up the Section

The author has been elaborating on the significance of the person and work of Jesus Christ in the role of High Priest, especially in contrast to the work of the Levitical priests. In this section he continues and concludes that line of thought, reemphasizing some of what he has already said and adding new applications to the information he has been providing.

📖 **10:1–18**

AN ANNUAL REMINDER OF SIN VS. A CLEAN SLATE

One can be outside on a sunny day, able to see quite clearly while working among the shadows. But when the person steps into direct sunlight, the difference becomes evident. It is this image the author of Hebrews uses to contrast the old covenant with the new one. His reference to the law as a shadow of things to come (10:1) is not his first (8:5). And as he has pointed out previously, the law required that sacrifices be made year after year, again and again.

This time, however, he asks the logical question: If animal sacrifices were sufficient in themselves to remove the sins of the worshiper, why did they need to be continued (10:2)? This is the third of his it-seems-obvious questions. He had already asked why, if perfection could be obtained through the Levitical priesthood, scripture speaks of another priest yet to come (7:11, 17). Shortly later he asks his readers to consider the need for another covenant if there had been nothing wrong or incomplete with the first one (8:7). His question in 10:2 seems just as obvious.

The priests' sacrifices on behalf of the people were not an effective remedy for sin. In fact, the animal offerings were actually annual *reminders* of sin (10:3). The cleansing of the person was only temporary. It wasn't long before sin and guilt again returned to the lives of the worshipers. But those who fully understood the author's reasoning realized that this was not bad news. He isn't saying that the sacrifices were supposed to take away sin but were failing. Rather, what he is making clear is that the sacrifice of animals was never capable of removing sin and was never intended to be a permanent remedy (10:4).

His citation of Psalm 40:6–8 was taken from the Septuagint (10:5–7), and he understood it to be a reference to Jesus. The quotation is especially applicable at this point because it compares the Levitical sacrifices unfavorably with the work of Christ. The Old Testament writings contained numerous revelations that the Levitical rituals served no good purpose apart from the faith and obedience on the parts of the worshipers. The author has made the point before but needs to reiterate it in this context.

Critical Observation

Opinions differ as to whether certain sections of the Psalms should be considered "messianic." A messianic psalm is one that is a prophecy uniquely fulfilled in Christ. Many other psalms are called "royal" psalms. In their original context, these psalms concerned King David or the dynasty of Davidic kings that followed him. They apply to Jesus typologically rather than uniquely; that is, He is the ultimate and final fulfillment of a psalm that originally referred to others. The kingship of Israel, when properly understood and lived out, was symbolic of God's leadership. The king was supposed to be God's appointed person over the nation. David was the greatest model for this, and all the kings that followed him are compared favorably or unfavorably with him. Many psalms, therefore, speak of David's leadership, and these "royal" psalms point forward typologically to God's ideal leader and David's greater son—the Messiah, Jesus Christ. It is not surprising, then, that the early church members were able to see Christ throughout the Psalter.

The author is quite purposeful here (10:8) as he specifies sacrifices, offerings, burnt offerings, and sin offerings rather than grouping all sacrifices together. He indicates the entire sacrificial ritual of the Mosaic Law, aware that his readers were striving to use such methods to deal definitively with their sin before God. He has no quarrel with worshipers who offer sacrifices while acknowledging their trust in the Lord as the true Redeemer. He takes issue, however, with those who hoped that the act of sacrifice would itself cleanse them from guilt.

His perspective reflects God's outlook on sacrifices as well. The heartfelt offering made by a sincere worshiper was like a pleasing aroma that went up to God (Genesis 8:20–21). But when the offerings were made out of obligation or with an attitude of apathy, they produced no sweetness and had no effect (Amos 5:21–22).

The willingness of the first-century Christians to forsake the relationship aspect of their faith in order to practice a ceremonial religion instead was a clear step backward, which was another reason the author recalls Psalm 40:6-8 (Hebrews 10:5-7). It wasn't the animal sacrifice that God desired, but rather an offering of one's heart and faith.

The will of God (10:7, 9-10) that Jesus came into the world to fulfill was, of course, the offering of Himself for sinful humankind. And again, what need would there have been for such a sacrifice if the Levitical sacrifices had been adequate to take away sin and guilt? Christ established a better solution for the sin problem of the world, and in doing so He set aside the prior system (10:9).

As the author begins to wrap up this portion of his argument, he repeats a number of key points in summary. He again uses a favorite phrase to describe Jesus' sacrifice: once for all (10:10). He reminds his readers that the work of the Levitical priests was never really done, yet Jesus completed His work and sat down at the right hand of God the Father (10:11-12). He even repeats his scriptural basis (Jeremiah 31:31-34) to show that his viewpoint is not out of line with God's Word (Hebrews 8:8-12; 10:15-17).

His point is clear: Those who insisted on animal sacrifice as a means of salvation would never find God's favor. But those who place their faith in Jesus will experience the true salvation that God promises and Christ guarantees—a permanent and full forgiveness of sins.

📄 **10:19-39**

RESPONDING TO THE PRIESTHOOD OF CHRIST

After a lengthy section of exposition, the author turns to another segment of application before moving on to his next thought. The "Therefore" used in verse 19 is a clear indication that he desires his readers to do something about what he has been writing.

No amount of animal sacrifice would ever entitle a worshiper to enter the Most High Place, yet the blood of Jesus was sufficient to allow people to be in God's very presence (10:19-22). It is a renewed and cleansed person who is invited to stand before God. The invitation includes the criteria of sincerity, assurance of faith, and cleansing from a guilty conscience.

Yet once again, it is important not to read this new way (10:20) as contrast between the old way of the Mosaic Law and the new way of Christ and His apostles. It is a common interpretation, but one that violates the author's entire viewpoint. He insists that there had always been but one way, one gospel, and one salvation. The Old Testament saints drew near to God as New Testament Christians did—through faith (11:6).

The old way was not the way of Moses, but the way of death. The new way is the way that produces a new creation, brings a person into a new covenant with God, and provides a new life, heart, and name. The new covenant is not a matter of a better degree of access to God, but of real access, when before there was none. Faithful believers always had access to God, even before the institution of the rituals of the law. In and of themselves, those rites could make no one perfect and bring no one to God.

Demystifying Hebrews

The references to baptism in 10:19–21 (hearts sprinkled and bodies washed) are less about the ceremony of baptism than to what baptism signifies and seals. It is sometimes said that the Israelites were "baptized" as they walked through the Red Sea, although the experience certainly didn't save them or change them in any significant way. Yet the author's statements demonstrate how vividly baptism represented spiritual cleansing to the first generations of Christians in the early church.

And in response to this recent evidence he has presented, the author again presents his persistent theme: the necessity of holding unswervingly to one's faith, ever looking ahead to what has been promised (10:23). He also notes that Christianity was not intended to be a solitary religion; it is a fellowship of saints. Believers are *collectively* looking to the future. As they do, they are to spur one another to deeper love and positive actions (10:24) and to continue to encourage one another and meet together (10:25).

People who call themselves Christians yet show little or no interest in others do not realize what is at stake or how vulnerable they are to fatal errors of thought and life. The author's warning that follows is stark and grim. To choose to continue sinning has terrible results. Committing intentional sins effectively declares oneself an enemy of God (10:27) and tramples underfoot Jesus and everything He has done (10:29). Such people have only the judgment of God to look forward to (10:27), which, without the salvation provided by Jesus, is a dreadful thing (10:31). This warning is stronger than the one previously stated (6:4–8) and will be repeated yet again (12:25–29).

But the author isn't merely trying to scare his readers. He desperately wants to turn them around and prevent them from making a decision that will ultimately harm them. He is aware of the good they have done and reminds them of it (10:32–34). Their hope in everlasting life had motivated them to stand up for the gospel, even when they had to suffer as a result.

Shrinking back from one's faith has always been a problem, as the author points out by quoting from Habakkuk 2:3–4. He takes the liberty of transposing the two lines to place more emphasis on the warning (Hebrews 10:37–38). The quote also reinforces his point that the righteous have always lived by faith—both in the Old Testament system and after the completed work of Christ.

Even though his readers were flirting with spiritual danger, the author is confident that most of them will stand fast. He is being brutally honest with them and very frank about the potential consequences, yet he is convinced that they will continue to believe and be saved (10:39).

Take It Home

What gets more of a response out of you: the motivation of a positive reward, or the threat of the worst that could happen if you fail to act? Why do you think the author uses both positive reinforcement and no-holds-barred warnings of potential consequences?

HEBREWS 11:1–40
NOTEWORTHY FAITH

Faith: Two Definitions and Three Examples   11:1–7
Examples of Faith throughout Israel's History   11:8–40

Setting Up the Section

After a lengthy and somewhat complicated plea for his readers to strengthen their faith and hold out for all the wonderful things God had promised them, the writer now turns to their history as a means of persuasion. He provides example after example of people who demonstrated faith that led to positive results. They were all people who chose to be faithful despite never receiving what they had been promised—something he is asking his readers to do.

📄 11:1–7

FAITH: TWO DEFINITIONS AND THREE EXAMPLES

Hebrews 11 is one of the great chapters of the Bible. The writer has just completed a persuasive, detailed exhortation for his readers to continue their faith in Jesus Christ. Now he turns to a long list of flesh-and-blood examples of those who prevailed after trusting the Lord through thick and thin. He not only tells his readers how to live; he shows them through examples of those who succeeded.

He also provides two definitions for faith. The first is in verse 1: being sure of what we hope for and certain of what we do not see. This definition echoes Paul's observation that hope that is seen is no hope at all (Romans 8:24–25). The "people of old" mentioned in Hebrews 11:2 (NET) are the people who lived prior to the coming of Christ. Some of the examples go back considerably further than others.

The biblical narrative begins with creation, and perhaps the author thought he should start there as well (11:3). It was an event witnessed only by God, and it is a truth that can be known to humans only by divine revelation. Sometimes well-meaning people become so embroiled in debating the science of creation that they fail to emphasize God's involvement in the origins of humankind. According to the writer of Hebrews, that is no small breach of faith.

The author also provides insight into the Cain and Abel story (Genesis 4:1–16). Many people assume that God received Abel's offering because it involved a blood sacrifice and rejected Cain's because it did not. Yet both Hebrews and Genesis suggest that Cain's real sin was tokenism. Abel offered the very best of what he had, while Cain offered only a sampling when he should have given the firstfruits of his crop to God. It was a faulty attitude that led to the rejected offering.

The cryptic comment about Enoch in Genesis 5:24 is better explained here (Hebrews 11:5). Enoch walked with God and was no more because God took him away. The writer of Hebrews verifies that, indeed, Enoch did not face natural death as most everyone else does. (Another exception is Elijah, who isn't mentioned by name in this chapter but is likely one of the people referred to in 11:35 [1 Kings 17:17–24].)

The author's second definition of faith is in Hebrews 11:6: a belief that God exists and rewards those who diligently seek Him. Enoch was spared death because his faith pleased God, and Noah (and family) was spared because he believed God and acted on something he had not yet seen (11:7).

Critical Observation

It is interesting to pause at this point and review the first three examples on the author's list of heroes of the faith. Abel had faith and was murdered. Enoch had faith and did not die. Noah had faith, and everyone died except him. People are instructed to have faith, yet there are no promises or guarantees that they can predict or control the outcome of their lives as a result.

📄 11:8–40

EXAMPLES OF FAITH THROUGHOUT ISRAEL'S HISTORY

Throughout this letter the author has been urging his readers to keep looking ahead to what God has in store for them in the future. And perhaps no one personified such an attitude better than Abraham. His story dominates the section dealing with the patriarchs.

Several examples of Abraham's faith are mentioned. To begin with, he left his homeland solely because God promised to lead him somewhere else. He didn't even know where he was going! But when he arrived, and God promised him the land as an inheritance, he lived there as if it were his even though he never possessed it during his lifetime. (All he actually owned was a small burial plot.) He lived much of his life as a stranger in someone else's country (11:8–10).

A second example is God's promise to provide him with an heir. God waited until Abraham was one hundred years old, and Sarah ninety, to bless them with their son, Isaac, which explains the author's comment that Abraham was too old and as good as dead (11:11–12). By persevering in faith, Abraham saw God act even though it required a miracle for Him to do as He had promised.

A third example involves Abraham's willingness to offer Isaac back to God. There was an element of logic to his faith. After the miraculous birth of his son, Abraham believed that God would certainly honor His promise to provide numerous descendants through Isaac. So when it seemed as if God were going to have Isaac die, the only way the promise could come true would be for God to raise Isaac back to life again. No evidence exists that anyone had ever seen, or even conceived of, a bodily resurrection from the dead. Yet Abraham believed that was exactly what God would do if necessary to be true to His promise (11:17–19).

Tucked away within the stories of Abraham is an important observation that many people seem to miss. The author makes it clear that Abraham was looking for more than a piece of real estate when considering the promise of God. If he just wanted a tangible, physical country, he could have returned to his original homeland. Instead, Abraham was seeking a better, *heavenly* country (11:13–16). He was looking for the very same things that modern believers seek. That's what makes him such a noteworthy model. He never received the complete fulfillment of what he sought during his lifetime, and neither do New Testament believers. Faithful perseverance is just as important for first-century (and twenty-first-century) believers as it was for Abraham.

The examples from the other patriarchs are summed up in just a few sentences (11:20–22), but the readers of Hebrews would have been familiar with all of their stories from Genesis. The main point is that one generation after another died with the certainty that God would fulfill His promise and keep His Word.

Moses is another top figure in Israel's history. And as is the case in numerous instances, the faith of the parents is shown to be influential in the subsequent birth and life of an important spiritual figure (11:23). Of course, Moses didn't get off to such a good start. After being raised by Pharaoh's daughter, his murder of an Egyptian overseer declared his loyalty to the Israelites (Exodus 2:11–15). The short-lived pleasures of the Egyptian court were not to be compared with the eternal inheritance to be enjoyed by those who trust the Lord and do His will.

The author's striking reference to Moses' suffering disgrace for Christ's sake (Hebrews 11:26) is important. Clearly, *Christ* is not identified by name in Exodus, yet the writer of Hebrews informs his readers that it was, in fact, Jesus with whom Moses identified. He had already said that Jesus built the house in which Moses was a servant (3:1–6).

Moses' flight to Midian to escape Pharaoh is portrayed here (11:27), not as an act of desperation, but of discretion. He continued to persevere in his faith during his years in the wilderness. And when called to lead his people, his faith regularly inspired them—as they separated themselves from Pharaoh, as they walked across the dry path through the Red Sea and on to the Promised Land (11:28–29).

Faith was just as important after arriving in the Promised Land as it had been in getting there. Just two examples were provided: the falling of the walls of Jericho and the faith of Rahab, the woman who helped the Israelites and the only survivor (with her family) of the fall of Jericho (11:30–31). The first-century Jewish believers were most likely jolted a bit to be reminded of the faith of a Gentile prostitute—and God's vindication of her—as an example that they would do well to follow.

Even this late in the letter, the author still thinks of himself as speaking rather than writing (11:32). This is no typical New Testament epistle; it is a sermon.

The writer realizes he cannot provide much detail for all the historic examples of faith, and it's interesting to note which people and events he includes in his final summary. What follows (11:32–38) spans the period from the Judges (Gideon, Barak, Samson, Jephthah) to the kings (David) to the heroic resistance of the Maccabees.

Demystifying Hebrews

Some of the author's references to unnamed heroic figures are clear: Shutting the mouths of lions surely refers to the prophet Daniel; quenching the fury of flames points to Shadrach, Meshach, and Abednego; women receiving back their dead seems to indicate both Elijah and Elisha, who each brought a woman's son back to life. Other examples are less clear. For example, scripture says nothing of anyone being sawn in two (11:37), although tradition says that was the way Isaiah died.

The author's inclusion of people like Samson and Jephthah remind believers that living faith can coexist with great character flaws. (Their stories are told in Judges 10:6–16:31.) Faithful people need not be perfect people by any means.

And again, it is noted that faithfulness to God does not always have visible earthly rewards. In the closing verses of this section, the writer speaks of torture, imprisonment, stoning, and poverty. Yet those consequences of life weren't really important in light of the people's remarkable faithful commitment to God.

The final two verses of Hebrews 11 are often misunderstood. The author's clear statement is that the faithful people of Old Testament times did not receive what had been promised to them (11:39). The assumption many people make, then, is that modern believers *have* received it in full.

But the author is not here distinguishing between the situation of believers in the ancient epoch and believers in the new epoch. Rather, he uses the Old Testament heroes as examples because he wants modern believers to identify with their situations. Like those on his list, all believers continue to look to the future for a better country, a better resurrection. One of the last things the author will write is that all believers continue to look for the city that is to come (13:14). All who place their faith in God are to be made perfect *together*—old and new (11:40).

Take It Home

Responding in faith to believe what can't be seen is still essential to the Christian experience. We cannot see into the past to verify God's love for us before we were even born. We cannot see into heaven to ensure it's as good as scripture says. We cannot see the soul. We are still awaiting the return of Christ after two thousand years. None of these things are provable in a laboratory but must be taken on faith. Of all the examples provided in this chapter by the writer of Hebrews, which person(s) most inspire(s) you to continue to persevere in your faith? Why?

HEBREWS 12:1–29

THE LOVING DISCIPLINE OF GOD

Setting Up the Section

This section of Hebrews continues the author's thought from the previous section. The reason he has just listed so many exemplary people of faith is so his readers would be inspired to imitate them. Here he provides practical insight for what to expect as his listeners begin to recommit themselves to Christ and return to the faith they were being lured away from. He begins with a positive petition but adds a severe warning for anyone who continues to resist God.

📄 **12:1–13**

A POSITIVE APPEAL: THE BENEFITS OF SELF-DISCIPLINE

After providing such an abundant and commendable group of examples in Hebrews 11, the author tells his audience to imagine being surrounded by those heroes as they lived out their faith in the first-century world (12:1). The historical figures could be perceived as a cheering section that would give the modern believers a home-field advantage of sorts.

Those who are serious about persevering in faith are called to a sometimes-challenging level of self-discipline. The conditions of their spiritual "race" are similar to those of a literal marathon. The first step is to rid oneself of all unnecessary hindrances, and the second is to set a pace that will enable the runner to persevere to the finish line. It is also helpful to remain fixed on Jesus. He has already run the race and knows all about pain, shame, and trials, as well as the joy to be experienced by those who endure (12:2). He is proof that faith will be rewarded.

The first-century believers were starting to give up on their faith with very little effort to persevere. They hadn't come near to suffering to the extent that the faithful people in the past had done—much less to be able to compare to what Jesus had gone through on their behalf (12:3–4). As soon as their faith became a little difficult, they were ready to revert to old familiar ways but would forfeit a genuine relationship with Christ in exchange for mere rites and ceremonies if they did so.

As he was wont to do so frequently throughout his letter, the author pulls out an applicable scriptural passage, this time from Proverbs 3:11–12 (Hebrews 12:5–6). It is a reminder that some of the difficult things in life—godly discipline, rebuke, and even punishment—are in fact necessary and beneficial. Even the correction of God is always carried out in love.

But then, why let it get to the point where God needs to enforce the rules? The author exhorts his readers to take it upon themselves to discipline themselves while enduring hardship (12:7-8). No loving father would stand idly as a child endangered himself or settled for less that what was best for him. First, an involved father would attempt to persuade and encourage the child to excel. If that didn't work, the father would surely impose some means of discipline. And no father is more loving than God, so believers should expect Him to respond if they wander from the security of His will and calling. In fact, discipline is a sign that the person is part of God's family (12:7-9).

No one enjoys being disciplined by an authority figure. When God takes action to get a person's attention, it is not usually pleasant. But neither is it lasting. As soon as the person responds, the disciplinary action is quickly replaced by righteousness and peace (12:10-11).

📄 12:14-29

A WARNING FOR THOSE WHO REJECT DISCIPLINE

The author seems to realize that some people might need a stronger argument, so his encouragement to endure hardship and appreciate discipline turns into a warning for anyone who doesn't take his words to heart.

Peace within the Christian community is not something that occurs automatically or should be taken for granted. Believers are to make every effort to ensure they have a holy lifestyle on an individual basis and a peaceful coexistence with others in the church. Otherwise, people lose sight of God and the things that matter (12:14).

Each Christian must seriously pursue holiness and help other believers do the same. It is important to deal with sin as it arises, or it will quickly become a bitter root that spreads quickly to affect many (12:15).

Sexual immorality is one obvious entry point for sin into the community (12:16). But just as insidious is the attitude of Esau, who personified the Jewish believers beginning to desert the church. Esau had foolishly exchanged his future inheritance for the immediate gratification of his hunger. Similarly, the first-century believers were willing to trade what they had been promised for the readily available pleasures of the world. The writer reminds the church that when Esau realized what he had given up, he tearfully attempted to regain the blessing but was unable to do so (12:17). Esau's tears reflected remorse for the consequences of his actions but not a godly sorrow that leads to true repentance. The first-century believers would do well to consider their attitudes and actions before making a similar mistake.

Demystifying Hebrews

The juxtaposition of denouncing sexual immorality along with the godlessness of Esau may appear awkward. But there was a belief in Jewish tradition that Esau was a sexually immoral person, and the author may have been referring to that line of thought.

The description in verses 18-21 is of the Israelites at Mount Sinai as God gave the law to Moses. The first-century believers were beginning to romanticize life under the old covenant, and this was a reminder of the tremendous fear that had been a part of that system. Those who knew Christ had the benefit of the new covenant with a heavenly perspective rather than an earthly one, and had Jesus as their mediator rather than a human priest (12:22–24). They belonged to the assembly of the firstborn, meaning that they were saints set apart to God and privileged to receive all He offered. They were eligible for the very blessings Esau squandered.

Critical Observation

The same word translated "begged" in verse 19 is translated "refuse" in verse 25. Such an observation suggests that the Old Testament Israelites weren't so much awed by the presence of God as resistant to hearing His Word. Perhaps they didn't make the request (to hear no further Word spoken to them) out of reverence for God, but rather out of the craven fear that comes from unbelief. This view can be supported by their behavior with the golden calf less than a month later. In addition, the quotation by Moses (12:21) was not taken from the Exodus account on Sinai, but from Deuteronomy, where Moses was reflecting on the sin of the people with the golden calf. It seems he was not expressing fear about being in the presence of God, but about what would happen to Israel as a result of their unbelief and disobedience.

Yet those very privileges make the writer's warning even more significant. The notion that God is terrifying and distant in the ancient epoch but is more kind, loving, and accessible to His people after the life of Christ contradicts any number of statements in scripture. With all the additional information about the importance of Christ's sacrifice and ongoing priestly work on behalf of God's people, it is even more egregious now to ignore the Word of God than ever before (12:25–27).

Israel in the days of Moses experienced the grace of God and suffered when they forsook God in disbelief and apostasy—just as was true for believers in the first-century church. God's anger and judgment are still realities, as the author has already reminded his readers in 2:1–4; 6:4–8; 10:26–31, and elsewhere. He is making no attempt to side-step these serious considerations.

The writer has confidence in the genuineness of the faith of the Jewish believers but is not reluctant to warn them of the dire consequences of apostasy. He never strays far from his focus on the end of time and the salvation that comes in its fullness only when Christ returns. In the context of his current warning, he quotes from Haggai 2:6 to show both the surety and severity of God's power (Hebrews 12:26).

The image of heaven and earth being physically shaken is quickly contrasted with the one thing that is never in danger of being lost or disturbed—the kingdom of God (12:28–29). God is rightly described as a consuming fire (12:29), which is ample cause for those who disdain His work and His Word to fear. But for those who remain reverent and worship Him, the result is thanksgiving and ongoing expectation of all He has promised.

(⌂)

Take It Home

"Fear of the Lord" is a phrase common in the Old Testament and is found in the New Testament as well. It is usually defined more as "respect" than "fright," although people draw the line at different places. How would *you* define a proper fear of the Lord? Do you think most believers today have a proper fear in their spiritual relationships? If not, what do you think ought to be different?

HEBREWS 13:1–25

PRACTICAL APPLICATIONS FOR PERSEVERING FAITH

Setting Up the Section

This section appears to take an abrupt turn. It seems strange that the writer pauses in the delivery of his long sermon on the absolute necessity of having a persevering faith in Christ to list some specific duties that may not seem to bear directly on what he had previously written. Yet it is characteristic of the Bible to specify particular ways in which a believer should practice and work out the faith to which he or she has been summoned in any given passage. Hebrews is no different in this respect.

🖹 13:1–16

THE SACRIFICE OF PRAISE AND GOOD WORKS

There is a sense in which the message of Hebrews—the sermon portion—could be regarded as finished at 12:29. This closing section, then, becomes something of a postscript one might add to a personal letter, but not necessarily an oral sermon.

Much of this section is merely a clarification of the opening statement to persevere in brotherly love (13:1). Most people like to believe they exemplify love for humankind, yet those noble thoughts aren't borne out in everyday actions. It's one thing to "love" a group of unknown or unspecified people; it's quite another to consistently demonstrate love to the specific people one interacts with on a daily basis.

Most likely, the author's comments are in regard to believers, since he begins with the mandate to continue loving one another as brothers. So the strangers that the Hebrew Christians were to entertain (13:2) were probably fellow believers from other places. Whether fellow Christians or not, it is clear that believers should not confine Christian love only to those they know well.

Critical Observation

The author's reference to entertaining angels (13:2) is reminiscent of Abraham and the hospitality he offered three men who turned out to be the Lord and two angels (Genesis 18). Similar hospitality by Samson's parents toward a divine messenger was also rewarded (Judges 13). And there were other instances. The author's point is that hospitality shouldn't be perceived as an obligation or something done in order to receive a return on one's efforts. Rather, hospitality should be offered with the awareness that the host never knows what might be the result. Sometimes he or she will be very surprised.

Similarly, the command to visit prisoners (Hebrews 13:3) might be primarily in regard to believers who had been imprisoned on account of their faith. Underlying all these commands is the golden rule to treat others as one would like to be treated (Matthew 7:12). Brotherly love is more than verbal expressions of regret for others' situations; it requires putting oneself in the situation of another and responding the way one would desire to be treated.

Christian charity in the early church was not always convenient. Believers were bringing others into their homes and going out into their culture to meet others and respond to their needs. Of course, if their faith was beginning to flag (as the author has suggested on numerous occasions), their brotherly love for other Christians might be withering as well, necessitating this closing afterthought.

Certain statements in the New Testament reveal that the early church was troubled by certain ascetic teachers who strongly promoted celibacy—especially among spiritual leaders (1 Timothy 4:3). Other philosophies were much too lax regarding sexual relationships (1 Corinthians 5:1–2). In a single statement (Hebrews 13:4), the author of Hebrews first endorses marriage and then demands that it be given the respect that God intended for such a vital relationship.

He follows with a similar exhortation for a proper attitude toward money, extolling contentment over greed (13:5). God's presence in a believer's life should be the all-important priority that allows a better perspective on life (13:5–6). His readers served a God who would never forsake them and who was always there to help.

The leaders he refers to (13:7) were the first generation of people who had taken the gospel with them as they responded to all that Jesus had taught and had modeled (previously mentioned in 2:3). They had themselves become models of faith and worthy of imitation.

The frequently quoted statement in verse 8 is usually cited to affirm that amid all the uncertainties of this world, the character and promise of Jesus Christ are absolutely unshakable certainties. This is what the first-century believers would have taken it to mean. However, in the context of the New Testament in general, and the other arguments by the writer of Hebrews specifically, the statement is also an important theological confession. Christ is the same *yesterday* as today and forever. It is true that at a particular moment in time, the Son of God appeared as a person in the world to die and rise again, redeeming His people from their sin and guilt. Yet as eternal God, He had been involved with creation, with Abraham, with Moses, and throughout the history of Israel. The blessings and benefits of His redemption have been spread backward as well as forward in time.

Demystifying Hebrews

Any correct understanding of the theology of Hebrews—and scripture as a whole—must acknowledge that Christ did not begin to be His people's savior or object of their faith when He came into the world as the son of Mary. What He accomplished by His incarnation, suffering, obedience, death, and resurrection was the basis for the relationship He had held with His people since the days of Adam and Eve. Otherwise, it could not be said that Christ is the same yesterday, today, and forever (13:8).

As he nears the end of his letter, the writer once more lays out his grand theme (13:9–16). Again he warns his readers of the fatal error of attempting a compromise with Judaism. It wasn't that their rites and ceremonies were worthless (13:9), because numerous church leaders continued to observe them. But in a church that was increasingly Gentile, those old Jewish ways were of no value in providing salvation for anyone. In terms of justification before God, it was dangerous to require *anything* in addition to the work of Jesus Christ.

For believers coming from a Jewish background, the situation in the first-century church must have been quite difficult. They were being asked to downplay the importance of the temple and all its ceremonies. Christians had none of the visible accoutrements that signified a religion to most people of their time—including temples, altars, or priests. Their pagan neighbors thought they were atheists, and their Jewish peers would have scorned their faith without all the outward signs of religious ceremony. So the author of Hebrews reminds his readers that they did indeed have an altar, a priest, and a temple. . .in heaven (13:10–14).

Previously in Israel's history, God had once taken up station outside the camp (Exodus 33:7–11). Similarly, Jesus' sacrifice of Himself outside of Jerusalem rather than in the temple becomes an enacted parable expressing God's judgment on the people's unbelief. The exhortation is clear: It is wrong to continue to attempt to stay connected to the old ways. The time had come to make a clean and permanent break with the way of thinking that considered salvation a matter of the blood of bulls and goats.

Animal sacrifices were no longer necessary. Rather, believers were to offer God a sacrifice of praise (13:15–16)—a confession of His sufficiency and a commitment to do good works. The good deeds have nothing to do with acquiring salvation, but are in response to the forgiveness and righteousness God provides. The language of the Old Testament is brought into the New as yet another proof that the liturgical teaching of the Old Testament is still a valuable model for principles and practices of worship. Offering sacrifices to God is still completely appropriate, but the blood of animals is no longer necessary. Sacrifices of praise connect the worshiper's daily life with his or her worship of God. It is an offering far greater than some cash or a check dropped into the passed plate each Sunday.

PROPER SUBMISSION TO AUTHORITY

In retrospect, seeing how determinedly the author has tried to explain the dangers of reverting to old ways and rejecting Christ, and his persuasive argument to convince his readers to remain true to their faith, it seems safe to assume that the near-schism within the church had already created some tension between those members and the leaders. So the author issues a clear call for obedience to those who were watching over the spiritual integrity of the church (13:17). Their work was demanding enough without a lot of opposition from within.

One result of faithfulness and obedience is a clear conscience (13:18)—something that had become quite rare, and still is. Such a claim is certainly no boast of sinlessness. Rather, a clear conscience is produced by having integrity while establishing one's desires as a Christian and maintaining a fundamental commitment to live in keeping with those desires and high ideals. A clear conscience is achievable only when the believer gratefully receives God's grace and help on a regular basis.

The author has given his audience a lot to think about. His final benediction (13:20–25) is a beautiful summary and reminder that Jesus Christ's shed blood and resurrection are the foundation of God's work in saving people and enabling them to live holy lives. The distinction he makes here is what separates Christianity from all other faiths and philosophies: the conviction that Jesus Christ is *the* way, *the* truth, and *the* life.

Hebrews is one of the longer books of the New Testament, yet the writer considers it a short letter (13:22). He wants his readers to prayerfully consider what he has written, because he plans to follow up his letter with a personal visit (13:19, 23). His brief, final comments confirm the historical nature of the witness of the New Testament with references to real people, times, and places. Yet they do little more than tantalize. The New Testament says nothing else about Timothy's imprisonment (13:23). The author himself remains unknown. And it is impossible to determine whether he is writing *in* Italy, or writing *to* Italy from elsewhere and including the greetings of expatriate Italian believers who were with him (13:24).

Yet the message conveyed in Hebrews comes through clearly, emphatically, and repeatedly: It is essential to keep persevering in faith, looking ahead to the return of Christ, and anticipating the completion of salvation along with the complete rest and promise of God.

🏠

Take It Home

The writer of Hebrews was able to declare a clear conscience and a desire to live honorably in every way. Can you say the same thing? If not, what are the areas of life you need to work on? What might you need to confess or address in order to make your conscience entirely clear?

JAMES

INTRODUCTION TO JAMES

AUTHOR

James was the natural son of Joseph and Mary and the younger half brother of Jesus, since they shared a mother but not a father. James is always mentioned first in the lists of Jesus' siblings (Matthew 13:55; Mark 6:3), indicating that he was most likely the eldest of Jesus' half siblings. He is also mentioned in Acts 15:13; 21:18; 1 Corinthians 15:7; Galatians 1:19; 2:9, 12; James; and Jude.

Although he did not believe in Jesus during Jesus' early earthly ministry (John 7:5), after the Resurrection James became the leader of the Jerusalem church from AD 44–62. He presided over the Jerusalem Council (Acts 15), and he was considered by Paul to be a pillar of the church, alongside Peter and John (Galatians 2:9). According to Josephus, a first-century Jewish historian, the Jewish Sanhedrin sentenced James to a martyr's death in AD 62.

PURPOSE

The book of James is one of seven letters in the New Testament called the "general" or "catholic" Epistles (catholic meaning "universal") because it is addressed to a general Christian audience, rather than a specific congregation. Its tone is one of pastoral exhortation. More than fifty of the 108 verses in the letter are imperatives, but James writes his commands in a way that is filled with care and concern for his brothers. Because of its teaching flavor, many scholars consider James more of a sermon in written form than a letter.

OCCASION

James was a Jewish Christian writing to a Jewish Christian audience. The letter is replete with Old Testament teachings and allusions, but it is clear that James wrote from a distinctly Christian perspective and from the experience of one who had spent time with Jesus. The audience was a group of Christians who were experiencing persecution for their faith. James wrote to them to encourage them in the face of trials and to help them know how to stand firm in the faith.

THEMES

James's letter is a pragmatist's dream. He gives his wise instruction in a distinctive rubber-meets-the-road way that only a firsthand witness can. He shows that it is not good enough to have faith without works, but believers must do right acts for the right reasons. James's overall concern is consistency in practicing faith through obedient acts that produce results—truly hearing God equals obeying Him. Submitting to God means living out what one says he or she believes. Loving one's neighbors affects the tongue. Caring for the oppressed is a result of obedience to a just God. James calls for submission to Christ in genuine faith that works.

HISTORICAL CONTEXT

Many scholars date James as early as AD 45–48, which would make it perhaps the earlest New Testament epistle. There are several reasons for this conclusion:

1) The Council of Jerusalem took place about AD 50, yet it is not mentioned in James. In fact, there is no reference to a conflict about requirements for Gentile Christians, the well-known debate of the Council, so it is assumed that James's letter predates it.
2) Church leaders are called by Jewish terms, *teachers* and *elders*, rather than later church terms, *overseers* and *deacons*.
3) The synagogue is mentioned as the meeting place of Christians (2:2).
4) James addresses his letter only to Jewish Christians ("the twelve tribes scattered among the nations" James 1:1 TNIV), which suggests that the mission to the Gentiles had not yet begun. James may well be writing to the Jewish Christians who were dispersed from their homeland during the persecution described in Acts 8.

CONTRIBUTION TO THE BIBLE

James's instructions echo those found in the Old Testament, but they also repeat Jesus' own teachings. James is teaching new believers what it means to live out their faith in Christ as Lord. (The Greek word *pistis*, translated "faith," appears fifteen times in the letter.)

Critical Observation

There are several strong similarities between James's teachings and those of Jesus in His Sermon on the Mount. Besides pointing to the likelihood that James, the half brother of Jesus, is the author of this letter, they show that James's letter works to teach believers a specifically Christian worldview.

James 1:2	Matthew 5:10–12
James 1:4	Matthew 5:48
James 1:5	Matthew 7:7–12
James 1:22	Matthew 7:21–27
James 2:12–13	Matthew 6:14–15
James 3:11–13	Matthew 7:16–20
James 4:11–12	Matthew 7:1–5
James 5:1–3	Matthew 6:19–21
James 5:12	Matthew 5:33–37

OUTLINE

JAMES 1:1–27

FACING TRIALS AND LIVING OUT FAITH

Setting Up the Section

Early in the church, Christians were gaining their own identity apart from Jews, but this new identity came through much persecution. James urges the believers to persevere in the midst of trials in order to strengthen their faith so they may become righteous in their actions. The call in this chapter is to live with unconditional obedience to God.

📄 **1:1**

GREETINGS

The writer of the letter simply introduces himself as James. As the most prominent leader in the first-century church in Jerusalem, he would not have needed to explain who he was. Yet instead of clinging to his position, or even to his blood relationship with Jesus, James calls himself a servant. His authority doesn't come through his position as leader or apostle (Galatians 1:19), but as a servant of God and of the Lord Jesus Christ.

The use of the phrase "Lord Jesus Christ" should not be read lightly. James writes to Jewish Christians, and the use of *Lord* indicates deity. Adding *Christ* emphasizes Jesus' role as Messiah.

James addresses the letter to the twelve tribes "dispersed abroad" (NASB) or "scattered among the nations" (NIV). The phrase describes the *diaspora* (scattering), or dispersion of the Jews. While the literal twelve tribes of Israel (the descendants of Jacob's twelve sons) no longer could be traced, references to these tribes had come to represent a regathered Israel. James primarily uses the phrase to represent the Jewish Christians living outside of Palestine, perhaps due to persecution after the stoning of Stephen (Acts 8:1–3).

📄 **1:2–4**

THE WORK OF PERSEVERANCE

James addresses his "brothers and sisters" (Greek: *adelphoi*) fourteen times in his letter, setting the tone of both pastor and fellow believer. He moves quickly from a joyful greeting to a difficult command—be joyful in the midst of trials (1:2). James's message is clear: Even (or perhaps especially) while suffering, believers should live out their faith. The command echoes Jesus' words in Matthew 5:11–12.

James is writing to people facing trials because of their faith in Jesus. The label "all sorts of" (NET) indicates trials that occur as part of the common human experience, as well as those that come in the form of persecution or difficulties for those who follow Christ.

How can joy and trials coexist? The one experiencing the trial knows that the end result is a stronger character and faith. James says perseverance is developed through trials. God gives believers the ability to endure with patience, and the testing develops perseverance and a stronger faith. It's a lifestyle that leads to a mature and whole spiritual journey. The word *perfect* (1:4 NET) does not mean without fault, but "whole," "complete," or "mature."

📄 1:5–8

ASK AND BELIEVE

Wisdom is a key tool to knowing how to deal with difficult situations. In acknowledging the need for wisdom, James points believers toward God's grace (1:5). God's nature is to give generously and without reservation. His call to live by faith goes out to everyone.

God requires that people ask in faith, believing without doubt. One who doubts is someone with divided loyalties—between depending on self and depending on God. Doubting that God is good and loving makes a person unstable (like being tossed by a wave), which shows up not only in his or her prayers, but also in his or her life.

Demystifying James

Throughout his letter, James uses metaphors to create word pictures for his readers: wind-tossed waves (1:6); withering plants (1:10–11); self-inspection using a mirror (1:23); a dead body (2:26); bridling of a horse (3:3); turning a ship (3:4); forest fire (3:5–6); taming wild beasts (3:7); impossible fountain of fresh and salt water (3:11); impossible vine of grapes and figs (3:12); ephemeral mist (4:14); clothes consumed by moths (5:2); rust behaving like fire (5:3); farmers waiting for rain (5:7); rain watering the earth (5:18).

📄 1:9–11

HIGH AND LOW POSITIONS

James introduces the topic of wealth and materialism, something he expounds on throughout this letter. James is not encouraging poverty and cursing wealth. He is talking about perspective and where believers find their security.

Humble circumstances were a trial many first-century Jewish Christians faced. Many had been forced to leave their homes, losing their property and their source of income. Many possibly also faced self-inflicted poverty when they refused to participate in unethical business dealings. But believers should take pride in their high position because their worth and security are found in Christ.

When singling out the rich (1:10), James references those who abuse wealth and oppress the poor as a means to gain more. (This is something he explores further in chapter 4.) The rich will fade away because money does not bring security. James uses the same wildflower imagery that Jesus uses in Matthew 6:25–34. The rich place their stock in this world, but that beauty will be lost forever. Wealth births the illusion of power, which births the illusion of invincibility, but true security is found in God alone.

HOW TEMPTATION WORKS

Verse 12 serves as a summary statement of ground that James has already covered in chapter 1:

> "Blessed is a man (an echo of Jesus' Beatitudes and reason for joy in 1:2)
> who perseveres (1:3–4)
> under trial (1:2);
> for once he has been approved (stood the test, 1:3),
> he will receive the crown of life which the Lord has promised to those
> who love Him" (NASB).

James's words give believers the courage to face difficult choices and to choose the way of Christ.

James is clear about two things in verses 13–15:

1) Temptation does not come from God. This passage speaks to the holy character of God. God is not tempted by evil, and He is never the source of temptation.

2) Temptation is not sin. Responding inappropriately to temptation is sin, and unconfessed sin brings death. But simply being tempted is a different matter.

James tells his beloved brothers and sisters to stop being deceived (1:16). God is a loving God who wants to help His children, not harm them. God is not the source of temptation, but the source of every good and perfect gift. Not least of these gifts is salvation. God gives new life using the message of truth. This brings believers to a choice: Either sin can be the master (as implied in verses 12–16), or the Creator can be the master (as expected in verses 17–18). God is contrasted with the unstable believer here, because with Him there is no variation or shifting shadow. He is unchangeable, immutable, and unwavering. Believers can rest in knowing His character remains the same, and so His gifts will always be good.

Demystifying James

The Old Testament teaches Jews to bring their "first fruits," or the first and best of their harvests, as an offering to God (Exodus 34:22; Leviticus 23:9–10; Deuteronomy 26:9–11). In verse 18, James calls himself and the believers he writes to "a kind of first fruits among His creatures" (NASB) because they are a new creation, a new people, in Christ.

HEAR AND DO

James condemns dormant, unapplied knowledge. He calls for people to listen to a message of truth and then live a life consistent with that message, and he offers guidelines for what that might look like.

He introduces here the theme of controlling the tongue (he continues to emphasize this theme in chapter 3). The pressure that trials create may make believers quick to react in anger; James says to act differently. Verse 19 is a key verse for the letter because it points to a faith that results in changed behavior.

In verses 21–22, the "message" (NET) refers to Old Testament scripture, but James adds Jesus' teachings to this understanding of the message, which is why it is able to save souls. This is the same meaning James intends when he uses the phrase "perfect law of liberty" (1:25 NET). When James tells readers to hear ("understand," "know," "be aware") this message, he means more than a passive listening; he intends a proactive response on the part of his readers. To hear the Word but not allow it to change one's life is self-deception (see 1:16). If believers listen to the message without allowing the message to grow roots and effect change, they are only fooling themselves. Christians cannot claim new life in Christ while pursuing sin that brings death, and they cannot commit their lives to Christ while continuing selfish living. That is the same as looking in the mirror with no more than a passing glance (1:24–25). James calls for believers to look intently into the perfect law. He is repeating Jesus' teaching in Luke 11:28, which says that those who hear God's Word and obey it are blessed.

🔍

Critical Observation

The word translated "peers" in verse 25 (NET) carries the idea of examining something in order to understand it. The word is used of Peter, John, and Mary Magdalene (on three separate instances) looking into Jesus' empty tomb for the first time. In fact, for them, and for us, it involved stooping down to get a closer look. It is with that intensity that we should seek understanding from the scriptures.

James says one's religion is worthless if it is without fruit. As just one example, he says that if faith doesn't change the way a person speaks, then that believer deceives himself (1:26–27). James mentions three areas in which genuine faith will be demonstrated, though it is by no means an exhaustive list: the tongue (1:26), caring for the unfortunate (1:27), and purity (1:27). Pure faith is to care for those who are powerless and defenseless (a theme that is prevalent throughout the Old Testament) and to live in a way that is not influenced by the things of the world.

As believers in Christ, the question isn't *if* we will experience trials and hardship in life, but *when*. So we should prepare as best we can for when the time comes. The Bible is filled with examples of men and women who faced trials and responded in a variety of ways. In order to properly endure and weather hardships, we need to know what we believe—and to live it out. When trials come your way, will you persevere and grow in faith? Or will you resist what God wants to teach you?

JAMES 2:1–26

LOVE, FAITH, AND ACTION

Setting Up the Section

In the second chapter of his letter, James again calls for consistency in living out faith. The first half of this chapter deals with consistency in loving others regardless of their socioeconomic status; the second half calls for consistency in one's works and words.

This chapter in James has seemed troublesome to some. At issue is the relationship between faith and works. James agrees that one is saved by faith alone and not by works, but he emphasizes that genuine faith produces fruit. James concludes that workless faith—like faithless works—is unmeritorious before our heavenly Father.

📄 2:1–7

NO FAVORITISM

James introduces a hypothetical situation involving two people who receive two different responses: The one who appears rich receives preferential treatment; the one who appears poor is treated like a lesser-class citizen. James argues that everyone is worthy of preferential treatment, and those who provide it selectively are guilty before God. He concludes this section with a powerful passage that describes one of the clearest—and most difficult—ways to love one's neighbor as oneself: by extending mercy and forgiveness. Thus, James continues his emphasis on living out faith.

James does not have a problem with the rich, though taken out of context it may seem like it. He does, however, have a problem with financial gain that comes through exploitation. He states that the rich who are receiving favoritism are the same people who oppress and dishonor the poor and drag debtors off to jail. What's more, they are also slandering the name of Christ and persecuting Christians. James is not suggesting a *reversal* of discrimination by treating the poor well and the rich poorly; he is teaching a *removal* of discrimination. Preferential treatment has no place among Christians who serve a just God; to be holy as God is holy means treating others as God would treat them—with value and dignity.

James also shows that the fundamental advantage of the poor over the rich is their awareness of their powerlessness. This sentiment echoes James's own words (1:9-10) and echoes Jesus in Matthew 5:3—Blessed are the poor in spirit. Awareness of our own powerlessness is essential before we can trust Christ to do what people are unable to do: save themselves.

Demystifying James

The Jews had started a practice of seating those with privilege or position closer to the front where the Torah and other scripture were kept on scrolls, while other "less important" people were seated in the back. This practice continued in some Christian churches in the first century. Similar preferential treatment takes place in churches still today, but James says it should stop.

📄 2:8–13

LOVE YOUR NEIGHBOR

James writes about the "royal law," the same law he speaks of in 1:25. James refers to the Mosaic Law but adds the definer *royal* to reiterate the significance of the law of Christ, the King—the One who fulfilled the Old Testament law.

To love your neighbor as yourself is an Old Testament command (Leviticus 19:18), and it is an imperative that Jesus gave new meaning to in Matthew 19:19; Mark 12:31; and Luke 10:27. Where the Old Testament law gave instructions on how to treat other Jews, Jesus broadened the meaning of *neighbor* to include even enemies. Jesus' command to love God with all oneself and to love others as oneself is the underpinning of all other commandments. Favoritism, for example, is sin because it isn't in keeping with the law of love. Christians cannot claim to love God and then mistreat the people made in His image.

James argues that showing preferential treatment is no small infraction. He uses adultery and murder as extreme offenses against the royal law to love one's neighbor as oneself (2:11). James explains the law as a unit, so that when someone disobeys one part, he or she has disobeyed the entirety. The Mosaic Law showed the Israelites their need for God and their inability to live holy lives on their own. Jesus, on the other hand, issues a law that brings freedom (2:12). There is freedom from sin's penalty and freedom to serve God by speaking and acting in accordance with Christ's teachings.

James calls for mercy, not judgment (2:13). Mercy and forgiveness are supernatural activities. They are extreme demonstrations of loving our neighbor as ourselves.

DEAD FAITH

The Greek construction of James's rhetorical question at the opening of verse 14 implies a "no" answer. He is not saying that believers are not saved by grace through faith, but he is saying that no one finds salvation through a dead faith. James is clear: Faith must affect every area—and action—in a believer's life. In the same way that Jesus condemned a fruitless fig tree (Matthew 21:18-19), James says that faith without works is dead. *Claiming* to have faith is different from *actually having* faith, because genuine faith is evidenced by actions.

James does not advocate a works-based salvation, though. Workless faith and faithless works are equally dead. James's main concern is consistency of faith, evidenced by its fruit. True faith is active belief and active trust, which result in a changed life. The example in James 2:15-16 shows that action is necessary; otherwise words are empty. What use are words without obedience?

In verse 18, James argues for theological unity: faith *and* works. He essentially says faith without works is impossible. The way people see someone's faith is by how he or she lives it out.

THE SIGNIFICANCE OF FAITH AND DEEDS

James emphasizes the uselessness of faith without its accompanying deeds by saying that even the demons believe in the Triune God—but they do not obey (2:19). He points instead to the example of Abraham, who obeyed out of trust and belief in God. In the beginning of Abraham's narrative, he showed that he trusted God by leaving his home and traveling to an unknown destination (Genesis 12:1-7), and later Abraham showed his faith by preparing to sacrifice Isaac, his son. His faith was made complete (as opposed to a hollow faith) as a result of his obedience. Even the prostitute Rahab acted in obedience that resulted from trust and belief (Joshua 2:4-15; James 2:25). Christians can find narratives throughout the Old Testament of people demonstrating that genuine faith is always accompanied by obedient actions.

ⓞ

Critical Observation

Many scholars find James's theology of justification (2:24–25) problematic because it seems to contradict Paul's theology (Romans 4:1–3). However, understanding that the two apostles use the word *justification* in different ways shows that they are not in conflict. According to James, *justified* means believers are shown to be righteous for having lived a life of faithful obedience.

Paul refers to an initial justification in a moment of gaining righteousness by faith, where James means a final justification, or ultimate declaration of a person's righteousness. It wasn't Abraham's act that made him righteous, but Abraham had an active faith, and that made him accepted by God. Paul sees works as something people do to try to earn salvation, so that faith is an initial saving faith that then leads to obedience; James sees works as a natural outpouring of genuine faith. Paul makes it clear that believers enter the kingdom of God by faith, but James adds that once in the kingdom, obedience is necessary.

JAMES 3:1–18

WISE LIVING

Setting Up the Section

This passage includes James's famous teachings on the power of speech. He refers to the combination of thought and speech, and the precariously instantaneous connection between the two by talking about the power of the tongue.

James says the tongue is challenging to tame. It is as unmanageable as a raging fire and as harmful as poison. What's more, it is disproportionately influential: It bears tremendous weight for its relatively small mass. Usually this influence is negative, but when managed properly it can wage a significantly positive force.

📄 3:1–6

THE TONGUE'S POWER

James opens chapter 3 with an instruction that not many should become teachers. His address is to those who seek positions of leadership in the church, likely those who would presume to teach primarily for prestige. His warning is against pride, reminding those who think they should have authority to stay humble.

Critical Observation

There is a parallel of this teaching in Matthew 18:6, when Jesus warns against those who teach others to sin, and in Luke 12:42–48, when He states that much will be expected from those to whom much is given. The truth is not that teachers should be without fault of any kind, but they should be aware of their need to rely on God. James would have recognized the importance of the role of teachers, because Christianity was new. Teachers would be discipling new believers and providing instruction for the fledgling church.

James follows this specific address with general thoughts on living with wisdom and humility. He uses the tongue as an example of being able to control oneself and live wisely. The idea in this passage is that the tongue is seemingly unimpressive, yet it has disproportionate influence on the rest of the body. All are at risk to stumble, but teachers may be at greater risk for judgment because their tongues are their primary means for educating. The ability to control one's words is a mark of maturity for a believer.

To make his point, James uses a series of illustrations, or word pictures, that would have been familiar to his audience. James repeats the imagery of 1:26, suggesting that in the same way a small bit, or bridle, controls a large animal, the tongue can control a person (3:3). In the same way a small rudder directs a large ship at sea, so the tongue can set the course for a person's entire life. And just as a small spark can create a raging fire that would destroy a large forest, the tongue can corrupt the whole person (3:4–6).

Although the illustrations James uses are morally neutral, he is clear that the influence of the tongue is often negative. The image of fire that James uses conveys the potential of an uncontrolled tongue for widespread destruction, perhaps through gossip or slander or boasting. In the same way, the tongue's influence cannot be disconnected from the rest of a person. A person's words reflect his or her heart and character. In its ability to corrupt the whole body, the tongue can easily keep a believer from pure and undefiled religion (1:27).

📄 3:7–12

TAMING THE TONGUE

Verse 7 references the first chapter of Genesis, in which God gave humans the ability to rule over animals. The taming of animals is a common practice, but James shows that humans have trouble controlling their own tongues.

The tongue is restless, meaning it is unstable and its ability to do evil can never be fully restrained (3:8). It is important for believers to be aware of its power in order to avoid careless words. The tongue is also a deadly poison, which is a reference to Psalm 140:3. Words can harm those who speak them, poisoning them through bitterness, and they can harm those they are spoken to or about by wounding like a snake's bite.

By referring to God as "our Lord and Father" (3:9)—a phrase used nowhere else in the New Testament—James reminds his audience of their relationship to God. He also circles back to the topic of consistency by saying believers cannot use their words both to bless and to curse, referencing the creation account by pointing out the problem with believers using words to curse those who are made in the image of God. Because God values all people and has created them in His likeness, believers are to treat other people as though they have value, not use words to assault or destroy. In fact, Jesus said that believers are to bless those who curse them (Luke 6:28).

The tongue reflects what's in a person's heart (Luke 6:45). James uses the inconsistency in both praising and cursing to point to a deeper inconsistency in a person's heart. A pure spring does not produce both freshwater and salt water, and a fig tree does not yield olives (Matthew 7:16; James 3:11–12). In the same way, one who is pure in heart cannot produce words that curse. The idea of cursing is not something to be taken lightly. It is more than using "dirty" language or harsh words to express anger at a person. To curse someone is to proclaim them damned, or cut off eternally from God. To bless God and to curse someone that He made in His image are two actions that cannot go together.

Purity in speech is a natural outpouring of a genuine faith and nonnegotiable for the believer. This is a truth that James undoubtedly would have heard from Jesus when He said that people will have to give an account for every careless word they speak (Matthew 12:36–37).

Demystifying James

While *blessing someone's heart* may be a common colloquialism in some parts of modern culture, the kind of blessing that James wrote of would have had deep meaning to his readers. Blessing would have been part of the daily prayer life of Jews and, thus, Jewish Christians. One of the most common descriptions of God in Jewish literature is "The Holy One, blessed be He," and in the "Eighteen Benedictions," a Jewish liturgy, each ends with a blessing to God.

3:13–18

WISDOM VS. SELFISHNESS

James opens here with a question about wisdom (3:13). He comes back to this subject, tying this passage to the previous section on the tongue, by challenging those who think they are wise to show their wisdom through their actions. True wisdom produces humility, a result of understanding who a person is in relationship to God.

James again highlights the problem of inconsistency in the life of a believer. One who is truly wise cannot harbor bitterness and envy or selfish ambition (3:14). Twice he mentions envy and selfishness, two sides of the same coin. Envy comes when someone selfishly wants what another has, and this leads to strife, a point James makes further in chapter 4.

Wisdom is not something simply to *be*, but rather something to be demonstrated by conduct and actions. However, genuine faith is not something believers can accomplish on their own; wisdom for right living comes from God. And that wisdom from God results in actions that are pure, peaceable, gentle, accommodating, full of mercy, producing good fruit, impartial, and sincere. Worldly wisdom, on the other hand, seeks self-glory and personal gain (3:17–18).

"Wisdom from above"	"Wisdom from below"
Pure	Mixed motives
Peaceable	Ready for a fight
Gentle	Abrasive
Accommodating	Demanding
Full of mercy	Unforgiving
Full of good fruit	Full of bad fruit
Impartial	Prejudiced
Sincere	Manipulative

Take It Home

James is the "show me" book. If you think you are religious, show it by your speech. If you think you have faith, show it by your actions. If you think you have wisdom, show it by your conduct.

What are you showing the people around you? Are you longing for wisdom from above (Proverbs 16:16)? Are you asking the Lord for wisdom from above (James 1:5)? Are you demonstrating the wisdom from above (Colossians 1:9–10)?

JAMES 4:1–17

PUT IT IN PERSPECTIVE

Setting Up the Section

James is writing to believers who did not always find it easy to get along. There were pockets of disunity, arguments, disagreements, criticisms, and personal attacks taking place among these believers. His words go to the heart of the problem and address what is probably the most basic human sin: pride. He challenges believers to submit to God wholeheartedly.

📄 4:1–6

A CHOICE TO MAKE

Following his comments on wisdom that comes from above (3:15–17), James shows how false wisdom that stems from selfishness leads to fighting. The word translated *conflict* (NET) carries with it a violent image of a battle involving weapons. It's the image of an armed battle, a struggle for control. The word translated "quarrels" indicates an angry dispute without weapons.

Internal battles lead to external battles. The internal battle is a war of evil desires versus a Christian's soul, or the desire to follow selfish nature versus following God's will. The result of choosing these passions or desires (words that come from the same word that can be translated "hedonism") leads to external relational battles that take the form of verbal assaults.

When given over to selfish ambition or pleasures, division and fighting occur. In verse 2, James suggests that people fight because they don't get what they want. Here James also references Jesus' words in Matthew 5:21–22 when he says that the believers murder and envy.

James suggests the problem is a divided loyalty. Without turning to God and to His desires, even believers are left to their own selfish desires. He echoes the necessity for dependence on God by asking Him and trusting Him for needs (James 1:5). He adds that the believers either do not ask, or they ask with selfish motives, pointing again to the necessity for submission to God (4:3).

Take It Home

Can you name five people with whom you genuinely get along? Perhaps you have a great deal in common with them or you've shared many wonderful experiences together. Your friendship runs deep below the surface in these trusted relationships. Now think of five people with whom you do *not* get along (for some, this list is much easier to construct!). Perhaps you've had conflicts with them in the past or personality clashes. Do James's words about the reasons for conflicts lend any understanding to the conflicts that you experience? Do you find yourself engaging in the quarrel, or are you turning your selfish desires over to God?

In 4:4, James exchanges his comforting greeting "my brothers and sisters" (TNIV) with a serious "adulterous people" (NIV). The word he uses would have been understood by his Jewish audience as *adulteresses*, a female form of the verb denoting that they have been unfaithful to their groom, God. By using this powerful word, followed by the imagery of enmity with God and friendship with the world, James is accusing his readers of spiritual unfaithfulness. Echoing Jesus' statement in Matthew 6:24, James makes this strong point: Christians have to make a choice; they cannot love both God and the world's values.

Demystifying James

The concept of God as a groom and the idea of spiritual adultery would have been clear to James's Jewish-Christian audience. The Old Testament is filled with references to the Israelites' covenant with God using marriage images. When God's people turned to other gods, the prophet Jeremiah compared them to an unfaithful wife (Jeremiah 3:20). It is the theme of the entire book of Hosea, in which the prophet's marriage to an unfaithful prostitute mirrors the Israelites' turning away from God. Jesus, too, used this kind of language in calling the Jews who rejected Him an adulterous generation (Matthew 12:39).

James 4:5 opens with a rhetorical question in which James expects a "no" response. The verse is difficult to translate, as it is unclear whether *spirit* should be the subject or the object, and whether the human spirit or God's Spirit is in view. Two possibilities are (1) God, who placed His Spirit in us, is jealous for our loyalty or (2) the spirit that God placed in humans is prone to jealousy. In context with verse 4, it seems likely that verse 5 is a reminder that God is a jealous God (Exodus 20:4–5) and desires the unreserved love of His people.

James 4:6 is a reference to Proverbs 3:34. God gives grace to help believers love Him more when they humbly acknowledge their need for Him. Even if humans are, by nature, sinful and prone to turn from God, His grace is greater.

📄 **4:7–12**

SEEKING SUBMISSION

In verses 7–10, James presents a series of ten imperatives. He begins by calling believers to submit to God and ends with a repetitive echo to humble oneself before Him, both continued references to Proverbs 3:34.

Between these imperatives come commandments that offer an image of repentance. In each there is an act of will on the part of the believer, combined with an act of God's grace. To give into selfish desires is to yield to the devil. Through Christ there is no need for a human intermediary, so believers can draw near to God. To clean hands and make hearts pure reflects the connection between transforming both hearts and behavior; one without the other is insufficient (Psalm 24:4). James 4:9 is a call to take sin seriously and to seek heartfelt repentance. As God comes near, believers are painfully aware of their shortcomings and the need to depend fully on Him. After repentance, God lifts up believers, something they cannot do on their own.

Humility also leads to the exaltation of others (4:10). Those with a sense of arrogance and self-sufficiency feel worthy to judge. This is a necessary message for James's readers; he has already addressed those who think they are religious but are not, those who think they have faith but do not, and those who think they are wise but are not. Verse 11 continues an emphasis on relationships among believers. James highlights again the importance of controlling the tongue by refusing to harm another's reputation, something that would break a relationship.

God alone is the lawgiver and judge, and at the heart of His law is love (Mark 12:30–31; 4:11–12). James is concerned with condemning speech that divides believers and breaks the law of love. His question, "Who are you to judge?" follows Jesus' words in Matthew 7:1. It's a sharp question that gives believers a proper perspective of who they are in relationship to God.

📄 **4:13–17**

IF IT IS GOD'S WILL

James offers a powerful warning to those who think they are in control of their lives: Presumptuous living is dishonoring to God. It is not only those who confront God and demand equality with Him who offend Him, but those who often take matters into their own hands.

James's words here are likely addressed to those in business who travel (4:13). Because believers were dispersed, there would likely have been many who had to find a new way to make a living, and traveling to trade was a common first-century practice. The problem James points to is the tendency *not* to include God in the planning. It reinforces the message about submission by pointing to another example of self-sufficiency rather than dependence on God and a desire to do His will. This passage isn't about knowing the Lord's plan and deciding to make other plans; it is about making plans without consulting the Lord at all and taking the future for granted through self-made travel plans and business plans. James calls this arrogant boasting.

Verses 14–16 put believers in the proper place in the divine order, reminding readers that even a "long" life is but a mist. James is not suggesting literally adding the phrase "if it is the Lord's will" at the end of every sentence, but he is giving an imperative to acknowledge that no one should presume even to have the opportunity to travel, conduct business, and pursue success without recognizing that life itself is a gift from God. Self-sufficient boasting is evil because it disregards a need for God.

James ends this chapter with a reminder for believers to live out what they believe—to do the good they know to do (4:17).

Take It Home

"My life is my own." Few Christians would have the audacity to say those words, but most of us live as though we believe them. We often plan our days, our weeks, our months, and our years with a great deal of presumption. We sense that we are in control of our time and activities. In a results-oriented culture, we have convinced ourselves that the secret to success (in our education, career, family, future, and more) rests in the right formula. James reminds us that we are not in control of our lives. How seldom we acknowledge that our every breath is an unearned gift from God. Time is not our own, business is not our own, and the results of our efforts are not our own. In fact, our very lives are not our own (1 Corinthians 6:19–20). Let us live every day with that on our minds and make every plan contingent on, "If the Lord is willing."

JAMES 5:1-20

WEALTH, WAITING, AND PRAYER

Setting Up the Section

In the final chapter of his letter, James continues his focus on having an eternal perspective. He begins with a focus on material wealth and a warning to the rich who find their security in the here and now. Then he encourages believers to endure in the present by focusing on Christ. Finally, he points readers to trusting in God by praying earnestly.

📄 **5:1–6**

A WARNING TO THE RICH

In warning rich people, James is most likely addressing wealthy nonbelievers, possibly the oppressive landowners he references in 2:6. The misery that is coming is the future suffering on the Day of Judgment. It is important to note, though, that James does not single out everyone with wealth, but only the *unrighteous* rich.

Demystifying James

James's words to the rich reflect God's heart for the poor. His Jewish audience would have been familiar with the many passages in the Old Testament that direct God's people to care for the poor. They would also have been aware that those laws were often ignored. Old Testament prophets such as Amos and Isaiah spoke out against mistreating and ignoring the poor. James's use of the words *weep* and *wail* echoes the language of those prophets (5:1).

In verses 2–3, James highlights the impermanence of this world and all it has to offer and emphasizes the foolishness of placing security in earthly possessions. The word *riches* indicates more than just money and points to the many things that it can buy: clothing, gold and silver, treasures, indulgence in luxury, and crops and livestock.

Verse 2 echoes Jesus' words in Matthew 6:19–26. The warning is against hoarding wealth while others have need. Crops and hoarded food are rotting while others face hunger; excess clothing (a first-century luxury) is eaten by moths while the poor go without; and precious metals tarnish in storage instead of going to help others.

In addition to hoarding, James speaks out against people who acquire their possessions by unjust means. Workers lived day to day, so withholding pay might mean a laborer could not feed his family, possibly leading to eventual starvation (the murder referenced in 5:6).

The rich also often used the legal system to gain wealth and condemn the poor. God hears the cries of workers because He hates injustice and values human life.

James's words of warning in verse 5 again emphasize an eternal perspective. He condemns self-indulgence in the present, reminding the rich that their luxury comes at a greater price than they are willing to realize.

🏠

Take It Home

The Bible has a lot to say about money. We are encouraged to be financially responsible and have financial plans (Proverbs 21:20; 24:3–4; 27:23–27), but we are also encouraged to be generous givers (Proverbs 11:24–25; 21:13; 28:27; Luke 12:33–34). Jesus said, "What do you benefit if you gain the whole world but lose your own soul?" (Matthew 16:26 NLT). Are you hoarding, or are you saving wisely and giving to others in need? Do you allow others to use what you have? Are you aware of the needs of others within your community? Do you have an eternal perspective on wealth? Do you trust God for your future, or do you trust money for your future?

📄 5:7–12

PATIENT WAITING

James focuses again on his Christian "brothers and sisters" who are facing poverty and political oppression, exhorting them to be patient and strong in the midst of hardships. To suffering saints, James calmly whispers, "Wait."

This message continues to point to an eternal perspective. James uses the farmer as an example. The early, or spring, rains occur soon after a crop is planted; the late, or autumn, rains occur just before harvesting. It is not the rains that the farmer waits for, though, but the crop itself. He has planted, labored, and invested a great deal, and then he waits. Just as the farmer waits patiently for the fruit of his labor, so must Christians wait patiently for the return of the Lord.

It would be easy to grumble against or turn against other believers during difficult times, but James urges his brothers not to do this (5:9). James reminds believers that the Lord's coming is near. He is the judge standing right at the door, and He is coming to vindicate the righteous and to hold the unrighteous accountable.

The word translated here as "patience" occurs four times (5:7, 8, 10) in this letter. James uses the prophets as an example of exhibiting patience while suffering as a result of following God's will.

In verse 11, James returns to the notion of perseverance. Job's endurance is the same word used in 1:3–4, a strong perseverance in the face of trials.

Critical Observation

Job complained, but he remained faithful to his God. In the end he was blessed. James does not promise material blessings, but he does point to the promise of God's mercy and compassion. The word for "mercy" in 5:11 is only used elsewhere in Luke 6:36: "Be merciful, just as your Father is merciful" (NIV).

In verse 12, James warns briefly against oaths, echoing Jesus' words in Matthew 5:33–37. Oaths were commonly forfeited by legal loopholes, but Christians should be consistent in their honesty, avoiding even half-truths. Again, James emphasizes the weight of words and consistency. The oaths, in this context, were more than words. They were promises, often promises made before God within a worship setting.

📄 5:13–18

FAITHFUL PRAYER

In closing, James circles back to his opening call for prayer. He points to praying in all circumstances: whether facing trouble or in happy times (5:13). He also directs those who are sick to call church leaders to pray. Notice that it is not the faith of the sick person that James mentions, but the faith of those who pray. Presumably, the sick person exercises faith by calling the elders.

Demystifying James

Interpretations of 5:14–15 vary. One view that has strong support is the notion that the oil referenced (5:14) had medicinal properties in New Testament times, such that even Luke, a doctor, records its application in the parable of the Good Samaritan (Luke 10:30–37). The same Greek word for *oil* is used in Luke 10:34 and James 5:14. Another view is that the oil could have had a symbolic purpose of anointing, or setting someone apart, for God's care. Either way, the main focus is still prayer, emphasizing that it is God who does the healing.

James also dispels a widespread belief that illness is caused by a person's sin. He writes "if," indicating that sin could be a factor contributing to one's sickness, but it is not necessarily the cause (5:15). He also gives the opportunity to confess sins to one another, reminding believers of their call to bear one another's burdens (Galatians 6:2; James 5:16).

James calls the prayer of a righteous person effective and uses Elijah as his example (5:17). In 1 Kings 17:1, the prophet Elijah spoke with Ahab, the wicked king of Israel. As a sign of God against Ahab's wickedness, Elijah prophesied that there would be no rain for three years. Three years later, in 1 Kings 18:1, God sent him back to Ahab promising rain again. Elijah was not supernatural; he was human. What set him apart is that he prayed earnestly.

BACK FROM WANDERING

James 5:19 describes someone who wanders from the truth. This is the same word Jesus uses in Matthew 18:12, in reference to the one sheep who wanders away from the ninety-nine. The idea is more than just an unintentional straying from the path, but a complete departure from faith in Christ.

James does not want Christians to misunderstand prayer and think that the purpose is primarily for themselves. Instead, he emphasizes focusing on others' relationships with God in prayer. He offers a picture of Christian community in which members are accountable to one another. James's letter closes with a continued concern for living out a faith that works and also with concern for the welfare of others.

1 PETER

INTRODUCTION TO 1 PETER

First Peter is a great book to shatter any false expectations about who God is and what it means to serve God. It gives us realistic expectations about what this world has to offer and what perspective can help us through the tough times.

AUTHOR

This letter was written by Peter, one of Jesus' twelve disciples, who became a leader of the first-century Christian church. Because of the high quality of the Greek language used in this letter, some have doubted that Peter, the common fisherman, could have been the author. This argument is not strong, however. Greek was widely spoken in Galilee, and so Peter may well have been fluent in the language. Peter also notes at the end of the letter that he wrote "with the help of Silvanus" (or, Silas; 5:12). Like other New Testament writers (see Romans 16:22; Galatians 6:11), Peter may have dictated the letter to Silas, who improved the style and quality of the Greek.

OCCASION AND PURPOSE

Peter writes to believers living in Asia Minor to encourage them to faithfully endure persecution in light of the glorious salvation Christ has accomplished for them, and to see their suffering as a normal part of their service to God.

Peter addresses this letter to "God's elect, strangers in the world, scattered throughout Pontus, Galatia, Cappadocia, Asia, and Bithynia" (1:1)—the provinces of Asia Minor (present-day Turkey). The churches in this region were made up of both Jewish and Gentile Christians, though they were primarily Gentile. Several of Peter's statements suggest his audience is mostly Gentile (1:14; 2:10; 4:3-4)

Peter's purpose is stated in 1 Peter 5:12, where he tells the believers to stand firm in the true grace of God. The believers were experiencing a great deal of opposition and persecution because of their faith (1:6; 3:13-17; 4:12-19). Peter addresses them as "strangers" (NIV) or "exiles" (TNIV), living in a world that was growing increasingly hostile to Christians. By standing firm in the grace of God, they would be able to endure their "fiery ordeal" (4:12), knowing that there was a divine purpose behind their suffering and pain.

The letter was probably written in the early to mid AD 60s, shortly before or during the severe persecutions instigated by the Roman emperor Nero. Some have said that the context of the letter is the later empire-wide persecutions of Domitian (AD 81-96) or Trajan (AD 98-117). But in Peter, the persecutions seem to be local trials and hatred, not official state-sanctioned persecution. In later persecution, sacrifices to the emperors were a key issue. This does not appear to be the case in this letter. While Christianity had not yet been banned officially, there was a growing hatred for Christians, especially because (1) they lived differently, (2) they refused to worship pagan gods, and (3) they boldly preached the gospel. Peter says, "Do not be surprised" at such persecution, because you are resident aliens in this world (2 Corinthians 5:20; Philippians 3:20; 1 Peter 4:12).

Peter claims to be writing from "Babylon" (5:13), which is probably a cryptic reference to Rome. The reasons for this are as follows:

1) Literal Babylon on the Euphrates was almost deserted by New Testament times.
2) "Babylon" appears to be used as a symbolic title for Rome in Revelation 17:3–6, 9, 18, and in other literature.
3) Church tradition says nothing about Peter's travels to Babylon but tells us he went to Rome and was martyred there.
4) John Mark is with Peter when he writes this letter (5:13). Mark is mentioned with Paul during his first imprisonment in Rome (Colossians 4:10) and probably came to him there during his second imprisonment (2 Timothy 4:11).

THEMES

Major themes in 1 Peter include submission to authority, suffering because of faith in Christ, and shepherding the flock of believers. In these themes we are given the proper expectations that we are to have when we consider what it means to be a Christian.

OUTLINE

1 PETER 1:1–2:3

GOD'S PLAN FOR HUMANITY

Setting Up the Section

This letter begins with the traditional greeting, identifying Peter as an apostle of Jesus and stating to whom he is writing. The author is the same Peter who was called by Jesus to be an apostle and the same Peter who struggled with learning how to follow God by faith and not in the power of his own emotional zeal.

📖 1:1–12

OUR ENCOURAGEMENT

Verses 1–2 function as an introduction to a core foundation truth: God has called every believer to be conformed to the image of Jesus. As that is happening, the person being transformed will be different and, at times, persecuted.

Peter wrote to churches made up of both Jewish and Gentile Christians, who reside as "aliens" throughout the region of Asia Minor. All of the provinces mentioned in this verse are located in modern-day Turkey (1:1).

Critical Observation

Some say that this letter was written primarily to Jewish Christians, because Peter uses the word *scattered* or *dispersed* to describe the readers. This word often refers to the scattering of the Jews from their homeland to all parts of the Mediterranean region. Yet while Peter draws on this and many other terms that are elsewhere applied to Israel, here he uses them with reference to the church made up of both Jews and Gentiles—the new people of God in the present age. Statements in the letter concerning the believers' past life suggest that the majority of them were Gentiles (1:14; 2:10; 4:3–4).

The most important thing in this introduction is not the list of provinces, but the description of the people:

- Alien—someone living temporarily in a land that is not his or her home.
- Scattered—the people of the church who are dispersed throughout many regions.
- Chosen—selected with a purpose in mind.

Notice that the calling Peter refers to in verse 1 was a result of the foreknowledge of God, by the sanctifying work of the Spirit (1:2). The word *foreknowledge* does not mean that God knows the future as much as He actually *makes* the future.

The calling of God was accomplished by the sanctifying work of the Spirit. The word *sanctifying* denotes an ongoing process. The Spirit of God is constantly working in the lives of believers, conforming them to the image of Jesus.

There is a final part of this process. This calling and sanctifying are done so that people might obey Jesus and be cleansed by His blood. In this world we take our marching orders from Jesus Christ.

Demystifying 1 Peter

After Moses first read the Law of God, the Israelites affirmed that they wanted to obey. Moses sprinkled some blood onto them (Exodus 24:3–8). The picture here in 1 Peter 1:1–2 is that these Old Testament Jews had the blood of the covenant applied to them, and so they became children of the covenant.

Verses 3–12 reveal the future, present, and past encouragement of God's salvation. Verse 3 begins with praise. The word that is translated "praise," or "blessed," is the same word from which we get the word *eulogy*. It means to tell how great someone is.

Critical Observation

The fact that Peter refers to God as Jesus' Father is significant (1:3). A first-century Jew would have said that Abraham was his father. This meant that he shared in the blessed nature of Abraham. In saying God was Jesus' Father, Peter's wording stresses the fact that Jesus shared in God's nature.

Mercy is the part of God's nature that causes Him to look with compassion upon the most vile of sinners (1:3). As His great act of mercy, God caused us to be born again into a living hope.

In verse 4, Peter highlights the point of inheritance. The believer's hope is not simply in going to heaven, but in the inheritance awaiting there. It is imperishable; it cannot be destroyed. It is also undefiled, or sin-free. It is unimpaired by time and will not lose its value. Finally, it is unconditionally reserved—guarded. The point of a reservation is that it's guaranteed.

Believers not only have a protected inheritance, they are also a protected people (1:5). If God is going to protect their inheritance in heaven, then He is going to protect them on earth as well.

The salvation that will be revealed in the last time is the final part of salvation (1:5). In this case, the term *salvation* is referring not to the moment of salvation, but to the final salvation, when believers go to live with God forever. Until that day comes, believers are protected by God.

Peter's point is that in this world there will be trials, but these trials are momentary in the grand view of eternity (1:6). The faith displayed during trials will be the faith that will one day deliver us from this world.

Peter states that his readers greatly rejoice (1:6). These believers really did believe that waiting for them was the eternal inheritance that is far beyond any possession on earth. Whenever we think of this inheritance, our hearts can shout for joy, because what we have in heaven has been given to us out of the great love and mercy of God.

Verse 7 is a continuation of the truth of verse 6. Suffering is a tool in the hands of God to bring about revelation and glory. Jesus is our example. Through Him, God revealed His character and put His glory on display.

The overall point in verses 8–9 is that believers love Christ and believe in Christ even though they have never seen Him. As a result, they will gain the salvation from the world that they are living in.

Take It Home

Peter describes trials as lasting a little while (1:6). This is a perspective check. When you are in a trial, it seems as if that is all there is. Yet, compared to heaven, any trial is only momentary. What do you do while you are suffering? Keep your eyes on the person and work of Christ. Believe in what He has done for you and trust in the provision that He has given you that will be revealed in the last days.

To show the great value of the understanding that we have because of Christ, Peter makes four points of comparison between the prophets and his readers.

1) The prophets longed to know what we know (1:10).
2) The message of the prophets was consistent with the New Testament message: grace as well as judgment.
3) Not only did the prophets talk of God's grace, but the Spirit of Christ was within them (see 2 Peter 1:21).
4) The words of the prophets serve us more than them (1 Peter 1:12). When you read their message in light of the Cross, then you can see the fullness of what is written without the hindrances that the prophets had when they wrote it.

At the end of verse 12, we read that this gospel that has been preached to us is a message that the angels longed to look into. The word *long* means to crave. It is the idea of looking at something with deep desire.

1:13–21

OUR BATTLE

In verse 13, Peter uses the metaphor of someone "girding his loins" to illustrate working in the field or preparing for battle. In the first century, if a man wanted to work in the field, he would gather up his robe and pull it between his legs, then tie it around his waist. This would get the excess cloth out of the way so he could work. Similarly, a warrior would gather up his clothes and tuck them into his waist to fight more effectively.

In comparison, our minds are filled with excess thoughts about the cares of the world. The thoughts of our minds must be disciplined so that the focus is on the things of heaven.

Next, Peter tells his readers to keep sober. This is the idea of self-control, not having a mind or a heart that is inebriated with the love of this world.

As part of being obedient children, Peter tells his readers not to be conformed to their former desires. Now they need a different way of living—holiness (1:14–15). As believers, they are to reflect the very character of God in everything they do.

Critical Observation

Peter does not mean that your holiness will be equal to the perfect holiness of God. Instead, the holiness of God is now to be the pattern for how you are to react and respond to the world. Instead of justifying sinful responses to the world, we now place the holiness of God as the standard for our responses.

In verse 16, Peter quotes Leviticus 11:44, a verse from the passage outlining the dietary laws that set the Jews apart from the cultures around them. Today, we are not bound by these laws. Instead, we are bound by our commitment to imitate the character of Jesus.

In the context of verse 17, the word *judge* holds more the meaning of evaluation than condemnation. Peter is saying you cannot fool God; He knows how you are living. Since that is true, live reverently.

Critical Observation

One of the themes throughout Peter's letter is the idea that Christians are citizens of heaven, not earth. Verse 17 supports that theme by referring to Christians as strangers, or exiles, here on earth.

Verses 17 and 18 work together. In 17 we are told that God sees us for who we really are, and in verse 18 we are told that after seeing us exactly as we are, He redeems us, or purchases us out of slavery. Rather than mere human effort, redemption came in the form of Jesus' blood. In verse 19, Peter draws on the image of the Old Testament sacrificial system, offering animal sacrifices to maintain peace with God. The animals offered were to be without any blemish (Leviticus 3:1)—in His perfection, Jesus fit the bill.

Because of that redemption, we have faith and hope in God (1 Peter 1:20–21). We can partake of this faith and hope because of the resurrection of Jesus. The Resurrection was the sign that God was satisfied and redemption was complete.

🕮 **1:22–2:3**

THE FIRST ACTION OF FAITH—LOVE

In verses 13–21, Peter gives us the theological application—to keep our minds fixed on our inheritance, our behavior centered on being set apart from the world, and our hearts focused on who God really is and what He has done for us.

Critical Observation

Verse 22 serves as a transition to how our salvation should change our response to others. Peter makes a connection for us between obedience to the truth and the purification of our souls. This purification doesn't mean we no longer sin, but God cleans up our souls and makes us responsive to Himself.

How does this purification occur? We obey the truth. The word *obey* carries the idea of listening to something and then responding to it. Peter is saying that since we believed the message of the gospel and confessed that Jesus is who He said He is, that belief caused our souls to be purified. And the result? Love for one another.

The love mentioned here is unhypocritical love, a genuine, self-sacrificing affection that comes from the care and love that we have received from God. Our purification is not just about what we do and do not do; it is about why we do and do not do those things.

Verse 23 is a point that Peter has made already in this letter (1:4, 7, 18)—our salvation finds its source in the eternal Word of God. To illustrate his point, Peter quotes from Isaiah 40:6–8 (1 Peter 1:24–25). Just before this quote appears in Isaiah, God had declared judgment on Israel for rejecting Him, but in chapter 40, His message of salvation emerges.

The first few verses of chapter 2 are a continuation of the close of chapter 1. Peter says we must put aside our natural responses to the world around us. The sins listed here are the enemies of love. When we see what God has done for us, it should humble us and cause us to reach out to others with the same love. We should crave this new way of life.

Understand in verse 3 the importance of us tasting the kindness of the Lord. If one has not been touched by the grace of God, then he or she has not experienced the love Peter is saying we should offer to others.

1 PETER 2:4-25

GOD'S PLAN FOR THE CHURCH

Setting Up the Section

How do we live out this purification of our souls? How do we identify ourselves to the world around us? How do we relate to the governmental structure of our cultures? These are the kinds of questions Peter addresses in this passage.

📄 2:4–10

UNIFIED FOR A REASON

When we come to Christ, we come to Him not just as our Savior but as our living stone (2:4). This image of the cornerstone carries the idea of Jesus being the centerpiece of our lives. According to Peter, the world has rejected Jesus in this role.

Peter calls Jesus a *living* stone, just as he wrote about a *living* hope in 1:3 and the *living* Word in 1:23. Why? Because the cornerstone aspect of Christ's ministry was set in place by His resurrection. Since we get our lives from Him, we have identities that come from this relationship (2:5)—we, too, are living stones, pieces of a building that God is making. This speaks to our corporate identity.

We are called to be a spiritual house for a holy priesthood. A major role of the priest in the Old Testament was to offer sacrifices on behalf of the people. Our role is to offer spiritual sacrifices (2:5). Within the context of the church, when we love each other, care for each other, and sacrifice for each other, we are offering up to God the sacrifice and praise that He finds acceptable.

The truth that Peter has just proclaimed about Christ is not new. Both Isaiah 28:16 and Psalm 118:22 teach that there will be those who reject this stone and those who accept this stone (2:6-7). Rejection can lead to injury. To stumble means to get hurt (2:8).

Some have interpreted Peter's words at the end of verse 8 about destiny to mean that those who don't believe have been doomed to that fate. That is not necessarily so. It could just as easily mean that their rejection has been predicted by God because God said that there would be those who disobey. Their doom is simply the consequences of their choices.

Unlike those set apart for doom, the believer is different. The terms Peter mentions in verse 9 are terms that were used to describe the Jews in the Old Testament. Peter uses them to describe all Christian believers, even Gentiles.

We have an identity, mission, useful purpose, and a new lifestyle because of Christ. We are to tell the world about how God transitioned us from death to life and that this transition is a transition of love, mercy, kindness, and compassion. This is what we are to proclaim to the world.

INTEGRITY THAT LEADS TO PRAISE

Notice how Peter describes the believers: aliens and strangers (2:11 NIV). The word *alien* means a person who is not a part of the life of society in which they are presently living. In a spiritual sense, this is true of Christians.

The term *stranger* carries the idea of temporarily dwelling in a land with no intention of putting down roots. Certainly, this is how Christians look at their sojourn on earth.

The way Christians should be distinct is through their lifestyles—distancing themselves from sinful desires as an ongoing part of their spiritual walk. It is the role of the believer to maintain excellent behavior so that any false accusations of wrongdoing would ring completely untrue (2:12). While Christians may often be attacked because of their faith, their own behavior should not provide any fuel for the attack. We are not commanded to be free of accusation, but free of being guilty of accusations.

God wants our good deeds to be revealed so that our lives point the way to Jesus. The day Jesus appears is the Day of Judgment. On that day, the character of Jesus Christ will be the standard that will judge the world (2:12).

In this life, the attitude and action of the believer is to submit to human authorities. Our distinctness from our culture does not mean we are above the structure of the world. The government is sent by God to punish evil and praise good behavior, to keep lawlessness from ruling (2:14).

🔍

Critical Observation

Keep in mind which government Peter called these people to submit to—a government that did not respect Christianity, that supported practices that were offensive to God, and in months and years to come would begin a persecution of the church that would last for hundreds of years. Nevertheless, Peter wants them to see God's design for government and to submit for the Lord's sake. Of course there is a line in the sand—if the authority calls us to disobey God then we must reject their rule. But, short of that circumstance, we are not above the day-to-day ruling of the law.

Our response to government is designed not only to serve God but also to silence those who accuse us of wrongdoing (2:15). The *ignorance* mentioned includes the false understanding of Christianity spread among outsiders. The submission of the believers to government was meant to prove these foolish people wrong.

In verse 16, Peter tells the believers that they are free to be God's slaves rather than slaves of sin—they are free to uphold the laws of the state as God's servants. Peter wants his readers to see themselves as free from sin, free from having to please men, and free from the bondage of their own lusts *so that* they can be free to serve God and do what He says.

It is dangerous to see Christian freedom as a means to serve yourself. Your freedom in Christ is not a cover for evil. Freedom is the opportunity to be set free from the bondage of serving self in order to love and serve others (2:17).

Verse 17 is a summary statement of the preceding passage (1:17–2:16). When we use our freedom in this manner, God receives the praise and the world sees the power of the gospel at work on earth.

SUBMISSION AND SACRIFICE

According to most historians, almost half the population in the Roman Empire was some type of slave or servant. This was a key to the economic stability of the Roman Empire.

The slaves mentioned in verse 18 were not the slaves in the field but, instead, the domestic helpers. This is why many preachers apply this passage to employees.

If a servant became a Christian and began to put his or her priority on heavenly things, he or she could be tempted to take the job lightly or to judge an unbelieving master rather than submitting to him. Peter's point is that salvation in Christ is not an excuse to ignore the order and structure of the world. Peter is telling his readers to show respect and honor to their masters because the masters have authority—whether the master uses that authority well or not (2:19–20).

Why would we want to serve well in difficult situations? Because God is pleased when we obey Him, no matter the circumstances (2:19). This truth offers comfort to the servants who have to live in horrible conditions. They are in the favor of God as they suffer.

Peter clarifies the kind of suffering he is referring to by asking, "If you receive punishment for your own wrongdoing, is that suffering?" (2:20). Suffering because you were a bad servant does not offer the hope of God's blessing. Yet God rewards those who persevere through difficult times, revealing Jesus' attitude.

The first thing that we have to see is the relationship between suffering and Christianity. Verse 21 is a statement that the believers have been called for the purpose of suffering. God designed our salvation to include a life of serving others in this world. We do this by following Jesus' example.

In verse 22, Peter offers a snapshot of the service of Jesus in the face of suffering by quoting Isaiah 53:9, part of the description of the suffering Messiah. Jesus never sinned, yet He was accused and punished severely. In the midst of that, Jesus did not respond in kind (1 Peter 2:23). He was verbally and physically abused, yet He did not threaten abuse in return.

Jesus did this by continuing (not once, but over and over again) to *entrust* Himself into God's care. This *entrusting* is like walking onto an airplane and entrusting your well-being to the pilots and mechanics who manage the plane.

Jesus believed in and trusted in the fact that God would make all things right in the end. He was content to let the Father take care of the situation. In the meantime, Jesus continued to serve those who sought to kill Him—He prayed for their forgiveness and died to preserve their souls (2:24). He is the perfect example of someone who trusted God enough to continue to serve no matter the circumstances.

We were a straying people who wandered away from God (2:25). Jesus suffered for us so that we might be able to be pulled toward God and live for Him and live out His sacrificial love for this world.

⌂

Take It Home

God calls us to serve people and to love them, finding our place in the structure of the world. We do this because it pleases God, not because people deserve it. When we serve, we do so knowing that even though there might be injustice now, perfect justice will come one day in the future. It is not our job to dispense justice right now.

How can we better entrust our well-being into the hands of God when we face injustice?

1 PETER 3:1–22

GOD'S PLAN FOR THE CHRISTIAN

Setting Up the Section

What do the roles of husbands and wives reveal to the world about God? Peter reminds his readers not just of the acts of submission, but of the heart of submission— to God first, then within our relationships.

📄 **3:1–7**

THE HEART OF SUBMISSION

Peter begins this section by connecting these thoughts about marriage to the overall thought that he introduced in 2:11–12: Christians should live in every area so that they are showing the world the character of Jesus. He uses the phrase "In the same way. . ." (3:1).

Demystifying 1 Peter

There have been some who have tried to say that Peter uses the word *likewise* to draw a connection between verse 1 of chapter 3 with the last few verses of chapter 2. They teach that Peter's point is that just as Jesus suffered in life, so the wife must also be ready to suffer in marriage. But this is not Peter's point. His "likewise" is not referring to Christ's suffering (2:21–25), but to the life of reverence to God and submission to one another (introduced in 2:18) that Christians are intended to live.

Notice that the wives are to submit to their *own* husbands (3:1). Verse 1 is not a description of how all women are to relate to all men; thus you must read the remainder of this section within that context.

Submit means to honor the position of another. Its opposite would be to resist. Just as chapter 2 reveals how a Christian should act so that others will be affected, so here Peter reveals that as a woman functions within her marriage in this way, others will be influenced by her example.

Submission is an attitude that leads to an action; this is why Peter describes the attitude rather than the action of submission. In verse 2, Peter identifies the marks of a submissive life: a sincere and pure heart along with reverent behavior.

Just as the servants of chapter 2 were to honor their authorities out of obedience to God, here the wife is to honor her husband's position out of love for God. When the wife shows kindness and devotion to her husband, she is showing the world the kindness that God has shown her.

In the first century, often the women were the first to hear the gospel message, because the men were busy working. Yet, in that culture it was the custom for the women to adopt the faith of their husbands. Peter says in verses 1–2 that the evangelism of a woman's husband doesn't take place by her convincing her husband, but by her showing her husband the love and service of Christ.

In verses 3–4, Peter is not condemning a woman for dressing nicely, but he makes the point that women should not make their looks the sum total of their worth. He contrasts those who focus on external beauty with those who focus on the inner attitude. This part of the woman's life must be adorned with a gentle and quiet spirit.

In verse 4, Peter is describing a woman who doesn't have the need to push her beliefs on someone else. A quiet spirit is one that does not need to dominate a room.

Peter's idea here is not a new thought. Ancient women were known by this behavior (3:5–6). Sarah honored Abraham by referring to him respectfully according to the customs of the age in which she lived (see Genesis 18:12). Women today are the spiritual descendants of Sarah when they follow her example, unafraid of the vulnerability it might cost them to put someone else before themselves.

Next, Peter addresses husbands. They are to live with their wives in an understanding manner (3:7). The phrase translated "considerate" (NIV) or "in an understanding way" (NASB), can also be translated "according to knowledge." The husband is to be a student of his wife so that he can care for her and love her according to who she is specifically.

Peter's mention of the wife as the "weaker" partner is not an insult toward women or a statement of the moral or spiritual superiority of men (as some throughout church history have claimed). "Weaker" refers instead to the fact that women are generally physically weaker than men, and so a husband's role is to ensure that his wife is protected, cared for, and treated with dignity and honor. Another possibility, however, is that "weaker" means "less-empowered" and refers to the low social status of women in the first century. In this case, Paul would be saying that husbands should show honor and respect for their wives in contrast to a society that often demeans and abuses women.

The husband is to treat his wife with honor so that all will see that he values her, respects her as a precious gift from God. This honoring is not based on merit, but on the fact that she is a fellow heir of the grace of God.

The way that a man treats his wife has a direct effect upon his spiritual life. Love and respect your wife, Peter says, so that "nothing will hinder your prayers." We cannot have a harmonious relationship with God unless we are reconciled to others.

GRACE IN A GRACELESS AGE

Verse 8 opens with "Finally," and this signifies that Peter is coming to a logical conclusion. Thus far Peter has communicated in several different ways that the way we live in this world communicates the gospel—or not. In verse 8, he reviews the attitudes and the actions that must govern our relationships within the body of Jesus Christ.

All of these terms in verses 8–9 are products of grace. The assumption of this passage is that we are all in relationships with people who do not deserve kindness, yet God tells us to be kind and to treat people with compassion. When we do, we are giving them grace.

Humility is the only trait listed here that deals with self. It enables all the rest of the traits. It is impossible to show any of the above-mentioned qualities if one is not humble in the way that one lives.

Peter continues his conclusion with a "not" rather than a "do"—do not return evil for evil (3:9). Revenge is forbidden, but Peter goes further—we are called to give a blessing instead. A blessing is a gift that is meant to be an encouragement or investment into others; it's something that will benefit them.

Why offer blessing instead of revenge? Because God wants us to demonstrate the same grace we have received to the world around us. In verse 10, Peter illustrates this point by quoting Psalm 34:12–16, a psalm in which David realizes he does not need to retaliate against his enemies. The point of this psalm is to tell the believers that they must understand their responsibility in being committed to showing the world love rather than evil.

Demystifying 1 Peter

David wrote Psalm 34 when he ran for his life from King Saul and tried to find refuge in the city of Gath. There He escaped detection by pretending to be out of his mind.

In the midst of all this, David realized that those who understood how to live in this world are the ones who understand that peace and holiness are the keys to living.

SUFFERING PROPERLY

This passage picks up again Peter's central theme of enduring suffering for the cause of Christ.

Peter's first point is that we have been given protection from God. The heart of his question in verse 13 is a redefinition of being hurt. Yes, someone can harm us physically, but our souls are protected. Even if there is an earthly cost to serving and suffering, the cost cannot take away our salvation.

Peter's second point is that we are to remember God's promise (2:14). In the midst of suffering for doing what is right, we can think that God is hurting us because things are going badly. The point is that we have the very promise of God that He will see us through the suffering and repair us from any damage we might endure to bring us to the promise of heaven.

Verse 15 should be seen in connection with verse 14. The focus of our emotional and mental energy should not be fear or intimidation, but instead ensuring that Jesus has the center place in our lives. When we do this, our lives will stand out. It would be difficult to live for God in this manner and not have people ask why we are not afraid and why we keep serving those who hate us. We need to be ready to give an account of the hope that is in us. Then we will have the opportunity to share our hope in a spirit of gentleness and reverence. Our attitude must reflect the heart of the message that we are sharing.

Finally, we must have a conscience that is pure (3:16). To maintain that clear conscience, we must live with integrity in this world so any accusations against us won't stick.

Verse 17 reminds us that suffering that occurs as a result of seeking to serve Christ and love others is a tool in the hand of God. With this in mind, Peter points us to the suffering of Jesus as an example of the way God uses suffering (3:18). The first product of Jesus' suffering is redemption. The second is deliverance.

In verses 18–20, Peter explains that through His suffering, Jesus preached to spirits in prison who were disobedient during the days of Noah.

Some believe that these verses refer to the fact that Jesus went to Hades when He died and preached the gospel. Others believe the spirits in prison are the fallen angels (see also 2 Peter 2:4–10; Jude 6), and that Jesus' preaching was not to announce redemption, but to assert that all angels, authorities, and powers are in submission to Him and nothing can stop the deliverance that He provides. A third view is that Christ preached long ago to the people of Noah's day (either through Noah or in a preincarnate state), and that these people ("spirits") are now in Hades.

Whatever the case, Jesus' suffering brought about salvation. Just as Noah's family passed through the water and were delivered, when we pass through the waters of baptism and all that they symbolize, we are delivered (3:21). Peter rids his readers of any magical ideas about baptism by making it plain that the efficacy of baptism does not lie in the outward symbolism but in the inner response of faith toward God.

Jesus' suffering brought about redemption, deliverance, and salvation to a new life and a glory that is to be revealed. Suffering is a powerful tool in the hands of a mighty God.

Take It Home

First Peter 3:17 reminds us that if suffering comes, God has allowed it to come, but it is better to be in the will of God and to suffer than to be out of the will of God. We must stay the course and not use suffering as a signal to disengage from doing what is right. If you are in a situation where doing what is right will cause you to suffer, stay the course, because your suffering is not in vain. It is not a waste in your life; it is actually a part of God's will.

1 PETER 4:1–19

GOD'S PLAN FOR SUFFERING

Setting Up the Section

Peter's goal in both of his letters is to prepare the church to endure suffering. He does this by showing the reader the intrinsic value of suffering. When we suffer in this world, God uses it to mold us into the image of Christ. The reality of being molded into the image of Christ is a very important part of our formation. In this section, Peter wants us to see how suffering is used to achieve this goal.

📄 **4:1–6**

GOD USES SUFFERING IN HOLINESS

When verse 1 says a person is "done with sin" (NIV), this does not mean that person has become perfect. Peter is saying that the moment we share in God's understanding of suffering and we step up and begin to suffer for what is right, we are no longer pursuing the flesh but instead are living for the will of God.

The point that Peter is making in verses 1–2 is that suffering is the road or the path that God uses to deal with our sin. For this reason, suffering is not a liability in our lives; it is actually an asset.

There are two reasons we should embrace suffering:

1) The time is over for us to live for the lusts of the flesh. Every sin mentioned in verse 3 is a sin of personal pleasure. When people seek to live for righteousness in this world, they stop living simply for their own pleasure. They live, instead, aware that they will give an account to Jesus for their lives (4:2–5).

2) There is a reward that will follow—eternal life. Redemption cannot be stopped even if the world treats us like the scum of the earth (4:6).

Critical Observation

The term *Gentile* (NASB) is used in verse 3 to refer to not simply a non-Jew, but to a person who lives a godless life. That is why some translations simply say non-Christian (NET). In the Old Testament, the nations that surrounded Israel lived lives filled with pagan practices. These pagan practices could be summarized in the term *Gentile*. When Peter uses this term, he is saying that when people live solely for their own passions and flesh, they are not living as God's people.

GOD USES SUFFERING IN RELATIONSHIPS

With verse 7, Peter takes a turn in his teaching about suffering to show us how this news of judgment and mercy is meant to make us purposeful in our relationship with God. The first phrase—"the culmination of all things is near" (NET)—sets the stage for verses 7–11.

The word *end* denotes specifically the end of a plan—in this case, the plan of redemption. In light of all that will happen at the end of that plan, Peter mentions four priorities that should be a part of the Christian's life:

1) Prayer (4:7). Since God is bringing the world to His end, we must not stop communing with God. *Sound judgment* was a word used to describe people who were able to process the world through the eyes of God. The *sobriety* Peter writes of means to be vigilant and alert—the opposite of drunk.

2) Love (4:8). Notice the way verse 8 begins: "Above all." Love is the paramount quality that must shine in the life of the Christian, because it is at the core of the nature of God. We are to love deeply, with increasing energy. The language here is a picture of stretching forward with intense energy and effort—this is how God has loved us. This love that covers sins is not permissiveness toward sin, but more of a *dealing with* sin.

3) Hospitality (4:9). Hospitality means to show love to strangers—a high value in Ancient Near Eastern society (as it is today in the Middle East). In Peter's day there were many traveling preachers who moved from town to town and may have arrived unannounced at a believer's home. Since many Christians were very poor, having another mouth to feed would have been an enormous personal sacrifice. Hospitality is not just an act; it is a selfless act.

4) God's glory (4:10–11). We are to use the gifts that God has given us in the power of God so that God will receive the glory. Every believer has been given a special gift to use to serve others (4:10). Verse 11 places the gifts into two major categories: speakers and servants.

If we live according to these priorities, we can serve others, even in difficulty, because we believe that God is moving the world to His end and we can live for His glory rather than protecting our own glory.

GOD USES SUFFERING IN ENDURANCE

The remainder of chapter 4 focuses on persevering through suffering.

The reality is that suffering is intrinsic to living for Jesus (4:12). With this in mind, Peter tells us not to be surprised at the trials that come. We have to expect to have people resist us when we seek to do what the scriptures declare.

His description of trials is sometimes translated "fiery ordeals," which means "the burning experiences." The image is an ongoing trial that causes deep grief and heartache. Keep in mind, though, that fire not only burns, but it also purifies.

Some versions of the Bible use the word *testing* rather than *suffering* in verse 12. When a trial comes and a person has to endure it and keep his or her eyes on Jesus, that trial becomes a test for that person's own faith (see 1:6-7).

The result of our trials is revealed in 4:13. We all will suffer in many different degrees, and as we do, we must rejoice, because we are suffering more and more like Jesus. Since we know that Jesus is coming back and that His righteousness will rule, we can rejoice that we are in the effort with Him.

In verses 14-16, we find a message of hope—suffering in this world is not a sign of sin but a sign of blessing. The insults Peter mentions in verse 14 refer to being insulted for the name of Christ. The blessing has at its root the idea of being refreshed.

The idea behind God and the Spirit of glory resting on you is that God is applying His glory to your life so that when you suffer, His glory is being seen. In other words, your suffering is a usable moment in the hands of God, for God is allowing His glory to rest upon you. We can be agents of God's glory—in other words, the expression of His character and nature.

Verse 15 serves as criteria for the kind of suffering that blessing accompanies. Some suffering is a result of people doing evil, and as a result they suffer the consequences. Yet, if one suffers for the sake of Christ, then they must be encouraged.

The term *Christian*, which Peter uses in verse 16, was coined in the first century to refer to those who desired to follow Jesus. Verses 17 and 18 seem complex, but they make a simple point—if the trials the church is undergoing are severe, how much more severe will be the judgment awaiting the wicked. The word *judgment* used with reference to the church means the ongoing process of dealing with sin rather than the final pronouncement of judgment.

To make this point even clearer, Peter includes a loose quote from Proverbs 11:31 (1 Peter 4:18). In this proverb, the author states that the road to eternal life is not an easy road. If our life is hard as God's children, picture what life will be like for those without that life-giving relationship.

As we suffer, we must consciously place our souls into the hands of a faithful Creator (4:19). Peter uses the term *Creator* to remind us that we are going to get a new life in the next world, and that life is far better than the best that this world can offer.

⌂

Take It Home

To apply this passage, keep the following points in mind:

1) Seek to understand how God uses suffering.

2) Within the depths of your heart, believe that God truly is going to use your suffering.

3) Daily submit your mind, will, and emotions into the hands of God, trusting in the protection that He offers.

4) Press on standing for Christ no matter the resistance you face.

If you keep these four things in mind, you will endure the trials that come.

1 PETER 5:1–14

LIVING SOBERLY

Setting Up the Section

Peter begins this final section of his letter talking about the role of the elders with n the church. He also offers believers some final instructions concerning living in this world. By reminding the elders of their importance, mission, and future, Peter reveals the proper environment necessary for the flock to live soberly in a world that is drunk on its own pleasure and self-deception.

📄 **5:1–4**

ELDERS LIVING SOBERLY IN AN INTOXICATED WORLD

Prior to this passage, Peter said judgment is coming first to the household of God (4:19). In light of this, Peter presents the role of the elders within the context of the trials the flock will face.

Peter appeals first as a fellow elder (5:1). Peter is not only a fellow elder, but he is also a witness of the sufferings of Christ. This may mean that Peter literally saw Jesus suffer or that Peter has experienced the kind of suffering that is associated with serving Jesus. Both are true, and both give Peter credibility.

Peter also claims himself a partaker of the glory that is to be revealed. Just as we have to face the fact of our suffering, we also have the guarantee of the day of our vindication, the day that our reward is made ours, and the day that we inherit the kingdom of God fully.

The command to the elders is simple—shepherd God's flock. It is key to understand that God owns the sheep. This means that the elders are to care for the congregation in the manner the owner wants them to be cared for—the elders are overseers, not owners. God describes the elders this way:

- Willing (5:2). This is the idea of a mule that is being dragged by its owner. A proper elder does not have to be dragged into his work.
- Not greedy, but eager (5:2). The work is not merely a means to creating a certain lifestyle.
- Humble (5:3). To lord yourself over someone means that you will exact control or dominate that person.

Critical Observation

The position of a shepherd in the first century was not a position of honor. The fact that Peter uses this term to describe leaders brings an automatic idea of humility and service.

Rather than using the position to *tell* people what to do, the elder should *show* them an example of what to do (5:3). They must show the flock how they are to live. When Jesus comes, there will be a reward for all those who served the way Peter has described in verses 2–3. This reward is an unfading crown of glory; their work will not go unrecognized by God (5:4).

Peter identifies Jesus as the Chief Shepherd (5:4), a reminder that the elders are not the leaders of the church, but the stewards of it. When the Chief Shepherd appears, which refers to the second coming of Jesus, for all eternity the true elders of the church will have honor in heaven.

5:5–14

THE FLOCK LIVING SOBERLY IN AN INTOXICATED WORLD

Beginning in verse 5, Peter switches gears from the leadership of the elders to the response of the flock. The church needs to respond properly to the leadership of the church, each other, and ultimately to God.

First, the younger men. Verse 5 says "likewise" or "in the same way." Peter has given instructions to the elders as to how they should operate in the midst of suffering; in the same way, the young men are going to get their instruction.

The word often translated "young men" could be used to mean younger men, young men, or young women—someone who is younger than someone else. Therefore, even though many translations put the word *men* in the text, the clearest rendering is a young person.

The point is that the younger must submit to the older. In order for the elders to do their job, those who are under their care must receive and accept their shepherding. Peter offers his reasoning for this humility by loosely quoting Proverbs 3:34. God puts His hand out to the one who shows no humility and holds him back. In other words, God puts obstructions in the path of proud men so that they will have conflict until they humble themselves.

As Peter makes his case that humility is needed toward leaders and each other, then it stands to reason that we must be humble in our relationship with God (1 Peter 5:6–7). The mighty hand of God is an image that is used frequently in the Bible. Here it refers to what Peter stated in 4:17—namely, that God is at work in the lives of His children, using the trials of the world to deal with their sin. To humble yourself under the mighty hand of God is to acknowledge the trial that you are in and to surrender to the process rather than running away. We are to be ready to have God give us the honor in His time rather than fighting for it in our own schedule.

We humble ourselves under God's hand by casting all our anxiety upon Him (5:7). The anxiety that Peter is talking about is the feeling of pain, worry, and pressure that we feel when we are surrounded by people who cause us to suffer for our faith. If we cast our anxieties upon God, we are looking to God to provide the strength and hope that is necessary to do what is right in the midst of a trial.

In verses 8–9, Peter addresses evil. Even though God uses the evil in our lives, we must be careful as to how we are going to endure this evil—do we become anxious, or entrust ourselves to God? First, we need a sober spirit—characterized by self-control. Without that, we overreact and become derailed by suffering. We are also to be on the alert—to be ready for trials, to even anticipate them.

It is Satan who is seeking to overwhelm us when we live for God. Observe the way that the devil is described in verse 8.

1) The Adversary. An opponent who is out to get you, particularly in a legal scenario. This is someone who wants to take something away from you.
2) The Devil. This name means "slanderer." The devil is one who seeks to slander, lie, and deceive people.
3) A Lion. Consider a roaring lion. When a lion roars, it does so in order to dominate. A lion runs after a herd of animals to cause the animals to run until the weak and feeble fall behind. Satan does the same with the church.

In verse 9, Peter says to resist Satan. This is a picture of an army holding its ground so that the enemy cannot take possession of that land. We must stand firm in the same manner—but our faith is the valuable real estate we are protecting. Part of our power to resist is the knowledge that we are not alone in our suffering.

In verses 10–11, Peter offers one more piece of helpful advice—look to the future. This suffering is for a short time compared to eternity. This is such great news that Peter ends in words of praise (5:11).

Peter concludes this letter by saying that he sent this letter through Silvanus, a formal name for Silas who traveled with Paul (see Acts 15:35–41). Silas was faithful, which means that he, too, endured the trials of following Jesus.

While Babylon was a historic place in the history of Israel (see 2 Kings 24:8–17), Peter's reference to *Babylon* here in verse 13 was probably a reference to Rome. Some have suggested it may have been an attempt on Peter's part to conceal his own location. Others simply see it as an apt parallel given the antagonistic role of Rome at the time.

Mark, also mentioned in verse 13, was probably John Mark, a leader in the first century church who traveled with Paul and Barnabas (Acts 13:5, 13; 15:37–39; Colossians 4:10; 2 Timothy 4:11).

The kiss described in verse 14 was a typical greeting among Christians of this day.

Peter's final wish for peace would have echoed the hopes of all those who faced persecution. His teachings in this letter, if followed, provide a path to finding that peace in the midst of the turmoil of life.

Take It Home

Peter and Silas testified that this letter represents the true grace of God. In other words, this is the truth, so hold on to it.

1) We have been saved by God.

2) An inheritance is waiting for us.

3) In this world we will face trials for following Jesus.

4) In the midst of these trials, love the brethren.

5) In the midst of the trials, serve your enemies.

6) God uses the trials to work out our sin.

7) Walk humbly with God and people.

8) Walk soberly in this world prepared for suffering.

9) Remember that God will restore you before you go to heaven.

Let us remember these words so that we can walk faithfully with Christ.

2 PETER

INTRODUCTION TO 2 PETER

Late in the first century, the church was in an increasingly vulnerable position. In addition to the continuing threat of persecution, false teachers began to arise and distort the true message. At the same time, the apostles, who had established the church and provided its early leadership, were beginning to die off or suffer martyrdom. This letter deals with the problems that come when false teachers sneak into the Christian fold with the goal of turning people away from the message of Christ and enticing them with their own false message grounded in worldly wisdom and human achievement.

AUTHOR

The writer of this book identifies himself as Peter, one of Jesus' twelve disciples. Many have questioned Peter's authorship because of language differences with 1 Peter, among other things. However, conservative scholars still agree that while acknowledging the difficulties of the letter's authorship, Peter is a viable option.

PURPOSE

Peter's goal in writing is to fortify the church against false teaching. He wants to give the standard of truth to the church so that once he and the rest of the apostles are gone, the church will be able to stand strong against heresy. In order for the standard of truth to be established, Peter must show the true knowledge of God, the nature of the false teachers, and how to stand firm in the midst of both.

OCCASION

Peter is near the end of his life. This letter was probably written from Rome, about three years after Peter's first letter, around AD 67.

THEMES

Themes in 2 Peter include false teachers (2:1–22; 3:3–5) and Jesus' return (3:3–14).

HISTORICAL CONTEXT

False teachers had sought to overrun the church and destroy the foundation of the doctrine under which the church was established. Peter writes about the importance of the gospel so that the church would be strengthened and secure in the midst of false teaching. The letter has many words, phrases, and themes in common with the letter of Jude, and scholars debate which was written first and which author borrowed from the other.

CONTRIBUTION TO THE BIBLE

The trials that Peter deals with in his first letter focus on conflict against the church coming from the outside in the form of persecution. Second Peter is different in that it deals with the conflict and the trials that arise *within* the church because of false teaching.

OUTLINE

2 PETER 1:1–21
THE TRUE KNOWLEDGE OF GOD EXPLAINED

Setting Up the Section

In the first four verses, Peter declares that he is the true apostle, states the authentic message that is to be believed, and reveals what the authentic Christian life really is. He does this so the readers will not succumb to the perversion of the gospel that was being preached in their midst. The truths outlined in these verses, as well as in all of chapter 1, represent the core doctrines that were being twisted by false teachers.

📖 1:1–4

THE DIVINE POWER— THE KNOWLEDGE OF GOD GIVEN

The writer identifies himself in three ways (1:1):

1) Simon Peter
2) A bond-servant (NASB), or slave, in absolute submission to his master
3) An apostle, called by Jesus as one of the original twelve disciples

Next, Peter clarifies that he is writing to all believers rather than one specific church. He states that the faith the church has received is the same faith the apostles received. Not only is it the same faith, but also the same source of faith—the righteousness of Jesus Christ.

Peter wishes grace and peace for his readers. *Grace* is the unearned gift and favor of God (1:2). *Peace* is a term that means more than the absence of conflict; it means a right relationship with God. The fact that Peter wants grace and peace to be multiplied (growing exponentially) means he wants the believers to know the unending experience of God's blessing and peace.

The knowledge Peter refers to is an intimate and experiential knowledge of God (1:2). It is best illustrated in the kind of familiarity that comes through a marriage relationship. The more people know and experience God, the more they experience His grace and peace.

The divine power of Jesus is the power that dwells in God alone (1:3). When Peter refers to life in this text, he is referring to new life found in Christ alone.

Believers have everything they need for godliness. The life God calls His followers to live comes through the divine power of Jesus. Again, keep in mind the context of this letter; false teachers were extolling a system of works that leads to godlessness. Peter wants the readers to find their godliness in the power of Christ alone—not through human effort.

This life and godliness are given by the divine power of Jesus and come through true knowledge of Him. The idea in verse 3 is very simple—the new life and the godliness that believers need to please God come through a relationship with the One who calls them.

This divine power leads to a divine promise (1:4). One does not have to become holy to gain God's favor; He calls us when we are unholy so that we will become holy by partaking of the divine nature of Jesus. As a result, salvation leads to holiness, rather than the other way around. Believers should be growing in their reflection of the divine nature of Jesus Christ.

📄 1:5–11

THE DIVINE LIFE—THE KNOWLEDGE OF GOD GAINED

The point of 2 Peter 1:1–11 is to define for the readers the nature of true salvation. Peter's goal seems to be that his readers pursue what they have been given in Christ and, in light of their salvation, stand strong in the face of false teaching.

Notice that verse 5 is based on verses 3 and 4, which are not commands but rather a description of what God has done for us. Verse 5 states that one should apply all diligence—to pursue that which has already been given in Christ.

Peter mentions seven things believers are to add to their faith: excellence, knowledge, self-control, perseverance, godliness, brotherly affection, and unselfish love (1:5–7 NET). He does not offer these qualities as a checklist for holiness; instead, it is a grouping of character traits that believers now have the ability to live out because of the righteousness they have been given in Christ.

The word translated *add* in verse 5 originally meant to pay the expenses of a chorus in staging a play but came to mean providing support or aid of any kind (generally rich or lavish support provided at one's own expense). In the context of verse 5, it carries with it the idea of cooperating with God as He produces these important qualities in His children.

Peter says, in essence, if you are not pursuing these things and if they are not being fleshed out in your life, then your profession of faith is not valid (1:8). On the other hand, if you pursue them and are growing in them, then your profession is good. This is not a requirement for perfection, but a constant movement in the right direction. The Christian life is to produce a changed life so the whole world can see the character of God forming in a believer.

In verse 8, Peter refers to a believer's knowledge of Jesus. This is a knowledge that is forged in a relationship, not a simple acknowledgement or familiarity with a set of information.

In verse 9, Peter describes the fallout of someone who does not pursue the traits described in verses 5–7. That person is blind, shortsighted, and suffers from amnesia. He or she cannot see the reality of the present world, the inheritance that waits, or what Jesus has done for him or her in the past.

Verses 10 and 11 make it crystal clear what is at stake in such blindness and powerlessness and fruitlessness—the confirmation of one's calling into faith. The danger described in verses 8 and 9 is not the danger of slipping into the kingdom with no rewards. It is the danger of not being a citizen of the kingdom at all. The calling of God is a calling to transformation. Peter is saying that if one does not love and desire transformation, then he or she should question the calling.

📄 1:12–21

THE DIVINE MESSAGE—
THE KNOWLEDGE OF GOD AFFIRMED

In the first eleven verses of chapter 1, Peter lists the proper pursuits of the Christian life. Beginning in verse 12, he explains this focus.

Verses 12–15 are about remembering one's call and source of righteousness. The Christian life is the pursuit of the righteousness that one has been given in Jesus. As sin surfaces, God wants believers to remember that they have been given the righteousness of Jesus. Therefore, they can pursue a change of mind, will, and emotions through the Word of God, prayer, and their faith community.

The tenets of Christianity are not based upon people gathering to create a new religion. Instead, the tenets of Christianity are based upon what the apostles saw and heard—the majesty of Jesus Christ. They saw Jesus, touched Jesus, lived with Jesus, and saw the very glory of God shine forth from Him (1:16).

In verses 16–18, Peter refers to the event that is often called the Transfiguration (Mark 9:2–8). Jesus brought Peter, James, and John to a mountain, and He physically changed before them, revealing His glory. Elijah and Moses—both key figures in the storyline of the Bible—appeared with Jesus. This was a defining moment for the apostles.

Demystifying 2 Peter

Notice that in reference to the Transfiguration in Matthew, Mark, and 2 Peter, there is a difference in the wording of the voice from heaven. In Mark 9:7, God says to listen to Jesus. In 2 Peter 1:17, He declares He is well-pleased with Jesus. Matthew 17:5 records both statements. There is no contradiction here, since each writer selects what is important from his own perspective concerning the event.

After making the claim that what they received was from God, Peter draws the readers' attention to the prophecies of the Old Testament. His experience on the mountain with Jesus only verifies what was recorded by the writers of the Old Testament (2 Peter 1:19). Therefore, Peter calls the Christians to pay attention to the scriptures.

In verse 19, the dawn and the Morning Star refer to the time when Jesus comes back to establish His kingdom and to give people new bodies that can never sin. In Revelation 22:16, Jesus calls Himself the Morning Star. The picture here is that until the time believers enter into eternity, scripture is the source of direction for life.

The prophets did not come up with their teaching through their own wisdom (2 Peter 1:20–21). The prophets did not offer their own interpretation of God or what it means to be a child of God. The prophets were moved by God through the hand of the Spirit. In other words, the God who defined Jesus for the apostles is the same God who moved the writers of the scriptures, and therefore there is complete continuity in the message.

2 PETER 2:1–22

THE TRUE KNOWLEDGE OF GOD ATTACKED

Setting Up the Section

This section continues where chapter 1 leaves off, comparing the Old Testament prophets to the false teachers who had invaded the lives of Peter's readers.

📄 2:1–3

THE MISSION OF THE FALSE TEACHERS

False prophets had risen in Israel, just as they were appearing in the first-century church (Deuteronomy 13:1–3; Isaiah 28:7; Jeremiah 23:14; Ezekiel 13:1–7; 2 Peter 2:1). Note, though, that Peter switches quickly from the term false *prophets* to false *teachers*. These teachers were not prophets revealing God's truth.

Most certainly they will face judgment before God, since they have denied the One who bought them. They have refused the redemption offered them and influenced others to do the same (2 Peter 2:1–2). Peter's use of "the way of truth" may be an allusion to Psalm 119:30.

The opening verses of this second chapter offer six descriptions of these teachers and their motives (2 Peter 2:1–3). They are deceptive, Christ-denying, destroyed, sensual, slandering, and self-indulgent people who seek to care for themselves over God and the people of God.

📄 **2:4–9**

THE RESCUE OF THE GODLY

In verse 3, Peter announces sure destruction on these false teachers. He pulls from three examples in the Old Testament to make his point (2:4–6). He starts from Genesis 6 and then moves to Genesis 19 to call the people back to the scriptures.

His first example is from Genesis 6—fallen angels God judged for rebellion and immorality (Genesis 6:1–5; Jude 6). The fate described here is a reference to a place reserved for the most wicked to be held until they can be judged.

As a result of the angels' sin and all that humanity became in that era, God flooded the earth to wipe out the rebellious race—Peter's second example of God's judgment (Genesis 6–7; 2 Peter 2:5). God's protection of Noah and the survival of only a few faithful make this illustration particularly relevant to Peter's readers. Noah is described here as a preacher, contrasting him with the false teachers in this situation.

The final picture of God's judgment is Sodom and Gomorrah, cities renowned for their affluence and immorality (Genesis 19; 2 Peter 2:6). God's judgment took the form of fire from heaven, burning the cities to the ground.

Demystifying 2 Peter

Lot was Abraham's nephew and an inhabitant of Sodom and Gomorrah. He and his family were given warning to escape before fire destroyed the cities (2:7–8). Lot's story is told in Genesis 18–19, including the unfortunate fate of his wife. The Genesis account does not present Lot as an upright man as Peter seems to here. It may be that Peter's words here describe someone whose righteousness was affected by the wickedness around him rather than someone who was grieved by it.

Through these examples, Peter is demonstrating that while false teachers experience limited success, no one will have to endure them forever. God will judge the false teachers, and He will deliver the righteous (2:9).

📄 **2:10–22**

THE DESTRUCTION OF THE FALSE TEACHERS

Peter has now moved from the past to the present.

Verse 10 reveals the two main problems with the false teachers. First, they engage in overt immorality. And, second, they despise authority. Peter describes them as daring and self-willed (2:10). The idea around the word *daring* is that of recklessness. It carries the idea of a person who is so arrogant and so bold that he or she will do whatever he or she wants, no matter the cost.

Demystifying 2 Peter

To make his point, Peter describes one of the despicable acts of these teachers—insulting the "glorious ones" (2:10 NET; Jude 8–10). This is a puzzling statement. Who are the glorious ones? Some interpret this to mean church leadership. Others, and possibly the majority, interpret this as a reference to the fallen angels mentioned in 2:4. In both interpretations, the statement is made as an example of the brazen nature of these false teachers.

Verse 11 compares the insolence described in verse 10 with the actions and attitudes of heavenly angels. While they are agents of God and of heaven, and more powerful than the glorious ones, they are presented here as unwilling to cast judgment—a responsibility that belongs to God alone. The false teachers reveal their arrogance by taking liberties that even angels wouldn't take.

In verses 12–13, Peter compares these teachers to unreasoning animals. Rather than living by the Spirit, they simply follow their own fallen instincts—and, like wild animals, they are caught and destroyed. The fact that they are carousing in broad daylight would have been an offense not only to the Christian community, but to the first-century Roman culture at large.

The feast mentioned in verse 13 is regarded by many to refer to the love feast celebrated by the church. In this case, the immorality of these teachers was practiced in full view even at gatherings of the community of faith.

In a religious sense, a stain or blemish carries the idea of something that is not acceptable to God. Keep in mind that in Leviticus 21:21, God declared that no animal could be sacrificed to Him that had any spot or blemish.

Peter describes the nature of the false teachers as constantly immoral (2 Peter 2:14). When Peter says that these teachers have eyes full of adultery, he doesn't mean they are looking to commit adultery as much as the fact that all they can see is adultery. They believe that everything in the world belongs to them, and they want to have it all.

Worse still, they prey upon the spiritually weak so they can seduce them into their sensual lifestyle. The word translated "entice" (2:14 NET) implies something caught with bait. It is an intentional fishing expedition. This intentionality is also captured in the next idea that they have schooled themselves in immorality. They have become experts in sin.

What these false teachers offer is immorality in the name of God, thus replacing the righteousness of Jesus Christ with sin. Because their hearts are greedy, they pursue money, power, and pleasure and then peddle this to others as gifts from God.

To sum up this point, Peter writes two words to describe the false teachers: "cursed children" (2:14 NET). They live under God's curse. To make his point even clearer, Peter associates them with the Old Testament prophet, Balaam, well-known for his desire to turn a profit based on his religious standing. In the same way, these false teachers have a gift for teaching, but they are not using that gift for the glory of God. Instead, they are using it to glorify themselves.

Demystifying 2 Peter

The account of Balaam is recorded in Numbers 22. Balaam was a prophet who was willing to take money in order to entice God to curse the Israelites. Balak, the king of Moab, at the request of the Midianites, tried to use Balaam's prophetic gift to curse the Israelites. At first Balaam tried to comply, but God would not let him. In the process of stopping Balaam, God used a talking donkey to confront him.

Peter uses more word pictures to sum up the character of these men—springs without water, mists driven by a storm that pass over a place but never drop any rain (2:17). Since many of the readers of this letter lived in desert climates, these pictures were vivid. Peter is showing the people that false teachers might appear to be helpful, but in the end they do not bring people to the water of life.

Verse 18 describes the true method of the false teachers and the content of their teaching. Their words are empty, sometimes translated "vain," or "vanity." They have no value. These teachers have nothing beneficial to say, yet they say it with great pride and arrogance.

Notice that they entice by immorality. They pull people in to desire money, possessions, and power, and tell them that this is God's desire for them. The objects of their teaching are not all Christians, but also those who "have barely escaped from a lifestyle of deception" (2:18 NLT). These people are just coming out of an immoral lifestyle, and they are being enticed by teaching that allows them to have a moral version of their same perversion.

Critical Observation

False teachers promise freedom, but the truth is that they are slaves to their own immorality (2:19). Peter explains that a person is a slave to that which he or she surrenders. These false teachers present themselves as those who have chosen liberty in Christ over the old Jewish law. But the truth is that their liberty has become a license to sin. That is not what freedom in Jesus is about. There are certainly ethical restrictions on the behavior of those who seek to live like Jesus, even if those restrictions are ultimately guided by love. It is within those restrictions that followers of Jesus find freedom from the sins that ruled their behavior in their old lives. Because the false teachers are in bondage to sin, their promises of freedom are empty.

Peter's words in verses 20–21 have prompted much debate. How could it be better for someone never to have known the way of righteousness? The answer is that knowledge creates responsibility (see James 3:1, where teachers are said to receive a stricter judgment). Those who have heard and understood the message, yet willfully reject it, will be judged more harshly than those who have never heard or understood. The false teachers had heard the gospel, knew the gospel, and could even speak the gospel message, yet they never obeyed it.

Verse 22, which is a quote from Proverbs 26:11, points to the fact that since the false teachers have not been truly converted, they will return to their way of unrighteousness. False teachers will return to the sin that they claim they have left because they do not order their hearts by the Word of God.

2 PETER 3:1–18

THE TRUE KNOWLEDGE OF GOD PROTECTED

The First Reminder—Judgment Is Coming	3:1–7
The Second Reminder—Mercy Is Here for a Time	3:8–10
The Third Reminder—Live Godly, Wait Patiently	3:11–18

Setting Up the Section

Chapter 3 transitions from a description of the false teachers to encouragement for the readers. It is a chapter of reminders meant to help the church understand who God is, how to stay true to His message, and how to live in a world with false teaching.

📖 **3:1–7**

THE FIRST REMINDER—JUDGMENT IS COMING

In verse 1, Peter mentions that this is the second letter he has written to these same readers. While we could assume this refers to 1 Peter, the description here doesn't seem to fit. First Peter isn't a letter of reminder in the same way this letter is. Therefore, this may be a reference to a letter that no longer exists.

Peter also says he wants to stir his readers' minds—to make them think. He describes them as sincere, or pure. This means that Peter seeks to strengthen the sincere minds that they already possess. How does Peter make sure their minds stay in the truth? By making sure that they remember the scriptures—the prophets and the teachings of Jesus as recorded by the apostles (3:2). Given that this letter addresses specifically those who deny Jesus' return, the commandment mentioned here is probably that which calls Christians to live their lives *according* to the reality of Jesus' return.

Critical Observation

False teachers will inevitably question the words of both the apostles and the prophets, and for this reason Peter knows that the saints must stay true to what the prophets wrote and the apostles spoke. The believers do not need more revelation; they need to order their lives by the existing revelation that they have been given.

"In the last days" is a common phrase in the New Testament, referring to the time marked at the beginning of Jesus' time on earth and continuing until His return (3:3).

In verse 3, Peter refers to the false teachers as "mockers" (NASB) because they deride, or attack, God's truth—starting with the return of Jesus. They ask in doubt, "Where is Jesus? I thought He said He would return" (3:4). Their implication is that God has not had an active part in the history of the world. Things have continued to simply go their way, and He has not kept His promise.

First, Peter offers an argument based on Creation, referring to the first chapter of Genesis. God spoke the world into being (3:5). He formed it out of water, but He also used water as a means of judgment. Next, he points to the flood, another example that things have not always gone on without any intervention from God, as the false teachers imply (3:6). The world is not on an unlimited fixed course but instead is being run by the sovereign hand of God.

Peter's final point is that God will intervene by judgment on the ungodly (3:7). Just as God has intervened in the past, so He can, and will, in the future. He spoke the world into existence, judged it according to humanity's actions, and certainly has the power and authority to do so again.

📄 3:8–10

THE SECOND REMINDER— MERCY IS HERE FOR A TIME

Verse 8 is a reference to Psalm 90:4. This psalm was written by Moses and was a foundational psalm in early Christian teaching. Within Peter's context, it emphasizes the fact that God is not bound by time. The false teachers are incorrect in their assumption that because Jesus has not yet returned, He isn't going to at all.

According to verse 9, the patience of God shouldn't be interpreted as a lack of involvement, but instead as the ultimate involvement, because God is using this time to draw humanity to Himself. When Peter says that God doesn't want anyone to perish, it does not imply that all will enter the kingdom of heaven—verse 7 reveals God's judgment. But Peter is saying that the Lord is patient toward those who are not mockers and not opposed to the will of God—as he has described the false teachers.

Demystifying 2 Peter

In the Old Testament, the Day of the Lord was the future time when God would vindicate His holy name, bring judgment on those who refuse to believe, and gather His people into a new kingdom of righteousness and peace (Zephaniah 1:14–18; Malachi 4:1–3).

In the New Testament, beginning with Jesus, the day took on the connotation of Jesus' final return and judgment (Matthew 24:42–44; Acts 2:20; 1 Thessalonians 5:2–4).

In 2 Peter 3:10, Peter makes the point that there will be an end to the time of mercy—the Day of Judgment. Peter's comment that this day will come like a thief refers back to Jesus' own description of the unexpected timing of God's judgment in Matthew 24:42–44.

No one knows when this day will come, though Peter reveals some events that will take place:

1. The heavens will pass away—the sky, sun, moon, and stars.
2. The elements will be destroyed—at the time of Peter's writing, these elements would be understood as earth, air, fire, and water.
3. The earth and its works will be burned—humanity and all it has built up to sustain itself as a civilization. This may be a reference to Malachi 4:1, which speaks of a day that will burn like an oven.

📄 3:11–18

THE THIRD REMINDER—
LIVE GODLY, WAIT PATIENTLY

If God's judgment is to come as described in the preceding verses, then how should Peter's readers live in light of that reality? In the final verses of this letter, Peter reminds them how they are to live their lives in light of who God is.

The words *holy* and *godly*, in verse 11 (NIV), are in the plural. Peter is not giving the people a checklist for their lives, but is instead saying that they must pursue holiness and godliness in a variety of ways.

The word *hastening* in verse 12 (NASB) means, just as it does today, to speed something up. Within this context, speeding up is not a reference to the amount of time in which we wait for Jesus' return, but rather *how* we live as we are waiting. We must be a part of what God is doing on the earth. Waiting for that day is not a lack of activity, but it is active waiting as believers participate in God's kingdom.

Peter again describes the judgment of God in terms of fire—an all-consuming and powerful blaze (3:10, 12). This is not something that should strike fear in his readers' hearts, though, because the destruction is meant for the ungodly.

In verse 13, Peter reveals two things: There is a new world coming, and righteousness will be a part of it. This "new heavens and new earth" is a phrase from the prophecy of Isaiah (Isaiah 65:17; 66:22). The faithful will not simply escape this world; they will live where righteousness lives.

It follows then, if God is preparing a new world in which righteousness is the controlling factor, those who want to live in that new world will desire righteousness in their current lives. Peter wants his readers to focus on the peace that comes from walking in full harmony with God. He also says to be diligent, spotless, and blameless (3:14). This is an image from the Old Testament. The Passover lamb could not have any spot or blemish. In regard to his readers, Peter is saying that when Jesus returns, He must find believers living pure lives on earth.

Demystifying 2 Peter

In verses 15–16, Peter refers to Paul's writings, saying he and Paul are preaching the same message. At the end of verse 16, Peter places Paul's writings in the same category as all of the scriptures—which in this case refers to the Old Testament.

We can't be sure which of Paul's letters Peter's readers would have seen. At this time, Paul's letters were not gathered into one body of work as they are organized in the New Testament today. We also can't be sure which specific passage, if any, Peter is referring to. But certainly throughout Paul's writing, he encourages believers to live holy lives in light of God's commands and Jesus' return, just as Peter is doing here.

Notice that Peter admits Paul's letters can be difficult to understand, and misinterpretations can lead to destruction, which is true of all scripture (3:16). The false teachers take the difficult concepts and twist them to their own use.

Peter's final words are of warning and direction: It is the responsibility of the believer to be on guard (3:17). This means a believer must be personally vigilant over his or her own spiritual life.

In closing, Peter turns his attention to the spiritual growth of his readers—in the grace and knowledge of Jesus. Verse 18 is the application point of Peter's second letter. He opens the letter praying that grace and peace will be multiplied to his readers (1:2). At the closing, then, he comes full circle, instructing them to continue to grow in grace and also in knowledge. His inclusion of knowledge here is a reminder that dealing with false teaching requires tending to one's own knowledge of the truth.

Peter closes this letter with a benediction. Because Jesus is Lord and Savior, He is the One who deserves all the honor. Peter's mention of "that eternal day" (3:18 NET) refers to the final Day of Judgment, the coming of Jesus.

Take It Home

To grow in grace means to grow in gratitude and expression of all that you have received from God. Not only must we grow in grace, but we must also "grow in the grace and knowledge of our Lord and Savior Jesus Christ" (3:18 NIV, NET). This is imperative.

This world gives only temporary happiness, but the world to come will give eternal joy. We must live for that day, pursuing peace and purity, joining in God's kingdom. We must continue to pursue our understanding of the gift of grace and the One who gives it. This is the only way we can avoid being led astray by a twisted gospel message.

1 JOHN

INTRODUCTION TO 1 JOHN

The New Testament book we refer to as 1 John is a letter to a community of faith. Much of this letter is written to combat heresy regarding the identity of Jesus. The conflict over this heresy caused part of the congregation to split from the rest. John writes to ground the community in a true picture of not only Jesus' identity, but the identity of the children of God in light of who Jesus is.

AUTHOR

Determining the author of 1 John is somewhat different from determining the author of 2 and 3 John. In the case of 1 John, no author is identified in the work itself. However, the author does identify himself as an eyewitness of Jesus' ministry. He also speaks with an apostolic kind of authority and writes in a similar style to the Gospel of John. There is good evidence, both historical and internal, that supports the traditional view of John the apostle as author.

PURPOSE

The purpose statement for 1 John can be found in 5:13. We can deduce from this verse that the author is writing to believers and that his purpose is to assure them that they do indeed possess eternal life. Although this letter is written in response to a specific situation (the false teachers who had withdrawn from fellowship), it has a relevant message for the church at large.

OCCASION

John appears to be writing to a community to which he is well-known (and to which he may belong). Because this Christian community has undergone a serious split, and a substantial part of the community has withdrawn from fellowship over doctrinal issues, John writes to reassure them of their faith.

The group that has split off is continuing to propagate its own beliefs, seeking to persuade more community members to join them. John writes to warn members of the community to resist the proselytizing efforts of these false teachers by bolstering their understanding of the truth.

THEMES

While this letter is written to combat theological opponents, the themes of walking in light and confessing Jesus as Christ are repeated throughout all of it.

In John's attempts to assure the believers of their eternal life (5:13), he also repeatedly emphasizes two basic components of that assurance: obedience to God and the love of fellow Christians.

1 JOHN 1:1–2:2

GOD IS LIGHT

The Prologue   1:1–4

Walking in the Light   1:5–10

Setting Up the Section

The use of a prologue to begin a work is characteristic of both the Gospel of John and 1 John. This section of John's first letter lays the foundation for the rest.

🖹 1:1–4

THE PROLOGUE

The prologue of 1 John opens with a reference to "that which was from the beginning." While there is agreement that this is a reference to Jesus, some see this as a reference to His eternality, while others view it as a reference to the beginning of His earthly ministry.

It has been suggested that John's use of *we* in the opening verse is simply a style preference rather than an actual reference to a group. However, since that preference doesn't continue throughout the letter, it is more likely that the *we* references in the opening of the prologue refer to a group of people, including all eyewitnesses of Jesus' earthly life and ministry. The group probably includes John and the other apostles.

Some question whether the use of *word* in the prologue is a reference back to the famous prologue in the opening of John's Gospel, in which John refers to Jesus as *the Word* (John 1:1–14; 1 John 1:1). Here, though, the verses that follow expound on the idea of *life* rather than *word*. So in this case, *word* probably refers to the message of Jesus rather than Jesus Himself.

Verses 2–3 clarify that it is the eyewitness testimony about the earthly career of Jesus that is being announced in this letter. Why? So that the readers might have fellowship with John and the other apostolic eyewitnesses. People who are in fellowship share some reality in common—in this case, the commonality is the life of Jesus. This commonality would have brought comfort to those who had just experienced a sharp doctrinal disagreement in their fellowship.

Demystifying 1 John

To those who are watching closely, much of John's wording is a jab at the false teachers (not referred to directly until 2:18–19), who not only split from the community of faith, but are still trying to convince members of the community to join them. This gives added significance to John's point in verse 3. The reason for proclaiming the truth about Jesus from eyewitnesses is for the sake of fellowship.

While this word (*fellowship*) will not be repeated throughout the letter, it does provide a kind of foundation. The fellowship John describes here among the community members is based on their own fellowship, not only with God the Father, but also with the Son, Jesus. This connection is made over and over again in a variety of ways—as we have been loved by the Father and Son, so must we love each other.

In verse 4, John states his purpose for writing: that the joy of all these witnesses might be complete. This joy will come from continuing fellowship with one another and with the Father and the Son, as opposed to breaking that fellowship by siding with the false teachers.

📄 **1:5–10**

WALKING IN THE LIGHT

The summary statement for the next section is the message defined in verse 5: "God is Light, and in Him there is no darkness at all" (NASB). This is a description of one of God's qualities—completely sinless. It is also the introduction of the imagery of light and darkness—important images in John's theology.

Verse 6 begins a series of six "if" clauses, which end in 2:1. These divide into three pairs, each pair consisting of a hypothetical "If we say. . ." statement that has a negative connotation and probably represents the ideas of the false teachers (1:6, 8, 10), and then a "But if. . ." statement with a positive connotation that probably represents the counterclaim of John (1:7, 9; 2:1).

John's problem with the false teachers is their contradictory behavior: They continue walking in darkness, yet at the same time, they are making the claim to have fellowship with God (1:6).

If we say. . .	But if. . .
we have fellowship with God, yet walk in darkness, we lie (1:6).	we walk in the light, we have fellowship with each other and are cleansed by Jesus' blood (1:7).
we have no sin, we deceive ourselves (1:8).	we confess our sins, we are forgiven (1:9).
we have not sinned, we call God a liar (1:10).	we sin, Jesus is our advocate (2:1).

In contrast to verse 6, verse 7 introduces the counterclaim—if we actually do walk in the truth, we will be assured of fellowship with God. In this context, fellowship is something shared between believers as a result of a righteous lifestyle.

Verse 8 bounces back to the claim of being without sin. This is the situation of the false teachers. They are deceiving themselves. The attempt of the false teachers to deceive others (2:26) begins with their self-deceit about being guiltless of sins at all.

In verse 9, the confession John writes about is an ongoing lifestyle of confession, not just a one-time confession at conversion (as this verse is often applied). John's readers have already experienced conversion.

Verse 10 contains the last of the three pairs of "if" statements. It is almost a repetition of the claim in verse 8 but is stated a little differently. The false teachers had apparently developed a version of perfectionism by which they were able to deny that, after professing to be Christians, they could be convicted of sin. John counters this by pointing out that the one who claims this makes God a liar.

1 JOHN 2:1–29

OBEYING THE LIGHT

Setting Up the Section

This section contains three claims to intimate knowledge of God (2:4, 6, 9). As with the three "if we say" clauses in chapter 1 (1:6, 8, 10), these claims indirectly reflect the claims of the false teachers. The focus of the subject matter shifts from awareness and acknowledgment of sin to obedience of God's commandments. The concept of fellowship, introduced in the prologue (1:4), is replaced by an emphasis on knowing and loving God along with one's fellow believers.

2:1–11

DARKNESS AND LIGHT

The seriousness of the claim of no sin in the last verses of chapter 1 causes John to break the pattern of "if" statements with a parenthetical note at the beginning of 2:1. This note makes it clear that John is not simply implying that occasional acts of sin are acceptable; the purpose here is that the readers not sin at all.

The latter part of verse 1 includes the final counterclaim to the "if" statements beginning in 1:6. In this case, the counterclaim is that if one sins, Jesus speaks in his or her defense. This is the picture of someone coming alongside to represent us, like a mediator.

The word John uses to describe the work of Jesus—translated "atoning sacrifice"— involves the idea of a sacrifice for sins that turns away the divine wrath (2:2). Jesus does not turn away God's wrath by ignoring one's sin, but by offering His own punishment in one's stead—His life.

Keep the situation in mind: A group has left the fellowship because of a doctrinal disagreement, and they continue to attempt to convince others in the fellowship to join them. There would certainly be those in the community who wondered if the group that left was right in their opinion. John is writing to bolster those remaining, not only in their doctrine, but in their practice. His point in verse 3 answers the question, "How do we know that we know God?" John's answer is that obedience to God's commands gives the assurance that one has come to know God.

In the first of three claims, John alludes to the false teachers by describing the one who says he knows God but isn't following His commandments (2:4). According to John, this person's claim to know God is false; it's those who obey God's Word who truly know Him (2:5). In this case, God's Word is a reference not only to the facts of the scriptures, but to God's ethical demands. It is these demands a believer will attempt to obey (but presumably the false teachers would not be concerned about obeying).

The second of the three claims appears in verse 6: The person who claims to reside in God should live like Jesus. This is the first occurrence of this concept of residing, but it appears often throughout the rest of the letter. The implication in John's claim here is that the false teachers do not walk as Jesus walked, so how can they claim to reside in Him?

The commandment John speaks of in verse 7 refers to the teaching specified as the "new commandment" of John 13:34–35 (that believers should love one another).

Demystifying 1 John

John describes what he is writing as *not* a new commandment in 2:7, then as a new commandment in verse 8. Most likely, John means that this commandment does not originate with him. Yet it still can be called a new commandment, since that is the way Jesus Himself described it (John 13:34; 1 John 2:8).

The light/darkness contrast in verse 8 is a little broader than in John's Gospel, where he writes that the "light shines in the darkness, but the darkness has not understood it" (John 1:5 NIV). In the Gospel, the light refers to Jesus Himself. In this context, though, the obedience of John's readers is a part of the light that is shining.

The false teachers claim to be in the light. But if someone hates his fellow Christian, as far as John is concerned, this person—regardless of his or her claim to the contrary—still lives in darkness (1 John 2:9). The opposite of hating one's fellow believer is, of course, the fulfillment of the new commandment—to love one another. This is an important theme in this letter (John 13:34; 1 John 2:10).

Critical Observation

The idea of making someone stumble (2:10) has been cited by some as a reference to the "stumbling block" in Leviticus 19:14. The idea of the stumbling block is used figuratively in the New Testament to refer to something that is a temptation to sin or an enticement to false belief (Romans 9:33; 1 Peter 2:8; Revelation 2:14), which fits the context here.

The use of the verb *hate* in verses 9 and 11 may seem strong, but for John the failure to show love for others in the Christian community to which one belongs is a very serious matter. Such a person may be described as spiritually blind (John 9:39–41). Some see the description in 1 John 2:11 as a reference to Proverbs 4:19, with its description of the wicked who stumble in the darkness.

Critical Observation

In the New Testament, blindness is frequently a spiritual condition associated with deliberate disbelief. Particularly applicable to verses 9–11 is John 12:39–40, where deliberate refusal to believe, in spite of the miracles Jesus had performed, led to an inability to believe. Just as those who refuse to come to the light are left in darkness, so those who refuse to love fellow members of the Christian community are said to be in darkness.

2:12–17

REASSURANCE

In verse 12, John addresses his readers directly as little children. He writes to assure them that their sins have been forgiven. This is a reference to the whole group (little children) followed by two subgroups (fathers and young people [2:13]). Whether these two subgroups are distinguished by age or spiritual maturity is not clear, but John's words are applicable to all.

John first addresses the fathers. The expression "him who is from the beginning" (2:13 NIV) could refer either to God or to Jesus. Since God the Father is clearly referred to in the next verse, a reference to Jesus is more likely. Those who are addressed as fathers have remained faithful to the apostolic testimony about who Jesus is. When John turns to those he addresses as young people, the emphasis is on their victory over the evil one (Satan).

Critical Observation

This is the first time we encounter "the evil one" in this letter (2:13). Here, as with the four remaining occurrences in 1 John, it is a reference to Satan (2:14; 3:12; 5:18, 19).

In verse 14, John repeats himself, probably for the sake of emphasis. There is a new thought introduced here, though: The Word of God resides in these believers.

John presents only two alternatives in verse 15: A person either loves the world or loves the Father. In this case, the *world* does not refer merely to creation or to the world's population for whom Christ died (John 3:16). Instead, this use of *the world* represents those who stand against John and the teachings of Christ.

In 1 John 2:16, John defines everything the world has to offer:

1) The desires of the flesh. This probably does not refer simply to sensual desires

(lustfulness or promiscuity). It refers to everything that is the desire of human beings—all that meets their wants and needs.

2) The desire of the eyes. This is more than merely human desires; this is related to what we want for ourselves. We see it, and we want to have it.

3) The pride of life (NASB) has to do with our possessions and accomplishments, those things we brag about, even if in our minds.

Verse 17 makes it clear that all these things are transitory. While it is true that the world and worldly desires will pass away in the future, for John they have already begun to disappear in the present. The person who does the will of God is the believer (in contrast to the false teachers). It is in doing God's will (obedience) that the believer demonstrates to himself and to those around him that he is a believer. This amounts, for John, to one means of assurance.

📄 2:18–29

FALSE TEACHERS

Critical Observation

Many interpreters see a new section or perhaps a new major part of the letter starting with verse 18. If so, the theme verse would be the opening phrase: "Children, it is the last hour. . ." (NET).

The arrival of the last hour (a period of time rather than a moment in time) is signaled by the appearance of the false teachers, described as antichrists (2:18). To understand John's use of the term *antichrist*, note that it is more than just someone who opposes Christ, but one who is hostile and seeks to replace Christ. This reveals how John sees the false teachers with their innovative but false view of Jesus.

Demystifying 1 John

The Letters of John contain the only New Testament uses of the term *antichrist*. Although the word itself is unique to 1 and 2 John, the concept behind it and the figure to which it refers are not. Paul describes this individual, in 2 Thessalonians 2:3, as "the man of lawlessness" and "the son of destruction" (NASB). Jesus Himself refers to "the abomination of desolation" in Mark 13:14 (see also Matthew 24:15). This individual is also referred to as "the beast" in Revelation 13:1.

John describes the departure of the false teachers from the community (1 John 2:19). John's point here is that the withdrawal of the false teachers reveals that they never genuinely belonged. He implies that their departure is part of God's sovereign purpose, perhaps intending this as reassurance to his readers in the face of the turmoil that may have followed.

The anointing in verse 20 refers to the Holy Spirit who indwells believers, rather than a ceremonial one-time anointing.

Verse 21 contains more reassurance for John's readers. Because of the false teaching, some may have come to doubt that they really know the truth concerning Jesus. John writes to reassure them that they do know the truth.

Critical Observation

The phrase "no lie comes from the truth" (2:21 NIV) refers to the teaching of the false teachers. The contrast between truth and falsehood is introduced in 1 John 1:6, where the person who claims fellowship with God yet walks in darkness is characterized as a liar. But here the line is drawn much more distinctively. The picture that is painted of a false teacher is not simply one who is ignorant, but one who is hostile toward the truth as it is taught by John.

The false teachers have already been identified as antichrists (2:18). They are now identified as liars (2:22). This is the first time in the letter that John explicitly states the position of the false teachers—they deny Jesus is the Messiah. Most often this is understood to mean that these teachers reject the orthodox interpretation of the Incarnation: that Jesus' divine and human natures were fully united. What logically follows for John, then, is that if the false teachers deny that Jesus is the Messiah, then they have no relationship with the Father (2:23).

Verses 24–26 include a wordplay in the Greek manuscript. The Greek word translated *remain* can also be translated *reside*. One is to stay somewhere, and the other is to take up residence. The teaching of the apostles must remain (reside) in the readers in order for the readers to remain (reside) in the Son and in the Father. If that happens, then they will have eternal life (2:25). Verses 27–28 continue the *remain/reside* wordplay. John reminds his readers that the Holy Spirit resides in them. The "anointing" they have received is the indwelling presence of the Holy Spirit. This provides assurance that they do also indeed reside in Him—Jesus.

Verse 26 focuses again on John's primary reason for writing: to protect his faithful followers from the false view of Christ espoused by these departed teachers.

Critical Observation

At the end of verse 27 is a statement that can be taken as a declaration of fact or as a command: "you reside in him" (NET). In this chapter it transitions between a section of encouragement and a section of exhortation. While the phrase is true with either interpretation, it most likely ends the encouragement and so should be read that way, as an assurance to the readers that they do reside in Jesus.

Verse 28 references Jesus' second coming. At this point, John switches from reassurance to exhortation. He wants his readers to remain in the truth so that they don't have to shrink away from Jesus in shame when He appears. Anyone who does not remain demonstrates that whatever profession he has made is false, and he is not a true believer.

The "If" that opens verse 29 is not to cast doubt on whether Jesus is righteous, but instead whether the readers of the letter have realized this fact. The expectation reflected here is that all those who are truly God's children will practice righteousness. For John, conduct is the clue to authenticity of this relationship.

Take It Home

John stresses ethical behavior as important for the Christian, in contrast to the teaching of the false teachers, who argue that a Christian's moral or ethical behavior is unimportant. This serves to remind the church that actions have always, and still do, speak much louder than words. Speaking for Christ is important. Living for Him is essential.

1 JOHN 3:1–24

GOD IS LOVE

Love vs. Sin	3:1–10
Loving One Another	3:11–24

Setting Up the Section

Within this section, the first 3 verses are a parenthesis in which John reflects on what it means to be fathered by God, a subject he has already mentioned at the end of 2:29. The flow of the argument against the false teachers is then resumed by verse 4.

📄 3:1–10

LOVE VS. SIN

Verse 1 begins a parenthetical comment that extends through the end of verse 3. John refers to believers as God's children. The last part of the verse asserts that the world's treatment of believers is a reflection and outgrowth of its treatment of Jesus Himself.

The concept that John uses here to describe God's relationship to believers, as a father to children, points on the one hand to God's personal, relational, and loving nature. On the other hand, it defines the status of Christians: They are members of God's household.

What believers will be is to be revealed at some later point (3:2). In light of the reference to Jesus' second coming in 2:28, this is probably what John refers to in verse 2, when believers see Him "as He is" (NASB).

Because of this hope, believers are expected to purify themselves; that is, to separate themselves from sin and live with moral purity just as Jesus did (3:3). The assurance of the previous verse, that believers will see Him just as He is, has moral and ethical behavioral implications for their lives in the present. This serves to further rebut the false teachers' claims that what the Christian does in the present life is of no consequence With this verse ends the parenthetical section that opens chapter 3.

Verse 4 opens with a statement on lawlessness, which carries the idea of opposition or rebellion. Keep in mind that the "law" for John is the law of love, as given by Jesus in the new commandment of John 13:34–35. This is the command to love one's brother, a major theme of 1 John.

Critical Observation

Those who sin (3:4) are sharply contrasted with those who reside in Christ (3:6), which is typical of John's writing style. John is referring to the false teachers in verse 4. The only specific sin in all of 1 John that John charges the false teachers with is failure to show love for fellow believers (3:17).

In verse 5, John reminds the readers of the basics they all know: that Jesus came to take away sins. He also affirms Jesus' sinlessness. This, in turn, leads into the issue of sin for those who reside in Jesus.

Verse 6, along with verse 9, can seem to mean that genuine Christians do not sin. Obviously, this is not the case, as John points out in 2:1. More likely, John is saying that genuine Christians do not continue to sin with no remorse.

Throughout this letter, the ones attempting to deceive John's readers, as mentioned in verse 7, are clearly the false teachers. The deception that John is guarding them from is a misunderstanding of this: The practice of righteousness is the evidence that a person is a member of God's family.

The strong contrasts that have characterized this section come to a head in verses 8 and 10. He who is sinful refers to the false teachers. They claim to be in relationship with God, yet they refuse to live righteously as Jesus did. Such people do not belong to God but to the devil.

Jesus, however, came to destroy the devil's works. This is not a figurative statement. Here, the verb *destroy* means to "bring to an end, abolish, or do away with."

As already stated in 2:29, in a spiritual sense, one's paternity (whether one is a child of God or a child of the devil) is revealed by whether one practices righteousness.

3:11–24

LOVING ONE ANOTHER

The message described in verse 11—loving one another—is a restatement of Jesus' command to the disciples in John 15:12, which is itself a restatement of the new commandment of John 13:34.

In 1 John 3:12, Cain serves as the example of what not to do—instead of loving his brother, he took his brother's life. Here John illustrates the stark contrast between righteous and evil actions, just as he contrasted darkness and light in John 3:19–21.

Critical Observation

The mention of Cain and his brother, with its allusion to Genesis 4:1–16, is the only direct reference to the Old Testament in 1 John.

Since the way Cain treated Abel is the way unbelievers generally treat believers, John tells his readers not to be surprised when the world mistreats them (1 John 3:13). In contrast to the hostility they may experienced in the world, however, followers of Jesus also have assurance that they have crossed from death to life. This assurance comes from the love of fellow believers (3:14). As in 2:3 and 2:5, obedience to the new commandment to love one another becomes the basis for this assurance. Love for fellow believers is in fact a form of God's love for us, because as far as John is concerned, all love comes from God (4:7–11).

But the person who refuses to love fellow believers remains in a state of spiritual death (3:14). Such a person is surely an unbeliever, as verse 14 makes clear. Ultimately, these verses will apply to the false teachers (3:17), and the fact that they remain in a state of spiritual death demonstrates (again, as in 2:19) John's belief that they were never genuine believers to begin with.

In verse 15, John writes that the person who hates a fellow believer is as guilty as if he or she had murdered him. This is strong language, but failure to show love to fellow believers is a serious matter to John. Failure to show love for fellow believers is an indication that eternal life is not present within the individual. Once again, one's behavior is a measure of one's spiritual status.

In contrast to the hatred shown by the false teachers for fellow believers, and the hatred of Cain for his brother, verse 16 states the standard of love is established by Jesus Himself—He laid down His life. Jesus' sacrifice on behalf of believers forms a strong motivation for them to lay down their lives for fellow believers. For John, this act of selfless sacrifice on Jesus' part becomes the very standard by which love is measured.

Critical Observation

References to Jesus "laying down His life" are unique to the Gospel of John (John 10:11; 15:13) and 1 John (3:16). From John's perspective, Jesus' sacrifice was a voluntary one; He was always completely in control of the situation surrounding His arrest, trials, and crucifixion (John 10:18).

John next describes the opposite of sacrificial love. The individual who has ample material possessions and yet fails to show compassion for a fellow Christian in need demonstrates that he or she does not have God's love residing within. John's point is made by asking a rhetorical question: How can the love of God reside in this kind of person? The question assumes the answer: The love of God cannot reside in a person who doesn't show God's love.

Verse 18 describes love in two pairs of words. In each pair, the first word is produced by the second: Words are produced by the tongue, and actions (deeds) that show a believer's love for another are produced by the truth. John exhorts his readers to love one another not merely with words, but with real actions that spring from their relationship to the truth.

The prepositional phrase that opens verse 19 ("by this" NET) refers to the previous verse: By expressing love for one another, Christians assure themselves that they belong to the truth, because the outward action reflects the inward reality of one's relationship with God.

Verse 20 describes believers condemning themselves because of a guilty conscience concerning sin (3:20). In this case, their actions in showing love for fellow believers will assure them that God will accept and forgive them even if their own consciences are guilty.

On the other hand, if a person's conscience does not condemn him or her, then that person can have confidence in prayer (3:21). This is not to say that an obedient lifestyle on the part of the believer merits or guarantees answered prayer. It simply means that, insofar as believers' consciences make no accusation against them, and they are living in obedience to God's commandments, their will and God's will coincide, and they can reasonably expect to receive answers to their requests. This combination of confidence and answered prayer appears also in 5:14–15.

This same word, *confidence*, also occurs in connection to Christ's second coming (2:28; 4:17). So this may also be a reference to the Christian's assurance of a positive outcome at the judgment when Jesus returns.

John closes the chapter specifying God's commandment to believe in Jesus and love one another. The person who does these things, the genuine believer, is in a mutual and reciprocal relationship with God. The assurance of this mutual relationship between God and the believer is God's Spirit. The believer's assurance in 1 John is based on three things:

1) Believing in Jesus (3:23)
2) Loving one another (3:23)
3) The gift of God's indwelling Spirit (3:24)

1 JOHN 4:1–21

UNDERSTANDING GOD'S LOVE

Setting Up the Section

Since the book of 1 John has a rather free structure, many interpreters divide it in a multitude of ways, breaking sections in a variety of places. With almost no exception, though, the opening six verses of chapter 4 are kept together as a section standing on its own. It opens this chapter, which focuses on understanding God's love.

📄 **4:1–6**

THE TEST OF LOVE

Since having the Spirit of God is a ground of assurance for the believer (2:27; 3:24), it is important to know how to test the spirits. Every spirit is not from God (4:1).

The false prophets mentioned in verse 1 is a reference to the false teachers and their false understanding of Jesus. These teachers claim to be inspired by the Spirit of God, yet John takes strong exception to their teaching. In light of all this, John proposes the test described in verse 2: Does the Spirit confess Jesus as having come from God? Note that this test is both confessional (concerning what a person believes) and Christological (concerning what a person believes about Jesus). Presumably, the false teachers would not be able to make this confession, since this is designed to test their truth.

Demystifying 1 John

While verse 2 describes how to recognize the Spirit that does come from God, verse 3 describes the other side of the coin. A spirit that does not come from God does not acknowledge Jesus' identity. This is where the false teachers probably had their problems. By the time John was writing this letter, many heresies and sects had begun to distort Jesus' identity. For example, some could confess the Messiah would come in the flesh but could not connect this with Jesus. John identifies this kind of spirit with the Antichrist. Earlier John had called the false teachers antichrists (2:18). Now he says the false spirit behind them is the spirit of the Antichrist.

While in verse 1 John addresses his readers as friends, in verse 4 he addresses them as children. He offers them the assurance of victory over the false teachers because of the power of the Holy Spirit.

He makes a slight change to his language in verse 5. Whereas in verse 1 he asserts that the false teachers had gone into the world, in verse 5 he claims that they are *from* the world. This determines their perspective and also ensures that the world pays attention to them. (Compare this with John 15:19.)

In verse 6, John introduces another way to test the spirits. Those who are of God include all the faithful Christians who have held on to the orthodox testimony about who Jesus is. Those not from God is a reference to the false teachers, who refuse to listen to this testimony about Jesus. John makes this statement, not as a lone man demanding ultimate authority, but as one of the apostles whose message is connected with all those who witnessed Jesus' life (1:1–2).

📄 **4:7–21**

THE ANATOMY OF LOVE

In verse 7, John addresses his readers again as friends. He also returns to the theme of loving one another, the major theme of the second half of the letter. By "everyone who loves," John means those who love fellow believers sacrificially, as Jesus loves us (3:16). He again connects one's behavior toward fellow believers to an indication of whether that person has come to know God. Since God is love, those who truly know Him will reflect that love toward fellow members of the Christian community. According to verse 8, the reverse is also true.

In verse 9, God's love is revealed in believers through the giving of His Son (compare John 3:16). While all Christians are children of God, Jesus is God's Son in a unique, one-of-a-kind sense.

Critical Observation

John uses the term *world* in a variety of ways, depending on the context. In formulas like the one in verse 9, which echoes John 3:16 and speaks of God sending His Son to be the Savior of the world, the term is used in a neutral sense. In other places, like 1 John 2:15, John uses the same term to refer to the opposition of the world. In this case, it holds a negative connotation and has in mind that part of the population that stands against John's teaching.

John reminds his readers in verse 10 that real love comes from God, and no one can love God without Him loving us first, providing His Son to sacrifice for us. The initiative lies with God.

For the sixth and last time in this letter, John addresses his readers as friends in verse 11. God's example of self-giving, sacrificial love—the giving of His own Son—serves as the model for believers to follow in loving one another.

Since no one has seen God at any time, how is it possible for believers to know that God resides in them? Verses 12–16 offer three grounds of assurance for the believer:

1) The indwelling Holy Spirit. This indwelling of the Spirit (4:13) leads a person to testify to what God the Father has done through His Son, who was sent to be the Savior of the world (4:14). This expression recalls the testimony of the Samaritan woman at the well in John 4, which led to the same confession about Jesus by the Samaritans (John 4:42).

2) The confession that Jesus is God's Son (1 John 3:23; 4:15). This confession insures both God's residence within the believer and vice versa.

3) Love shown to fellow believers (4:16). When a believer shows love toward another believer, this provides assurance to the first believer that he or she resides in God, and likewise, that God resides in him or her.

In verse 17, John switches topics to Christian growth or sanctification, the outgrowth of loving each other. As believers love one another, their love is perfected, and that in turn allows them to have confidence when Jesus returns. They will not fear punishment, but they will be like Him.

Fear and mature love are mutually exclusive (4:18). A Christian who fears God's punishment (on the Day of Judgment, mentioned in verse 17) needs to grow in his or her understanding of love.

Critical Observation

The phrase, "fear has to do with punishment" (4:18) could be understood several ways. In the immediate context of the Day of Judgment (4:17), it seems virtually certain that eternal punishment (or fear of it) is what is meant.

Although verse 19 appears to be a declarative statement, it contains an implicit exhortation Because God first loved believers, believers *ought* to love Him and others in return.

In verse 20, John reverts to hypothetical statements like those in 1:6 and 2:4. Like the former statements, this one almost certainly has the false teachers in view: They claim to love God but fail to love fellow Christians. This leads John to conclude that such a person is a liar. Why? Because the person who does not love his fellow Christian, whom he has seen, cannot love God, whom he has not seen. Once more, in closing the chapter, John stresses the connection between loving God and loving one's fellow Christian (4:21). The two go hand in hand.

1 JOHN 5:1-21

GOD IS LIFE

Setting Up the Section

In this section, John will explain that the means by which believers conquer the world (including, of course, the false teachers, who are now part of the world according to 1 John 4:5) is their faith: faith in what Jesus has done during His earthly life and ministry, including His sacrificial death on the cross. For John, this is a faith the false teachers do not possess.

📄 **5:1-12**

THE LIFE OF JESUS

Once again (echoing 4:2-3) John stresses that confession of Jesus as the Christ is the standard that determines whether or not one is fathered by God. The second part of verse 1 reads like a proverb: If one loves the parent, one will love the child. While this is likely a general statement applying to any parent, in the present context it has application to loving God and loving God's children.

At face value, verse 2 says just the opposite of 4:20. In chapter 4, John states we can know we love God when we love our fellow Christians. Here John seems to be saying we can know that we love fellow Christians by loving God. It appears the debate is really over two things at once: whether or not we really love God (addressed by 4:20 and aimed at the false teachers) and how we can know that we really love God's children (addressed here and aimed at the readers). These two verses are like looking at the same coin from two different sides. They both work together.

A believer's love for God is expressed by his or her obedience (5:3). The description that God's commands are not weighty or burdensome may be a reference to the words of Jesus in Matthew 11:30 (which are a reiteration of Deuteronomy 30:11). John can describe God's commandments as not being weighty, because the commandment is to love one another, and God Himself is the endless source of this love. It is the love of God living inside Christians that makes the commandments unburdensome.

In the first part of verse 4, John uses the word *overcome*. He has already used this same word to describe victory over Satan in 2:13-14 and over the false teachers (described as false prophets) in 4:4. Here, John most likely has in mind victory over the false teachers.

In the latter part of verse 4, John also refers to a past conquering. Although some interpreters connect this with the past victory achieved over the false teachers, it may refer to Jesus Himself, who has already overcome the world by His victory over death. Thus, when John says faith has conquered the world, he is speaking of believers' faith in Jesus, who overcame the world by His sacrificial death on the cross, resurrection and return to the Father.

Although verse 5 is phrased as a rhetorical question, the answer is clear. John now affirms that it is the person who believes that Jesus is the Son of God who has conquered the world.

In verse 6, John says Jesus came by water and blood. A common interpretation sees the water as a reference to Jesus' baptism, while the blood is a reference to Jesus' death on the cross. Others see it as a reference to the outpouring of blood and water that came forth from Jesus' side after He died on the cross (John 19:34). While this phrase is a bit puzzling to contemporary readers, the terminology was probably familiar to John's original audience. His contention that Jesus came not by "water only" would be a strike at the false teachers. It may be that they affirmed Jesus' baptism but not His death and resurrection.

In 1 John 5:7-8, John calls on three witnesses to support his claims about Jesus: the Spirit, the blood, and the water. In the previous verses, the Spirit was listed separate from the water and the blood, but here they stand together.

The mention that the three witnesses are in agreement (5:8) means that they work together to achieve the same result—to establish the truth that Jesus is Christ (Messiah) and Son of God. Many see in the number of the witnesses (three) the Old Testament requirement that evidence had to be confirmed by two or three witnesses (Deuteronomy 19:15; John 8:17-18).

The testimony attributed to humanity (1 John 5:9) likely refers to the testimony of John the Baptist at the baptism of Jesus (John 1:32; 3:31-33; 5:36), which the false teachers were quoting to support their claim that Jesus "came by water" at His baptism (1 John 5:6). In this case, John mentions a fourth witness in addition to the three mentioned in verse 8: God Himself. John is saying that the false teachers, in their appeal to the human testimony of John the Baptist, are wrong because God's testimony surpasses human testimony.

Critical Observation

Verse 10 is a parenthesis in John's argument, which is then resumed in verse 11. John, in this context, is not distinguishing between the person who has made a personal commitment to Jesus and the person who has failed to do so, but between the person who has made a true confession of Jesus as the Christ, the Messiah, and the person who has made a false one, referring to the false teachers.

In verse 11, God's testimony (mentioned in verse 9) is revealed. The testimony is the eternal life that John and his readers possess, while the false teachers do not. It is important to remember that in John's debate with the false teachers, the controversy is not over the *reality* of eternal life (whether it exists at all), but over which side in the debate *possesses* it. John began with a testimony that the eternal life had been revealed (1:2), and it is consummated here with the acknowledgment of that eternal life as the final testimony in his case against the false teachers.

Possession of eternal life is connected to one's relationship to God's Son (5:12). The contrast between the readers of the letter, who are being reassured that they do indeed possess eternal life, and the false teachers, who in the opinion of John do not, is once again portrayed in stark terms. Someone either has the Son—He is present in the person's life—and thus has eternal life, or does not have the Son, in which case he or she does not have eternal life.

📄 5:13–21

ETERNAL LIFE

John begins his conclusion by telling his readers why he has written the letter (5:13). The expression *these things* refers to what has preceded. Once again John writes to reassure his readers that they possess eternal life.

In verses 14–15, John asserts the confidence that believers can have regarding prayer. Asking according to God's will brings assurance that God hears believers when they pray, and this gives assurance that they will receive answers to their requests.

In verse 16, John asks his readers to pray for the fellow believer who commits a sin, described here as a sin that doesn't result in death. While John's readers were expected to be familiar with this description of sin (resulting in death or not resulting in death), there has been some question since the original writing about what this sin is exactly. Theories include:

1) This is a specific sin. If so, we can't know from the information here what it is.
2) The sin is falling away from the faith, rejecting God after having once believed.
3) The sin is the refusal to believe in Jesus as God's Son.

Since in most of this letter John's negative aspersions have shed light on the position of the false teachers, it seems that the sin resulting in death is the sin of the false teachers whom John has consistently regarded as unbelievers (2:19; 3:14–15, 17). Refusal to believe in Jesus as the Christ, the Son of God, is the one sin that cannot be forgiven, because it denies the only means of forgiveness.

In verse 17, John does not leave the impression that any sin is insignificant. He reminds his readers that all unrighteousness is sin. Without the atoning work of Jesus, all sin leads to death.

Demystifying 1 John

John's claim that anyone fathered by God does not continue in sin (5:18) is essentially the same claim he makes in 3:9. In the immediate context in chapter 3, John is contrasting the children of God and the children of the devil. Here John writes that Jesus, who is born of God, keeps His children safe from the evil one.

If someone continues in the practice of sinning, in John's way of thinking it calls into question that person's salvation. It is God's life within the Christian that enables obedience.

In verse 19, John affirms that the whole world is still under the controlling influence of the evil one. However, believers do not belong to the world any longer. They belong to God and His Son.

John's closing can seem rather abrupt. It is possible that he is offering a general warning against idolatry in verse 21. However, John has spent virtually the whole letter discussing, in one form or another, the false teachers who are continuing to trouble the community. It is likely that this is a reference to the false image of Jesus that these teachers are putting forth.

Take It Home

John's letter is a continual effort to call this group of Christians back to an accurate view of Jesus, and thus an accurate view of the life they are to live as believers. The evil one is still at work today. It remains necessary for God's children to take account of the life within them, and the manner in which they practice the faith they are called to.

2 JOHN

INTRODUCTION TO 2 JOHN

Second John is a personal letter written to warn a sister congregation some distance away. In its original Greek manuscript, it is shorter than any other New Testament book except 3 John (with 219 words). The length of both 2 and 3 John is governed by the size of a single sheet of papyrus, which would have measured about 25 by 20 centimeters.

AUTHOR

As with the Gospel of John, the author does not explicitly identify himself as the apostle John. Instead, he uses the designation *the elder*. He obviously assumes the readers know him. However, the style of writing is unmistakably similar to that of 1 John. Also, as early as the second century, Christian historians and theologians recognized the author as the apostle John, one of the original twelve disciples.

PURPOSE

The purpose of this letter is to warn its readers of the missionary efforts of false teachers and the dangers of welcoming them whenever they should arrive.

OCCASION

Both 1 and 2 John are written in response to the same kinds of false teachers. This letter offers specific instructions about how to deal with the traveling preachers who were being sent out to local congregations. There is no conclusive evidence for the actual date, but this book was probably written around the same time as 1 John (around AD 90), while John was in Ephesus.

THEMES

Second John has the same themes that can be found in other writings by John: how to know the truth, how to live a life of love within that truth, and how to identify false teaching regarding the Christian faith.

OUTLINE

2 JOHN 1-4

Setting Up the Section

This Second Letter of John is written in a format characteristic of first-century letters It begins with an introduction (verses 1–3), which mentions the sender and the addressee, and includes a greeting. Many letters of this period follow the greeting with an expression of thanksgiving or a wish for the health of the addressee. Although no explicit expression of thanksgiving is found in 2 John, John's expression of joy in verse 4 may be roughly equivalent.

📄 **1–4**

THE GREETING

In verse 1, John identifies himself as the elder. He identifies his original addressee as "an elect lady and her children" (NET), which refers to a particular local church at some distance from the community where John is living at the time.

He also refers more specifically to all who know the truth. This focuses on those members of the community who have held fast to a correct view of Jesus in the face of opposition by the false teachers described in 1 John (1 John 2:3, 13; 4:16).

In one sense, the truth mentioned here suggests a primarily doctrinal focus—a point of belief about Jesus. In verse 2, however, the connection of truth with the expression "lives in us" (NIV) suggests that, for John, the truth is personalized and is a manifestation of the Spirit who resides permanently with believers.

John's greeting, while it fits the standard format of a first-century letter, also contains a significant amount of reassurance for the readers. Rather than wishing or praying for his readers to have grace, mercy, and peace with them (for instance, "may grace be with you"), verse 3 is more of a promise that these three important elements of faith, specifically from the Father and the Son, will certainly be with his readers.

The fact that John acknowledges that *some* of the members of the church are living according to God's truth does not necessarily mean that he is leaving out those *not* walking in the truth. It simply means that he does not have personal knowledge of all the members of the church to which he is writing (verse 4).

The use of the verb *walk* in verse 4 refers to conduct, behavior, or lifestyle. It is common in the New Testament (1 John 1:6; 3 John 3–4). In the context of this opening to John's letter, it refers to the resulting conduct of an individual who has truth residing within.

📄 **5–12**

THE MESSAGE

Verse 5 is an echo of 1 John 2:7. Both verses refer to a commandment that the readers have had from the beginning. The new commandment (John 13:34) is that believers love one another.

In verse 6, John explains what the love of God consists of: obedience to God's commandments. (This coordinates with 1 John 5:3.) Believers express their love for God by obeying His commandments and especially by loving one another.

The deceivers (verse 7) refer to the false teachers described at length in 1 John (2:18–19; 4:1). These false teachers are compared to the ultimate deceiver (Satan) and the Antichrist. This is not to mean they are identified as Satan or the Antichrist described in Revelation, but they are like these individuals in that they accomplish Satan's work and prepare the way for the Antichrist. They "do not acknowledge Jesus Christ as coming in the flesh" (NASB).

In verse 8, John urges his readers not to lose what they have worked for, which refers to their pastoral and missionary efforts in their community and surrounding communities. If the false teachers are unopposed and allowed to recruit in the community to which John is writing, all the effective work accomplished up to this point by the recipients of the letter would be in danger of being lost. Thus, there would be no basis left on which to be rewarded.

Critical Observation

The *reward* that John wants the readers to receive is a term for a workman's wage—the payment he is due in exchange for his labor. The idea of rewards for Christians who serve faithfully occurs in a number of places in the New Testament (Matthew 5:12; Mark 9:41; Luke 19:11–27; 1 Corinthians 3:8).

In verse 9, the false teachers are described as those who have gone beyond the apostolic eyewitness testimony about Jesus. Such a person does not have God, as opposed to the individual who remains in the apostolic teaching about Jesus. To *have* in this sense means to be indwelt by the Holy Spirit, who is in a dynamic relationship with both the Father and the Son at all times. John does not regard this to be true of the false teachers.

The warning not to welcome those without the teaching of Christ (verse 10) could simply be a prohibition against showing hospitality to the traveling representatives of the false teachers. It is possible, though, that the house refers to a church. If that is so, then this is an instruction to prohibit the false teachers to speak to the house church and spread their false teaching.

John's command not to welcome, or greet, these individuals is not intended to represent an insult. In this context, to greet someone means to greet him or her as a fellow Christian, and this is impossible, because as far as John is concerned, the false teachers are rot genuine believers. Therefore, they should not be publicly greeted as such. Giving one of the false teachers' representatives a greeting in public could be construed as giving endorsement to that person's views about Jesus. This would be, in effect, to share in his evil deeds (verse 11).

In verse 12, John indicates he has much more to say but prefers to do so in person. This is a quick letter sent in light of the urgency he feels about the danger of these false teachers.

📄 13

FAREWELL

In verse 13, John sends final greetings. It is significant that it is the *children* of the elect sister, and not the sister herself, who send the greetings here. This probably refers to members of a sister church to which 2 John is written. Evidently, John is staying in that community while writing this letter.

Take It Home

John's letter reminds us of the importance of knowing what we believe, not for the sake of winning an argument, but for the sake of walking with God in truth.

3 JOHN

INTRODUCTION TO 3 JOHN

Third John, like 2 John, is written in the standard correspondence format for the first century. It is slightly shorter than 2 John and is the shortest book of the New Testament. It is the only one of the three New Testament letters to be addressed to a named individual.

AUTHOR

As with the Gospel of John, the author does not explicitly identify himself as the apostle John, but instead uses the designation *the elder*. As early as the second century, though, Christian historians and theologians recognized the author as the apostle John, one of the original twelve disciples.

PURPOSE

John wrote this letter to commend two church leaders, Gaius and Demetrius, and to send a warning about Diotrephes, a man who opposed John's leadership.

OCCASION

The problem with Diotrephes was not a problem with heresy (as in 1 and 2 John) as much as authority. He was evidently trying to diminish John's authority as well as censure those sent by John. It was this behavior that prompted John to write to Gaius.

THEMES

John's third, short letter deals with the themes of hospitality toward the traveling teachers who spread the gospel in the first century. It also speaks to pride and its affect on leadership within a community.

OUTLINE

3 JOHN 1-2

Setting Up the Section

Third John begins with an introductory formula (verses 1–2), that mentions the sender and the addressee. The greeting, a standard part of the introduction, is omitted, but unlike 2 John, the letter includes a health wish (verse 3).

📄 **1–2**

THE GREETING

As in 2 John, John refers to himself as the elder (verse 1). The addressee's name, *Gaius*, was common in the Roman Empire, and it is unlikely that the person addressed here is the same as one of those with that name associated with Paul (Acts 19:29; 20:4; Romans 16:23; 1 Corinthians 1:14). This individual is well-known to John, but it is not certain whether they had met in person, since the report of Gaius's conduct toward the brothers is heard secondhand by John. Nor is it certain whether Gaius belonged to the same local church as Diotrephes (3 John 9) or was himself the leader of another local congregation. It is clear, however, that John regards Gaius as a valuable ally in the controversy with the false teachers and their false view of Jesus (verse 3).

John affirms in verse 2 that Gaius is well-off spiritually. He prays that Gaius's physical health would match his spiritual health. Notice, it is the spiritual health that is to be the standard by which one's physical health is measured, not the other way around.

📄 **3–12**

THE MESSAGE

In verse 3, the word *truth* may refer to either doctrine or behavior. Certainly John makes no effort to correct Gaius's doctrine. But according to verse 5, it is Gaius's faithful work on behalf of the brothers—the traveling missionaries who need support—that is commended by John. Therefore, in this context, the emphasis is on Gaius's behavior rather than on his doctrine.

In verse 4, John may be referring to Gaius as one of his own converts (like Paul refers to his spiritual children in 1 Corinthians 4:14–15), but more likely John simply regards those under his spiritual authority as his children.

Addressing Gaius as a dear friend in verse 5, John commends him for his faithful service to the traveling missionaries (the brothers), even though he did not know them personally. The missionaries have returned and informed John of Gaius's support (verse 6). It seems likely that the church mentioned here is also John's church, where he is currently located.

John writes that the missionaries have gone out on behalf of the name of God (verse 7). They have been sent out to combat the false teachers and have accepted nothing from non-Christians, or pagans. Their mission is not evangelization but concerns an in-house debate over Jesus' identity as the Son of God.

Critical Observation

The word translated *pagan* here occurs only four times in the New Testament (the other three are in Matthew 5:47; 6:7; and 18:17). It refers to Gentiles. Since the issue here is support for the traveling missionaries and there is no indication that John would want to forbid receiving support from Gentile converts to Christianity, the word must refer to Gentile unbelievers. The traveling missionaries sent out to combat false teaching have been accepting nothing by way of support from non-Christians. Why support from non-Christians should be refused is not entirely clear, although a number of interpreters see the possibility of confusion with missionaries representing pagan deities.

The first person plural in verse 8 includes John himself, Gaius, and all genuine Christians, who should all support the traveling missionaries in their efforts to resist and counteract the teaching of the false teachers.

In verse 9, Diotrephes appears to be an influential person (perhaps the leader) in a local church known to Gaius, but to which Gaius himself does not belong. John's description of Diotrephes suggests an arrogant person who has refused to acknowledge John's prior written communication. This communication probably concerns the traveling missionaries mentioned in the next verse, and Diotrephes has refused to acknowledge John's authority to intervene in the matter. (For Diotrephes this may have been an issue of John's authority and local jurisdiction over such things.)

The church mentioned here, which John says he may visit (verse 10), is not the same as the one mentioned in verse 6, to which John apparently belongs (or of which he is in charge). It seems probable that Gaius belongs to (or is in charge of) one local church while Diotrephes is in another.

Concerning Diotrephes, John gives a warning in verse 10. Because Diotrephes does not recognize John's authority, if John visits he will expose Diotrephes' behavior. Since Diotrephes made unjustified charges against John, John will bring charges of his own against Diotrephes.

John's instruction not to imitate what is bad is clearly a reference to Diotrephes' behavior (verse 11). By implication, John calls into question the genuineness of Diotrephes' faith. In John's terminology, it is clear that the phrase "has not seen God" is equivalent to "is not a genuine Christian."

Demetrius, mentioned in verse 12, is apparently someone Gaius has not met. He has a good reputation, and it is possible he is the leader of the traveling missionaries. John commends Demetrius to Gaius.

Demystifying 3 John

Demetrius may well have been the leader of a delegation of traveling missionaries and may even have been the bearer of this letter to Gaius. The writing of letters of introduction to be carried along by representatives or missionaries in New Testament times is also attested in Paul's writings (1 Corinthians 16:3).

📄 13–15

FAREWELL

As in the closing of 2 John, John says that he has many things to write to Gaius but prefers to speak in person. It appears that John anticipates a personal visit in the near future. This may be the same visit mentioned in connection with Diotrephes in verse 10. Gaius's church and Diotrephes' church may have been in the same city or in neighboring towns, so that John anticipates visiting both on the same journey.

John closes with greetings similar to 2 John 13. *Friends* is an alternative to *brothers* as an early Christian designation, especially within John's community. It may have come about from Jesus' teaching in John 15:13–15, "You are my friends if you do what I command."

JUDE

INTRODUCTION TO JUDE

AUTHOR

The author of this letter is Jude, the brother of James. Most likely these brothers are the same brothers listed in Matthew 13:55 and Mark 6:3 as Jesus' half brothers (born to Joseph and Mary after Jesus' birth). It was common in the history of the church to shorten the name of Judas to Jude, in the interest of changing one's name from that of the great betrayer, Judas Iscariot. While these two brothers did not have faith in Jesus as Lord during His lifetime (John 7:5), they became leaders in the first-century Christian church, and each wrote a New Testament letter.

PURPOSE

This epistle is a passionate plea for the readers to contend for their faith. In light of a growing heresy in the church that understood grace as a license for immorality, Jude wrote to an unidentified group of Christ-followers to call them back to faith.

OCCASION

We don't know exactly when Jude was written, but many estimate around AD 65. The content of Jude and 2 Peter are closely related, and this has prompted discussion about which came first and which provided reference for the other.

While it had been Jude's intent to write to this particular group of believers on the topic of salvation (verse 3), what prompted this letter was news of false teaching.

THEMES

Truth and discernment are two key themes of this book. A believer's security in God's love opens and closes the letter, but the meat of the content pertains to the false teachers in the midst and the need for believers to stand firm in the truth.

OUTLINE

JUDE 1–4

Setting Up the Section

In this section, Jude gives his reasons for writing and a strongly worded identification of the enemies of the faith.

CONTENDING FOR THE FAITH

Jude describes himself as a bond servant (or, slave; Greek: *doulos*) of Jesus Christ (verse 1). A bond servant is a lifelong loyal servant of his master. He also identifies himself as the brother of James. In this case, James is the half brother of Jesus. This kind of introduction is an act of humility on Jude's part, not touting his familial connection with Jesus, but rather his faith in Jesus.

Jude's identification of his readers (verse 1), while it does not specifically identify the people or the community, paints a beautiful picture of those who follow Jesus: chosen, loved by God, and kept by Jesus.

In verse 2, Jude writes an encouraging prayer request that his readers would receive their full capacity of three things:

* *Mercy.* The mercy of God displayed upon His children when He comes to judge the world.
* *Peace.* Supernatural contentment no matter the circumstances one faces.
* *Love.* The love of God manifested to us so that we will one day stand in His presence.

Jude's original purpose for writing had changed (verse 3). Rather than being a relaxed letter to friends, this letter deals with a problem the introduction of false doctrine into the community.

Jude sounds like a general giving a passionate speech to motivate his troops or a coach to motivate his players. He encourages his readers to *contend* for their faith, to passionately struggle, to protect it from destruction. This is not a onetime event, but an ongoing effort. He describes this faith as something that has been once for all delivered to the saints. The idea behind the phrase "once for all" is the concept of finality. Jesus was the complete fulfillment of the truth, and there is no more to add to it.

In verse 4, Jude tells his readers that the enemy has infiltrated the camp. The idea is that these men have subtly slithered in, escaping notice. These men came in under the guise of Christianity but distorted the message.

Jude's description of these teachers is written in strong language. It is possible, because of the deceitful tactics of the teachers, that he is denouncing men who have become respected, perhaps even leaders. Yet, Jude states, they are without God.

JUDE 5–16

Setting Up the Section

Jude wants his readers to see the true nature of false teachers so that they will not try to please them or keep them close. False teachers are not people to be reasoned with; they are a danger to the congregation and, as Jude will point out, need be avoided.

5–16

THE DESCRIPTION OF FALSE TEACHERS

In verses 5-7, Jude offers three examples of God's judgment on those who failed in contending for their faith. In doing so, he sheds light on the nature of the false teachers.

First, in verse 5, Jude refers to the redemption of the Israelites from Egypt. God delivered His children from Egypt, but after that deliverance, the people failed to believe that God would give them the land that He promised. Thus they died without entering the land (Numbers 32:10-13).

Next, in verse 6, Jude points out God's judgment on the angels. This is not a description of Satan's fall, but more likely a description of the angels in Genesis 6:1-4 who interacted with humanity and took women for wives.

Sodom and Gomorrah are Jude's third example. They committed the same sin as the angels—immorality (verse 7). The words translated *sexual immorality* here describe extreme, unbridled sexual sin.

If Jude is using these examples to describe the false teachers, then we can assume that these men were once orthodox in their faith but had fallen away from that faith and into immoral living. He assigns the fall of these men to their dreaming (verse 8). This may refer to their claims to have had visions that distort God's commands as given in scripture and thus claiming license to live immorally.

Jude tells us that the angel Michael (verse 9) did not even speak in his own authority to the devil. This is a reference to a story not included in scripture, but that was probably well-known to Jude and his readers. The story centered on who had jurisdiction over Moses' body after he died, the angel Michael or the devil. The point Jude is likely making here is that Michael did not act on his own authority even against the devil, but rather left that task to God Himself. (The words attributed to Michael here may have been drawn from Zechariah 3:2.) If Michael was this careful in how he spoke and acted, how much more so should mortal men watch their words in light of God's power? Yet these false teachers were cavalier in their attitudes, theologies, and philosophies (verse 10).

Demystifying Jude

Jude lists three more examples from the Old Testament that shed light on these false teachers (verse 11):

1) Like Cain, who offered up his sacrifice to the Lord on his own strength without faith, the false teachers try to please God on their terms and seek to do their work in the flesh (Genesis 4:1–16).
2) Like Balaam, the prophet who led the people of God astray for money, the false teachers follow their passion for wealth at the expense of the people (Numbers 22:1–34).
3) Like Korah's followers, who rebelled against Moses and were swallowed up in the earth, these teachers will be judged (Numbers 16:1–35).

In verses 12–13, Jude describes these troublesome teachers as sunken reefs (concealed danger), self-focused feasters, waterless clouds (empty promises), fruitless trees (twice dead because they came to faith, then fell away), waves carrying impurities to the beach (see Isaiah 57:20), and shooting stars that fall into the darkness.

Demystifying Jude

Verses 14–15 announce judgment by quoting 1 Enoch, a Jewish book written between the Old and New Testaments and not included in the Christian Bible. The man Enoch, however, is mentioned in Genesis 5 as the descendant of Adam through Seth, Adam's son born after Cain and Abel. One of Enoch's claims to fame is as the father of Methuselah. The other is that rather than record his death, the scriptures say that he walked with God and God simply took him from the earth (Genesis 5:18–24).

While it may seem strange to hear a New Testament writer quote from a book not included in the scriptures, it is important to remember that this book was valued by both Jude and his readers, and that the New Testament canon had not been formalized when Jude was writing this letter. Jude does not claim that it is scripture, but simply describes a scene recorded in it.

Finally, in verse 16, Jude gives a further, colorful description of the false teachers, painting them as negative, selfish men out for their own profit. Rather than men guided by the truth, they are represented more as disgruntled scam artists.

JUDE 17–23

Setting Up the Section

Up to this point Jude has been making his case against the false teachers, but here he focuses on his main point. Discernment and mercy are requirements for this community—discernment so one does not get carried away by false teaching and mercy to reach out to those who have been influenced by heresy.

17–23

THE DEFENSE AGAINST FALSE TEACHERS

In verses 17–19, Jude warns the community of danger by quoting the apostles. We can't know which of the apostles' writings Jude's readers were aware of, but we can certainly see from the New Testament scriptures available to us that the apostles often warned of false teachers (see Acts 20:29; 2 Corinthians 11:3; Colossians 2:4; 1 Timothy 4:1–3; 1 John 2:18–19).

Jude next offers five ways to stay faithful (Jude 20–22). These are not onetime events, but ongoing requirements:

1) Build yourself up in faith.
2) Pray in the Holy Spirit.
3) Stay within the love of God.
4) Wait eagerly for the return of Christ.
5) Show mercy to those unstable in their faith.

In verses 22–23, Jude addresses three different kinds of people who need to be reached: those who doubt because of false teaching, those who have gone past doubt and committed themselves to a false system, and those who are completely contaminated by heresy. All need to be reached but require different tactics.

Jude tells us to hate the garment that has been polluted by the flesh (verse 23). The garment spoken of here is the undergarment, which is closest to the body. The image of garments, both blemished and clean, appears throughout the scriptures. In the Old Testament, the law required the literal garments of a defiled person to be burned, and perhaps Jude's comment is an allusion to that custom. In both the New and Old Testaments, though, garments often were used to talk about the lifestyle of a person, laying aside the old garments in exchange for the new.

JUDE 24-25

Setting Up the Section

As Jude brings his Epistle to a close, he focuses on the sustaining power of God.

📄 24-25

THE DOXOLOGY

God's children will survive the false teachers they face because of the person in whom they place their faith. Jesus is able to keep us from falling and help us to stand clean in His presence (verse 24). The idea behind the word *able* is the concept of power, which is the focus of these verses. God is powerful enough to protect His children's souls from the threatening sin that is in the world.

Not only will God's strength allow us to survive, but we will stand spotless before Him. Jude is describing the great work of redemption.

In his final words of praise, Jude describes God as worthy of all honor for eternity past and future (verse 25). Yet, in His completeness, He saves us, protects us, and uses us to reach out to others and share the lifesaving news of the gospel.

Take It Home

If we are going to be contenders for the faith and guard the gospel that we have been entrusted with, we must apply the survival skills that Jude offers. Are you doing what it takes to stay in the sphere of God's love? What is your attitude toward those who might be trapped in a false belief system? Will you reach out to them with mercy?

REVELATION

INTRODUCTION TO REVELATION

The word *revelation* means "unveiling," or "disclosure." This is a book that reveals how the person, righteousness, and judgment of Jesus are going to be revealed in all of the fullness and power of God.

Understanding a symbolic book like this requires putting together whole sections rather than reading select verses in isolation. The meaning of Revelation comes from unfolding the entire book chapter by chapter. The message is God's sovereignty over all.

AUTHOR

As with most New Testament books, through the centuries there has been discussion as to the author of this letter. While the writer identifies himself as John (1:1), some have wondered if it is safe to assume that this means the apostle John. Many of the arguments on this topic center around the language differences from the other New Testament books attributed to the apostle (the Gospel of John and 1 John). There has been no irrefutable evidence, though, to sway conservative scholars from accepting John's authorship.

PURPOSE

The church in the first century was suffering. Many of the original apostles had been martyred for the faith, and John had been arrested and placed in exile on the island of Patmos. The fires of persecution were burning, and the immediate future seemed to hold only increasing difficulty. The first-century Christians needed spiritual, mental, emotional, and physical stability to stand firm in their trials.

The overall purpose of this letter is to encourage those Christians. They needed to know that the kingdom of God would overcome the kingdoms of the world, and that all those who oppose God and oppress God's children would be brought to justice.

OCCASION

Since so many of the images in Revelation are often interpreted in relation to governments and political leaders, discussions about when the book was written focus on which emperor was ruling at the time. Many suggest that Nero must have been ruling, but most suggest that John wrote during the time of Domitian, which would have placed the writing of this vision letter around AD 90–95. One of the biggest supports for this date is the fact that emperor worship—which is repeatedly alluded to in John's visions—was a much greater issue during Domitian's rule than during Nero's.

THEMES

First, John's book reveals significant aspects of the character and future work of Jesus Christ, the Lamb of God.

Also, the eternality and sovereignty of God is a major theme. The idea that God is outside of time and sovereign over human history is encouraging, because we can know that He is above the things in the earth that drive us down. God is holding all things together, and therefore, no matter how much it looks like evil is winning, that is not the reality.

CONTRIBUTION TO THE BIBLE

Revelation is the only book of prophecy in the New Testament and the only book that focuses so heavily on the end times. It offers us a symbolic, but rich, vision of the end of the age that is mentioned in places in the other New Testament writings.

OUTLINE

REVELATION 1:1–20

ETERNAL HOPE

Setting Up the Section

The book of Revelation, while a type of literature known as "apocalyptic" (a Greek word meaning "revelation"), is written in the form of a letter. It opens with a greeting typical for a New Testament Epistle.

John opens his letter with the truth of God's power and eternal nature. This would have been an encouragement to his readers who were facing increasing persecution for their faith. The first-century Christians needed spiritual, mental, emotional, and physical stability to stand firm in their trials. They would have been strengthened by the knowledge that God has a plan, and no matter how much it looks like evil is winning, that is not the reality.

📄 **1:1–8**

GREETING AND INTRODUCTION

The first two verses of Revelation reveal three things:

1) The book is a revelation of Jesus Christ and His sovereign control of the universe.
2) John is the one who received this revelation.
3) The letter is an eyewitness account.

Verse 3 is a beatitude. In it John claims this book as a prophecy to be heard and obeyed. The word *prophecy* here does not mean a prediction of the future, though much of Revelation has to do with future events. Instead, it is prophecy in the sense that it is God's truth communicated to humankind.

Demystifying Revelation

Verse 4 begins a section of letters to seven churches in Asia. These seven churches are all located in the western part of what we know today as Turkey. They all face differing circumstances and struggle with a variety of issues. Though these letters address the specific situations of each church, all together they offer a wealth of application for the church at large today.

Letters in the first century typically had a greeting that identified the sender and the addressees. The greeting in Revelation is what theologians call a Trinitarian greeting. It starts with a description of the Father, the supreme sovereign Lord of the entire world, past, present, and future (1:4). The seven Spirits before His throne represent the Holy Spirit (1:4). And at the first part of verse 5, we have a threefold description of Jesus:

1) *The faithful witness.* Jesus was faithful in the past to carry out God's plan of

redemption, and He will be faithful in the future by bringing about the plan of God for the consummation of the ages.

2) *The firstborn of the dead.* Because Jesus was faithful to the plan of God, God raised Jesus from the dead. This is the ultimate in hope for the believer, because all those who place their faith in Jesus can be assured of rising from the dead as well.

3) *The ruler of the kings of the earth.* Even though John's readers were dealing with cruel rulers, and it would seem as if these rulers were in ultimate control, Jesus has supreme control and the earth is under His rule.

At the end of verse 5 and the beginning of verse 6, John states two things about Jesus. First, He loves us and releases us from our sins by His blood. Next, He allows each true believer to be a part of the kingdom of God, and thus to be a priest to God the Father. Because of Jesus, there is no longer need for any other human mediators to connect us to God. Therefore, all believers are the object of Jesus' love, released from sin, a part of the kingdom of God, and able to pursue God directly through Jesus Christ. That is why John offers praise in the form of a doxology at the end of verse 6.

As a conclusion to the work of Jesus, John finally states that this same Jesus who loves us, releases us, includes us in the kingdom, and makes us able to serve God will also come again (1:7). Notice that at the return of Jesus the people will mourn (an allusion to Zechariah 12:10). They will be mourning the judgment that is coming as a result of their sin.

There are several titles given to God the Father in verse 8, and each conveys the depth and the strength of God:

1) *Alpha and Omega*: This statement refers to the eternal and unchanging nature of God. *Alpha* is the first letter of the Greek alphabet, and *omega* is the last. This means that God lives in an eternal state.

2) *Who is, who was, and who is to come*: God, although living outside of time, still dwells in time and therefore simultaneously interacts with those living in the present, those in the past, and those in the future.

3) *The Almighty*: This refers to the fact that God has His hand on everything and, therefore, is able to completely rule the world.

John's readers can take hope in these truths—God is the One who secures us in time and space because He is eternally secure in heaven.

📖 1:9–20

THE REVELATION OF POWER

In verse 9, John reveals that he is writing from the island of Patmos, a place to which criminals were banished. John's crime was proclaiming the Word of God. He writes that every believer partakes of the following:

1) *Tribulation*—the trials that come when a person seeks to follow God.

2) *Kingdom*—the spiritual world that one experiences in part on earth and then experiences fully upon death.

3) *Perseverance*—the ability to persevere in the trials that come along with following Jesus.

There are some that say that the Lord's Day (1:9) is a figurative statement referring to the final judgment day (1:10). More likely it is simply the first reference to Sunday, the new day of worship (as opposed to Saturday, the Jewish Sabbath) based on Jesus' resurrection. So here, John is caught up in the spiritual world on the day commemorating Jesus' resurrection.

Demystifying Revelation

It is important to interpret John's letter of Revelation as apocalyptic literature, a type of Jewish literature that often used symbolic images to describe spiritual as well as historical realities. This vision of John is not necessarily meant to be a literal description of people and events (the Antichrist, for example, will not literally look like a "beast"), but instead it is meant to be a figurative description that bares light on the character of Jesus and the nature of the salvation He is providing. This metaphorical language happens in other passages of scripture as well, such as when Jesus calls Himself bread or a gate (see John 6:35; 10:7). We are not supposed to think that Jesus actually looked like a piece of bread, but are instead supposed to understand aspects of His character and mission from the illustration. So it is with Revelation.

In verse 10, John says he was "in the Spirit." This may imply a kind of trance, but it certainly describes a state of mind in which John was open to the Spirit's leading through visions. In this open and spiritual state of mind, John hears a voice that sounds like a trumpet. This voice instructs him to write down his vision and send it to the seven churches listed in verse 11.

Verses 12–13 introduce a new image—seven golden candlesticks, or lampstands, which represent the churches John will address. And in the midst of those candlesticks is the Son of Man.

In John's vision, Jesus' description and even position are telling. The fact that He was standing in the middle of the churches signifies that the churches belong to Him (1:13). The term *Son of Man* (Daniel 7:13–14; Revelation 1:13), when used about the Messiah, refers to the fact that Jesus not only had a divine nature but a physical body as well. John is saying that he saw a man, but not just any man—He is a God-man. Jesus' full-length robe with a golden sash was the apparel of a priest. His white hair signifies both age and wisdom. In fact, it is the same type of description used of the Ancient of Days, a reference to God Himself in Daniel 7:9. This paints the picture of someone who has the wisdom of the world because He has existed forever (Revelation 1:14).

The fire images introduced in verse 14 and continuing into verse 15 are pictures of judgment. In this vision, Jesus is looking at the world with the eyes of judgment. The feet of Christ represent the reality that Jesus can judge the earth and will execute that judgment personally. His feet are glowing with the power of justice and righteousness.

The fact that His voice sounded like roaring waters implies that Jesus spoke with authority and power (1:15; see Ezekiel 43:2). The seven stars in Jesus' hand refer to the Spirit of God at work in each of the churches, and the sword from His mouth is a symbol of God's Word with the continuing connotation of judgment (Revelation 1:16). Jesus' shining face implies His glory (1:16).

John's response to this vision is not simply a reverent bow, but rather a complete collapse caused by the overwhelming glory he has experienced. Jesus tells him not to be afraid but to remember that He is eternal ("First and Last," mirroring verse 8), resurrected, and in control (1:17–18). These are three key truths that John can cling to so that he does not need to fear for his life in the presence of Jesus.

The use of *Hades* here refers to the realm of death, which Jesus triumphs over. This is a different meaning than hell, the place of punishment.

John's role, as described in verse 19, is to describe this vision, reveal the state of the churches, and communicate the later description of the future to come.

The angels (1:20) of the churches may simply refer to the spirits of those churches as opposed to an actual type of guardian angel. It is important to note that the churches are described as lampstands—not the light itself, but that which reveals the light.

Take It Home

While Revelation is apocalyptic in nature, it is important to remember that, like any New Testament book, it serves to reveal Jesus to us. We make the most of studying this book when we stop trying to figure out the "when" of Jesus' return (which we have already been told is impossible; see Mark 13:32–36) and instead focus on who Jesus is and who we are to be in light of that revelation.

REVELATION 2:1–3:22
LETTERS TO THE CHURCHES

Setting Up the Section

While some see these churches as only symbolic, it is more likely these were messages to specific congregations. What we do know about the cities addressed here meshes with the specific messages John writes. The situations of these churches vary, and thus John addresses many issues that churches face still today.

These letters do not represent a collection of letters that were once circulated separately, but were from the beginning part of the book of Revelation. The whole book was meant to circulate among the seven churches.

EPHESUS—PASSION FOR CHRIST

The church at Ephesus is committed to doctrinal purity; the believers have persisted as disciples of Jesus (2:1–3). Yet their love for doctrine and truth is stronger than their passion for the person of Jesus (2:4). The concept of not staying true to their first love may include not only their love for Jesus, but also their love for each other, which is to mirror their love for Jesus.

Demystifying Revelation

The Ephesus of John's day was the most important city in the Roman province of Asia, located in what is today western Turkey. It was home to 250,000–500,000 people. Because it stood at the crossroad of many trade routes, it was an eclectic city with many religions present.

The apostle Paul spent more than two years in Ephesus establishing this church. The New Testament book of Ephesians is his letter to the congregation. According to tradition, Ephesus is where John spent his later years.

The Ephesian church receives two commands (2:5):
1) They must consider how far they have fallen.
2) They must repent.

If they don't comply, Jesus will pronounce judgment, and their effectiveness as a church of God will be lost (2:5).

The Ephesian church is credited for standing against the Nicolaitans. All that is known of this group is found here. While it is clear from this passage that the Nicolaitans represent a heresy, we have only speculations as to the origin and specifics. Some have argued that this was a heresy spawned from Nicolas, one of the seven servants chosen to serve the widows in the Jerusalem church (Acts 6), who later fell into heresy and used his position to lead many astray. Others think that this group is not associated with Nicolas and just used his name to gain credibility.

This letter to Ephesus ends with "The one who has an ear. . ." (Revelation 2:7 NET), a statement used throughout these letters to the churches. It means that if anyone understands the real meaning of what he or she hears, then he or she must respond.

While the close of verse 7 refers back to the tree of life from the Garden of Eden (Genesis 3:24), God's paradise refers to the future when God restores heaven and earth from the fall of humanity.

SMYRNA—DEPENDENCE UPON CHRIST

Jesus addresses this church from His role as the resurrected One. He identifies them by the distresses they have experienced—suffering, poverty, and slander. Christianity was outlawed at the time John was writing and was particularly held in contempt in a place known for its loyalty and worship of the emperor.

Demystifying Revelation

Smyrna was a beautiful city with much trade based on a well-protected harbor. It had been destroyed and rebuilt before 200 BC. After that, it was rebuilt according to a plan, much as a planned community today. Most likely, the church in Smyrna was a product of Paul's Ephesian ministry (Acts 19:10) and was founded by the apostle himself or one of his converts. At the end of the first century, life was difficult and dangerous for Christians in Smyrna. As a loyal Roman ally, the city was a key center for emperor worship, so any other religious loyalties could easily be perceived as political threats.

In Revelation 2:9, John makes reference to those who call themselves Jews but are not. What he means is that, in light of the revelation of Jesus, being a Jew has more to do with how a person lives than with his heritage or bloodline. This is key to one's interpretation of John's writing in Revelation. One who understands John's use of the Jewish nation to mean the new nation of faith—the church—will interpret passages relating to the Jews as symbolically to be about the church as a whole. How one chooses to interpret this affects many portions of this book.

In light of the persecution of the day, the reference to prison in verse 10 may infer more than simple containment. It may be a reference to a type of holding cell where a detainee awaits execution (2:10). The mention of ten days would have been understood by John's original readers as an allusion to Daniel's request to be tested for ten days in order to see that God's commands regarding food would make him and his cohorts stronger than the rest of the men taken to Babylon (Daniel 1:12–15). This was a test that proved God faithful, as would the test of the Smyrnaeans.

Jesus wants this congregation to be faithful until death so that they may receive the crown of life. The word translated *crown* here is not a king's crown, but the winning wreath given to the winner of a game. In the case of the Smyrnaeans, if they persevere in the midst of their difficulties, they will not be hurt by the second death—in other words, they will be the ultimate victors over hell (the second death [Revelation 2:10–11]).

📖 2:12–17

PERGAMUM—PERSEVERANCE IN THE TRUTH

In the letter to the church at Pergamum, Jesus is described as the One with a sword in His mouth, an image that symbolizes the Word of God. This symbol may have had multiple meanings to John's original readers in that the sword also served as a symbol of Rome. In light of that fact, this image could serve as a reminder that Jesus' authority exceeds any earthly power (2:12).

Demystifying Revelation

Pergamum was about a hundred miles north of Ephesus, with Smyrna located about halfway in between. As Asia's ancient capital, it was considered Asia's greatest city, not because of its position on trade routes but because of its governmental standing. It was a city with many pagan practices, renowned for its altar to the god Zeus as well as multiple temples to the emperor.

The people in this church remained true to Christ in the face of great temptation. The believers did not give in to the emperor worship that was rampant, but instead they remained true even in the face of martyrdom. No additional information is given about Antipas's identity, but it's obvious from verse 13 that he was faithful even in death.

The reference to Satan is a reminder that their persecution is a product of spiritual warfare rather than simple governmental persecution (2:13).

The accusation against this church is that they allowed false teachers to exist in their presence (2:14). The references to Balaam and Balak are from an Old Testament account in which a king named Balak tried to hire a prophet named Balaam to curse the Israelites. When Balaam's attempt failed (Numbers 22–24), he instructed Balak to tempt the Israelites to forsake their religious commitments so the ensuing consequences would have the same effect as a curse (Numbers 31:15–16). Both behaviors listed here in Revelation 2:14—food sacrificed to idols and sexual immorality—were related to idol worship.

The reference to the Nicolaitans offers no more explanatory information than in the previous letter to the church at Ephesus (2:6). In this case, though, there seems to be a possible connection to the idol worship mentioned in connection with Balaam (2:14–15).

Jesus calls the church to repent, at the risk of war if they don't, thus the apt vision with the sword—an image of God's Word, but also a military weapon (2:16). On the other hand, if this church prevails against their sin, they will have hidden manna (2:17). This refers to the manna that was hidden in the ark of the covenant by Moses, one of the most precious relics of the ancient Jews.

Demystifying Revelation

The white stone in verse 17 may refer to an invitation. In the Roman culture, a white stone was given to the winner of a competition. The stone had the winner's name inscribed on it, and it was used to get the winner into the awards banquet. The party that these believers are going to will be "by invitation only," and they will receive this stone as the invitation. On it will be a new name that no one knows.

In the Greek culture there was a thought that the gods all had secret names in which their powers were kept. Jesus may be using that imagery to illustrate that they will have a name that has power to it and this name is hidden from the world. It is a name that has to be revealed. This name is given to the people as their new name because they are given a new life in Jesus Christ.

📖 2:18–29

THYATIRA—PURITY OF LEADERSHIP

Opening the letter to the church at Thyatira is a vision of Jesus similar to the description given in chapter 1 of Revelation. This vision of Jesus' eyes and feet highlights His all-knowing nature and His commitment to hunt down and conquer evil (1:14–15; 2:18).

While this church's good works are acknowledged, the church is also accused of tolerating Jezebel (2:19–20). This is probably an alias John uses for this troublesome woman, relating her to the wicked queen of the Old Testament by the same name

(1 Kings 16:30–31). This woman's teaching pulls people away from the Word of God to immorality and idolatry. On one hand, this church has people who are serving God in a strong fashion. On the other hand, they have allowed a false teacher in their midst to lead them astray (Revelation 2:20).

Demystifying Revelation

Many speculate that the church at Thyatira was founded somehow through Paul's ministry in Ephesus. At the time of the writing of Revelation, the city of Thyatira was entering its greatest season of prosperity. As a Roman outpost city, it served a purpose of protecting the Roman Empire from invading forces from the north. The various businesses were divided into guilds that all had their own gods. In order to do business in the city, a person had to go through a guild. Thus, before business was conducted, one would have to perform the worship customs of the god of the guild.

Verses 21–23 reveal how God deals with evil. Those who follow this woman will join her in illness and suffering as an added prompt toward their repentance.

There are those in Thyatira who have not succumbed to Jezebel's false teaching, and they are commended (2:24–25). The additional burden that will not be added to them probably refers to anything further than the service they have already been called to as disciples of Jesus (2:24). The reward for their perseverance, though, will be authority in Jesus' name (2:26).

The iron rod probably refers to a shepherd's implement with a metal tip (2:27). While a shepherd is a gentle leader, he maintains ultimate control over his flock. This image coupled with the image of the clay jars broken to pieces implies judgment. This may mean that the authority given to the faithful will be participation in Jesus' final judgment.

The morning star, also a reward given to the faithful by Jesus, refers to the power of a new life, the resurrected life that Christ had shown when He rose from the dead (2:28).

📄 3:1–6

SARDIS—FAITH THAT LEADS TO LIFE

Unlike the preceding churches, the judgment against the church at Sardis appears in the first verse of the address. It is a church that thinks it is alive, but in all reality it is dead (3:1). Sardis, the city, had twice been overtaken by enemies because of its failure to remain on watch. So it seems apt that the command offered to the Christian church in that city is to wake up (3:2).

The church of Sardis has a noticeable difference from the other churches addressed so far. All of the other churches have some corrupt people but others who are faithful. In this case, the faithful are in the minority (3:3–5).

Demystifying Revelation

Sardis was a wealthy city full of gold taken from the nearby Pactolus River. The city was located on a high hill at the intersection of five roads. Like the other cities addressed in Revelation 2–3, the church of Sardis was probably founded through Paul's ministry in Ephesus.

Through the years there have been a variety of meanings suggested for the white clothing mentioned in verse 4. Most likely, the white clothes represent justification through faith in Jesus. These few faithful individuals mentioned here have done nothing to forfeit that justification, thus staining their clothes (3:4). Also, they will be confessed before the Father, which means they will be acknowledged as belonging to Jesus and thus allowed to enter into heaven (3:5).

Finally, they will not have their name erased. Some people think that this is a reference to them not losing their salvation, but that is not the case. In some ancient cities, everyone had their name in a book, and when they died their name was crossed out or erased from the book. Jesus is saying that those who overcome will not have their names erased, because they will never die. Eternal life is their destiny.

📖 **3:7–13**

PHILADELPHIA—DELIVERANCE THROUGH TRIALS

The descriptions in verse 7 apply to Jesus. He is described as the One who has the key of David, meaning He has all authority. Though Jesus' reference to an open door can be interpreted in a variety of ways, the fact that no one can shut the door is an obvious reference to the fact that no one can undo what He decrees (3:7–8).

The Jews will bow before the believers in this city as a testimony to the reality that Jesus is the Messiah (3:9). The implication is that with the life and death of Jesus, the definition of God's chosen people has changed. No longer is it simply a matter of family heritage, but of faith in Jesus.

Demystifying Revelation

Little is known about the church of Philadelphia apart from this passage. Like most of the other churches, it was probably founded through Paul's ministry to Ephesus. One interesting note is that this church lasted for centuries. The people stood firm in the face of major persecution.

The church at Philadelphia will be protected from the testing that will come. This may mean they will escape trials, but it can also mean that Jesus will see them through the trials they face. They will have protection from all of the evil that will come to the earth (3:10).

The crown mentioned in verse 11 is not a crown of royalty, but a crown of victory, much like the garlands or wreaths worn by the winners of an Olympic competition.

The comparison of one who conquers to a pillar in verse 12 is a reference to strength. Earthquakes were common in this region. Typically, the pillar of a building was all that remained after a quake. Because of this, a pillar is an excellent image for something that will remain secure no matter what happens around it.

Critical Observation

While later in Revelation John writes that there will be no temple in heaven, in verse 12 he refers to the temple. This is a reminder that John is recording a series of symbolic visions. Each image stands alone, supporting a specific point of truth. To find apparent inconsistencies between those visions is only to recognize that they, indeed, are separate.

The believers described in Philadelphia, those who will be kept through testing, will have three names written on them: the name of God, New Jerusalem, and Jesus. This means they will be claimed by these three things. In their earthly lives they may have been insignificant, but in heaven they will be members of the New Jerusalem.

📄 **3:14–22**

LAODICEA—DANGERS OF A LUKEWARM FAITH

In the opening of the letter to the church at Laodicea, several names are used for Jesus that have not been used yet in Revelation. All three stress His authority.

The judgment against this church is that they are lukewarm (Revelation 3:15). The water supply to Laodicea came from a hot spring, so the water in the city was indeed lukewarm. In this case, of course, it is the spiritual condition of the church that is being described. Rather than denying Christ, they made an empty profession. According to verse 16, this is nauseating to God.

Demystifying Revelation

Laodicea was an economic banking center for Asia. Due to its location, it became a major financial site for the Roman Empire. The city was famous for the soft black wool it produced. Laodicea was also known as an important center of ancient medicine. The nearby temple of the Phrygian god Men Karou had an important medical school associated with it. That school was most famous for developing an eye salve, which was exported all over the Greco-Roman world. All three of these industries (clothing, banking, and eye medicine) are used in Jesus' condemnation.

Verse 17 further carries the charge against this church, declaring that these people claimed to need nothing, yet they were poor, blind, and naked. These three assertions were direct hits at the industry of the Laodiceans: banking, medicine, and clothing. Banks cannot remove the bankruptcy of the soul. Wool cannot cover the nakedness of sin. Eye salve cannot remove the blindness toward the gospel. Thus, to trust in the things of the world is foolish. According to verse 18, only Christ can actually take care of spiritual poverty, blindness, and nakedness.

Verse 19 echoes a truth found elsewhere in the New Testament—God disciplines those He loves. The repentance referred to here is not an ongoing daily repentance, but a once-for-all, turning-from-your-old-ways kind of change.

Verse 20 is a well-known verse, including a word picture of Jesus asking to be let in. The words translated "share a meal" (NET) do not refer to a meal shared with a stranger, but with a meal shared among friends who know each other well.

The reward offered in verse 21 is unlike the wreaths or crowns already mentioned that are given to winners of a competition. Instead, this is the offer to rule with Jesus.

REVELATION 4:1–11

OH WORSHIP THE KING

Setting Up the Section

From this point on, John's writing transitions from the letters to the church to the vision of heaven. He begins with a vision of God Himself.

📄 4:1

THE DOOR OF REVELATION

Verse 1 opens with an introductory phrase that John often uses in Revelation to begin a new vision—"After this I looked. . ." (NIV).

The door of verse 1 is the third door mentioned in Revelation. The first is the door of opportunity in Philadelphia. The second is the door of fellowship in Laodicea. This door is one of revelation. John is going to pass through a door that will allow him to see the God of the universe and all of the glory that controls the world.

The voice that sounded like a trumpet is the voice of Jesus calling John into the vision. Notice that the revelation Jesus is about to reveal is of things that *must* happen. They are certain.

📄 4:2–3

THE GOD OF REVELATION

John saw the throne of the Almighty (4:2). His description of the throne is not meant to be literal. The images are used to describe the meaning of the throne. This symbolic language describes the universe from a heavenly point of view.

John describes God by using the names of jewels. Different versions of the Bible translate these names differently (jasper, carnelian, diamonds, rubies, etc.). Also, we can't be sure if the ancients used the same names for precious and semiprecious stones that we use today. Nevertheless, the importance of John's description is in the images of beauty and value that are attributed to God. John gives no literal, physical description of God, because God cannot be described. Instead, the character and nature of God are described, because that is what anyone could ever see of God (4:3).

There was a rainbow, or a halo, around the throne. This is reminiscent of the rainbow that signified the eternal covenant that God made with Noah (Genesis 9:12–13; Revelation 4:3).

THE REVELATION OF WORSHIP

In verses 4 and 5, John paints a picture of worship. The first picture is twenty-four elders sitting on thrones around God. There are many interpretations of this picture, ranging from the elders as a special class of angels to the elders as the church before God.

For those who make a case that these elders represent the church, John's description, then, is of the redeemed—they have white robes (19:8), they are wearing crowns (James 1:12), and they reign with God (2 Timothy 2:12). Why are there twenty-four? Some say there were twenty-four priests that represented the entire nation of Israel. And some have said that the elders represent the twelve tribes plus the twelve apostles. Each interpretation includes its own difficulties. However the specifics are interpreted, this vision reveals the majesty of worship.

Critical Observation

The key to understanding the picture painted of the throne of God in Revelation 4:5 is the account of the Jews at Mount Sinai in Exodus 19. When God descended upon the mountain, it shook with thunder and lightning. All of this was a picture of the holiness of God. John is telling us in this passage that God is holy and His holiness reigns in heaven.

John also sees seven lamps of fire. Unlike the lampstands mentioned in Revelation 1:12–13, these are outdoor torches. John identifies these torches as the seven Spirits of God, a phrase that denotes the Holy Spirit (see Zechariah 4:1–10).

Since there is no sea in heaven (Revelation 21:1), the body of water mentioned in verse 6 is not a literal sea. Instead, it is a descriptive term showcasing the brilliance of heaven. Today a clear glass or a large mirror is easy to come by. In John's day, though, a large glass as clear as crystal was an extravagance beyond imagination. This points to the immense glory and power of the One who sits on the throne.

There are also living creatures centered around the throne (4:6). Their positions suggest both their closeness to God and the fact that they attend to Him. One general description that covers all of the creatures is that they are full of eyes both front and behind. Eyes are used for seeing, and thus these angels are aware of what is all around them. Some have suggested that the creatures are cherubim, but this is not known for certain.

According to verse 7, each of these creatures has a different face: lion, calf, man, and eagle. Each symbol shows that all of creation is represented before the throne, and thus all of creation is worshiping God. Creation's purpose is to bring glory to God.

These creatures, representative of the creation of God, call out God's holiness. They repeat the word *holy* three times, emphasizing that God is holy. They also acknowledge that God is almighty and eternal; He began all things, and He will bring all things to a conclusion.

Verses 9–11 offer a picture of worship. The angels give glory, honor, and thanks to the One who sits on the throne. To give someone glory is to put that person on display. To honor is to praise someone for what he or she has done. To give thanks is more than simply recognizing an attribute of someone, but to go one step further and be grateful for who that person is or what he or she has done. The heart of the worship is centered on displaying God, acknowledging His attributes, and thanking Him for what He has done.

In addition to the angels, the elders also worship. They fall before God in reverence and lay their crowns before Him. All of their actions—throwing themselves down, offering crowns—communicate God's greatness. They are placing themselves below Him. This indicates that they do not look at God as a peer; instead, they see themselves as His servants. When they fall before God, they offer up words of praise.

Take It Home

The elders' song of worship gives words to their actions and acknowledges God as the source of all creation. There is no way to understand the judgment of God without understanding that God is the center of the universe. Everything bows to Him, putting Him in the position of granting His approval to all He has created. Giving that approval, or not, is the act of judgment.

REVELATION 5:1–14

THE LION AND THE LAMB

The Scroll and the Lion	5:1–5
The Lamb and the Salvation	5:6–7
The Worship and the Praise	5:8–14

Setting Up the Section

In chapter 5, John's visions transition from God the Creator to Jesus the Redeemer. Here the nature of Jesus will come into view when we see the final judgment of the world taking place. Jesus will be the Judge; thus He is called the Lion. Yet Jesus is also the Savior of the world; thus He is called the Lamb. As the Lamb, He took the sin of humanity so that they might stand redeemed before God.

📖 5:1–5

THE SCROLL AND THE LION

The scroll John describes has seven seals. Sealing a scroll was not an unusual practice. Some scrolls may have had seven seals on the outside that had to be broken in order to unroll the parchment. In this case, though, it seems the seals open each section of the scroll. The angel is looking for someone worthy to open the scroll, read it, and carry out the plan of God (5:1–2).

When no one could be found to break the seals, John weeps (5:4). The kind of weeping described here is a loud, wailing grief.

While John reveals in verse 1 that the scroll is in the hand of the person sitting on the throne, it seems that he doesn't fully see that person until verse 6. John has seen a vision of Jesus but not the revelation of Jesus that the elder is referring to. This elder begins to explain to John that Jesus is the One who is worthy to open the scroll.

The phrase "Lion of the tribe of Judah" is found only here in the Bible. In Genesis 49:9, Jacob speaks a prophecy over each of his sons. When he speaks of Judah, he refers to him as a lion cub. Jesus, of course, finds His ancestry in the tribe of Judah.

The "root of David" means that Jesus was born into the family line of David. Both Matthew and Luke give genealogies of Jesus, tracing Him through David's bloodline (Matthew 1; Luke 3).

📄 **5:6–7**

THE LAMB AND THE SALVATION

The lamb that appears to have been killed symbolizes Jesus' crucifixion (5:6). The fact that the lamb has seven horns and eyes suggests completeness. The number seven often carries that connotation in the Bible.

Horns are often a symbol of power; most powerful animals have horns. In this image, then, Jesus is represented as the One who possesses complete power.

In the same way, the seven eyes represent complete vision. According to the text here, these eyes are the seven Spirits of God. While this may be a reference to the Holy Spirit, it is more likely this all-seeing attribute is credited to Jesus.

Critical Observation

The lamb is the meekest of animals, the least fierce, and evokes the least amount of fear. Yet, it was through becoming a Lamb that Jesus conquered. Jesus proved His strength by being meek. The triumph of God does not come through power, but rather through love and meekness.

The end of verse 7 is the high point of John's vision—the Son of God takes the scroll from the hand of God. This means that the plan of God is ready to be carried out, and the person of Jesus Christ is the One who will implement the plan.

📄 **5:8–14**

THE WORSHIP AND THE PRAISE

The elders and the creatures fall down in worship of Jesus. The only appropriate response to this moment is praise. In this case, the instruments and implements they use are harps and bowls of incense (5:8).

Harps, possibly small lyres, are often associated with worship in Revelation. The bowls with incense symbolize the prayers of the saints who have been under the persecution of evil in the world and as a result of the persecution have been killed (6:10).

As with so many new things in Revelation, the elders and creatures are singing a new song (5:9). In this case, new is not a chronological designation but more so the quality of the song. This song is meant for this particular situation, not simply reused from another. The song celebrates the fact that Jesus is worthy to take the scroll. He is the One to accomplish the plan of God—dying for people from every nation in the world. Not only did Jesus die to bring humanity to God, but He also enabled believers to stand before God holy and just.

In both verses 9 and 10, the song acknowledges that the redeemed belong to God. In verse 10, they are appointed as a kingdom and as priests. This is similar to John's greeting in Revelation 1:6.

In verse 11, John's vision widens so that he sees and hears innumerable voices as one voice singing. His numbers are not meant to be equations of a specific number, but are instead a description of the vastness of those in the vision. The song itself claims Jesus' worthiness, as does the song in verses 9–10. The first four descriptive words are qualities of Jesus: power, wealth, wisdom, and might. The last three describe the response to Jesus: honor, glory, and praise (5:12).

Then, added to the innumerable amount of worshipers, every creature joins in the singing (5:13). The final "Amen" is added by the elders who began the song in verse 9. There is no distinction drawn in their worship between the One sitting on the throne (God) and the Lamb (Jesus). They worship them as one.

REVELATION 6:1–17

THE FOUR HORSEMEN OF THE APOCALYPSE

Setting Up the Section

Beginning in chapter 6, and continuing into chapters 7 and 8, the scroll is unrolled and its seals are broken. Rather than reading the scroll, John experiences it in visions.

The unrolling of the scroll marks the judgment of God upon the earth—justice brought to the world. The first four seals on the scroll reveal the sin of humanity unleashed on the earth.

📖 6:1–2

THE WHITE HORSE

Jesus, the Lamb, breaks the first seal on the scroll, at which point one of the four creatures shouts an invitation to come (6:1). This invitation is not directed to John, but to the white horse and the first horseman. This horseman holds a bow and is given a crown. As in Revelation 2:10, this is a crown of victory rather than royalty. The implication, of course, is that this horseman will find victory in his efforts.

This horse and rider serve the purpose of conquering. The idea here is simple: The first judgment that must come to humanity before the final consummation of the ages is that of military conquering. There are three popular views as to who will conquer or be conquered:

1) This horse represents Christ and the gospel in the world.
2) This horse represents the Antichrist.
3) This horse represents the spirit of conquest, or military figures.

We cannot know for certain, but we can note that the bow seems a significant part of the vision, and that a bow is not a typical Roman weapon. So this vision has implications beyond a political statement regarding the Roman Empire. This is a vision of a conqueror and destruction.

Critical Observation

Some associate this first vision with one group of warriors in John's day who were known for using bows—the Parthians. They were a feared group of warriors who tormented much of the East and Middle East for hundreds of years. The Parthians were noted for two things: their horsemanship and their skilled archery. They would ride into a city, shoot their arrows with deadly accuracy, and then ride out so fast they could not be killed. They rode white horses that they trained to jump and maneuver in incredible ways.

While John's vision is probably not intended to be this specific (one army or one country), the Parthians may have been the closest comparable image for John's original readers.

📄 6:3–4

THE RED HORSE

As with the first seal, the Lamb opens the second seal, and the second creature offers the same invitation to the next horseman to come (6:3).

The power to remove the peace that is on the earth is granted to this horseman on a red horse. Since God is sovereign over all things, it is He who grants the permission. The imagery here is not that this horseman does the butchering, but that he removes peace, and without that peace, humans butcher one another. The great sword is the image of the machines of war being unleashed on the earth, acted out by people left to their own devices without any divine intervention.

📄 6:5–6

THE BLACK HORSE

With the next seal broken by the Lamb and the next invitation from the third creature, a horseman rides in on a black horse with a scale in his hand. Since verse 6 reveals the exorbitant prices of wheat and barley, this horseman symbolizes famine. The scale is for measuring out food.

The announcement in verse 6 is not ascribed to any one of the four creatures. In fact, the announcement itself is only said to have been like a voice from among the creatures.

A quart of wheat was what one person needed in a day. According to the prices called out in verse 6, a person would work all day to simply get the grain that he or she needed. If there was one income for a family, the problem was obvious. In addition, barley was used by the poor to mix with their wheat to make it go further. According to the information given in verse 6, the market prices were well beyond what anyone could afford.

The oil and the wine were protected. These are basic ingredients for cooking and for purification. We see that they have been left out of the judgment, but no reason is offered for this. Because the olive trees and grape vines are still producing, this famine will affect the poor, but some will survive.

📖 6:7–8

THE PALE HORSE

The fourth horse and rider, also summoned by the Lamb breaking the seal and the voice of a creature, is described as pale, or ashen. This signifies a pale green color, the color of a corpse.

This horseman is not holding a weapon of any kind, but his name is Death, and he is followed by Hades, the place of departed spirits. As with the third horseman, permission is given for the destruction to take place involving 25 percent of the earth. This destruction will come by a variety of means.

📖 6:9–11

PRAYER IN PERSECUTION

The next seal marks a change. The first four reflect the coming of a particular kind of destruction. The fifth involves the prayers of a particular group of people—the persecuted (6:9).

The first evidence of the difference between this seal and the four preceding is that no one summoned the vision. In the first four seals, one of the living creatures called "Come," and the horsemen came. For the fifth seal, John simply notices the souls who have been violently killed for their faith.

These souls are under an altar—they are already dead. They have been persecuted to death. John gives two reasons why these souls have been killed: (1) because of the Word of God and (2) because of the testimony they had been given by Jesus.

The Word of God refers to the message of the scriptures (6:9). The central message is the redemptive work of Jesus Christ. The testimony that these souls maintained refers to the active and verbal faith that they lived out in the world. These people were distinctively Christian, and they were killed because of it. The lives of these people became offerings of worship; thus they are under the altar.

While their persecution is a reality, the focus is on their prayers for justice (6:10). Sin is running rampant, and many people are being killed for their faith in Jesus Christ. Those who have been killed want justice. In light of the teachings throughout the scriptures about vengeance and its place in God's hands (not humanity's), it would be a mistake to understand the prayers of these souls as merely a cry for revenge. It is, rather, a cry for God to rule. This is a prayer that longs to see the power in the hands of the One who rightfully controls the universe. The souls even address God as *sovereign*, a term often used for the master of slaves. They recognize His power and authority.

The answer to their prayers comes in two parts. The first part is in God rewarding them for their sacrifices. Their reward is rest. Once dead they are allowed to enjoy the peace of heaven. The other part of their reward includes a long white robe, which probably represents victory as it does in the vision of the white horse of the first seal (6:1–2).

They are told to rest until the "full number" (NET) of martyrs was reached. This does not imply that God has a certain quota of martyrs that have to die before He will enact His justice, but it does reveal the reality that more people will be sacrificing their lives for Him (6:11).

THE COSMIC DISTURBANCE

There are two parts to the disturbance of the sixth seal: first, the cosmic light show and, second, the response of the people.

The reason the sun and moon are both a part of this vision is that God is going to move at the same time all over the world; in some places it will be night and in other places it will be day. Notice the sun will be black as sackcloth. This is a reference to the black sackcloth worn by mourners. The garments were made out of the hair of black goats, so they were naturally very dark. If the sun ever became that dark, there would be no light. Without light, the entire world will be disoriented.

🔍

Critical Observation

Keep in mind that John's visions are not the first his readers have heard of the apocalypse. Jesus Himself spoke of terrible events at the end of the world (Matthew 24; Mark 13; Luke 12). The Old Testament prophets offered their own apocalyptic visions as well (Joel 2:11, 31; Zephaniah 1:14, 18; 2:2). It is quite likely that John's readers made a connection between his visions recorded here and the teachings of Jesus and the prophets. Rather than new and disturbing images, John is likely describing a confirmation of God's sovereignty from the ancient days to the ultimate future.

If the sun goes away, the natural fallout will be that the light given from the moon will also cease to exist, since it merely reflects the sun's light. John records that the moon looks like blood (6:12). The idea is that there is a covering of the moon to such a degree that it will give no light. Instead, there will be darkness and the moon will look as if it has been covered in blood. Remember that blood is maroon in color when in large quantities, so this describes a darkening of the moon more than a reddening of it.

The two images of sackcloth and blood are meant to convey the destruction that is coming. Blood symbolizes death, and sackcloth represents the mourning that comes along with it.

There are two ways in which the word *stars* can be translated in verse 13. It could mean the actual stars in the sky falling, but it more likely refers to meteors falling from the sky to the earth. While some have interpreted the result of the falling stars as a violent effect, like an earthquake, the illustration John actually gives is of ripe figs that easily fall when the wind shakes their limbs.

Verse 14 paints the picture of the sky opening up so that the atmosphere, the blue canopy that is over the earth, will split open and form a hole. Then verse 15 indicates that these events will affect everyone on earth and cause widespread panic. Verse 16 reveals the hopelessness of the situation. It is clear that no person has control of his or her own fate. Each is at the mercy of the powerful sovereignty of heaven and earth (6:17).

REVELATION 7:1–17

THE DRAMATIC PAUSE

Setting Up the Section

Chapter 7 describes a pause between the sixth and seventh seal. This pause sets up the events just prior to the wrath of God being poured out on the earth. It is a moment God stops the clock to provide divine protection.

📄 7:1–8

THE ANGELS AND SERVANTS

John describes four angels holding back the wind (7:1). The fact that they are standing at the four corners of the earth implies that they cover the whole earth.

To this point, John has not described any winds that need to be held back, so these angels may be holding back all that was released in the first four seals. At the least, they are stopping the natural order of the world. The sun is not shining, the stars are not shining, meteors are falling to the earth, and now the wind has stopped blowing.

In verse 2, another angel ascends and carries the seal of God's ownership. This angel instructs the four angels holding the wind to hold back their damage until the servants (slaves) of God are identified by a seal on their foreheads (7:3). This seal will mark them so that they will not be hurt during the judgment of God.

Critical Observation

According to Revelation 14:1–5, the servants marked with a seal are those who have kept themselves pure, followed the Lamb, been purchased by God, and been offered as firstfruits.

Many interpreters of Revelation hold that the 144,000 people represent Israel. Keep in mind, though, that John is sending this letter to dispersed Christians, not all of whom are Jewish. Also, keep in mind that John has made statements elsewhere that can be interpreted to mean that God's chosen people are no longer determined by heritage or ancestry, but by faith (2:9; 3:9). In light of this, others interpret this 144,000 as the faithful of the Christian church.

Verses 5–8 provide a list of the tribes of Israel. These lists are based on the sons of Jacob (whose name was later changed to Israel). While the tribes are usually listed in order of the age of the sons, in this case Judah is listed first, though Judah was not the oldest son. This is significant in that Jesus is from the tribe of Judah. This may have been intentional on John's part, though it is difficult to find an intentional meaning in the order of the rest of the list.

A tribe is missing from this list—Dan. Some say this is because of the idolatry engaged in by that tribe.

📄 7:9–17

THE BELIEVERS ARE RESCUED

What follows is John's vision of an amazing and diverse crowd in the serenity of heaven. Many think this refers to the Rapture, when God removes His church from the world. Others believe it refers to those who have been killed during the unleashing of evil. Regardless, these are people who have come from the world and are now rescued from their misery and are in the presence of the Lord (7:9).

These people are worshiping the Lamb. Their long white robes are more akin to glorious celebration than everyday clothing. The palm branches they wave are typical symbols of triumph (7:9). They are worshiping the Lord because of the salvation He has given (7:10). All the angels worship as well, proclaiming their own doxology to God (7:11–12).

In verses 13–14, an elder both asks and answers the question of the identity of this throng in white robes. His answer includes the now familiar phrase "great tribulation." This could mean simply the ongoing tribulation that these people have faced on earth, as opposed to the specific period now referred to as "the Tribulation." Undoubtedly these are the redeemed, because their robes have been washed clean in Jesus' blood.

The elder's description continues in verses 15–17 with the fate that awaits these worshipers. They will be provided for, and even shepherded, by the Lamb. Reminiscent of Psalm 23, Jesus will provide for them, and the sorrows and difficulties of this life will be left behind.

🏠

Take It Home

We can be encouraged by this vision in two ways. It signifies the following:

1) Believers will not face the wrath of God.

2) Enduring trials for our faith here in this life will not be forgotten in eternity.

For John's original readers facing persecution, this would have been a precious thought. For contemporary readers, it offers an eternal perspective in the midst of the suffering we face.

REVELATION 8:1–13
THE WRATH OF GOD

Setting Up the Section

What we have here is the beginning of the wrath of God. The judgment of Jesus is going to be carried out. This is the great moment of justice that suffering believers have been praying for.

📄 8:1–5

PREPARATION FOR JUSTICE

In John's vision, God is about to deal with the sin that is in the world. At the opening of the seventh seal, the response is silence (8:1). And a new vision begins.

The seven angels in verse 2 are specific angels. They are those who stand before God. And in this case, they are the ones with the responsibility of carrying out justice on the earth. The trumpets symbolize the instruments of that judgment (8:2).

Critical Observation

The difference between the seventh seal and the former seals is who is implementing the punishment. During chapters 6 and 7, humankind and nature are having their way. During this vision of the trumpets, it is the angels who have been given the role of executing the judgment of God on earth.

Verse 3 is a dramatic image of the prayers of the saints ascending into heaven. In 5:8 the incense embodies the prayers of the saints, but that is not case here in chapter 8. In chapter 5, prayers for justice are given to God from the martyred saints. The idea here is that all of the prayers for justice are given to God so that God can answer them all. He is going to begin the process of retribution for the persecution of the church.

In verse 4, the prayers ascend from the angel's hand. Heaven and earth are united in this request. And in verse 5, fire from the altar is added and the prayers are empowered. This can be seen as a picture of the power of God added to the prayers.

📄 8:6–13

THE FIRST FOUR TRUMPETS

As with the seals, the first four trumpets are distinguished from the last three. In this case, the first four are concerned with natural events and the last three with people. The trumpets are distinguished from the seals in that the trumpets are God's intervention rather than the world's actions upon itself. These trumpets do not describe the final judgment. In each case, only part of the world is affected. To John's original readers, though, they are reminders that God will indeed deal with sin.

- THE FIRST TRUMPET (8:6–7): The angels prepare to blow the trumpets, but only the first trumpet is sounded, followed by hail and fire mixed with blood. One-third of the earth is burned. In this case, *one-third* may not mean an exact amount, but instead may be a way of saying that a portion of the earth was affected, but not the majority.

Critical Observation

Each of John's visions stands somewhat on its own. An example is the first trumpet (8:7), in which one-third of the grass and trees are destroyed. Then in the account of the fifth trumpet, God commands that the grass not be destroyed (9:4). Revelation is best understood when it is read as a series of apocalyptic visions each standing on its own. While similar elements may appear in the visions, they are not meant to be treated as scientific facts that should be paralleled and measured. This is a vision, much akin to a dream—truth told in images for a first-century audience. These visions communicate over and over, in a variety of ways, that God will deal with sin in the end.

- **The Second Trumpet** (8:8–9): At the blowing of the second trumpet, something like a mountain of fire is thrown into the sea. We are not told exactly who did the throwing. This time a third of the sea becomes blood and a third of the creatures and ships are destroyed. This event is more than just pollution of the water, since ships are destroyed and sea life dies.
- **The Third Trumpet** (8:10–11): At the blowing of the third trumpet, a star falls from the sky and lands on a third of the rivers and springs, making a third of the water toxic. The plant with the same name as the star, *Wormwood*, is a bitter plant often used as a metaphor for something bitter to the taste, though it is not usually considered a poison.
- **The Fourth Trumpet** (8:12): The fourth angel's trumpet sound struck a third of the sun, moon, and stars. This affects the structure of the universe. Everything from the remaining plant life and even the tides in the oceans would be changed. Certainly, as described, the natural amount of daylight would be altered.

Thus far, the attacks have dealt only with the earth and have only indirectly affected human population. With each phenomenon, God is removing hiding places and protection in nature.

After the first four trumpets and judgments, a flying eagle proclaims three woes, perhaps in light of the three trumpets yet to blow (8:13). This is a curse and a proclamation of things to come. The appearance of the eagle (which may mean one of several kinds of birds of prey, as the term was used in the first century) provides an interlude in the trumpets.

REVELATION 9:1–21
THE DAY OF THE LORD

Setting Up the Section

Just as the last three seals pertain to things of heaven rather than earth, the last three trumpets deal with the realm of the supernatural—in this case, though, it's the demonic rather than angelic realm.

📄 **9:1–11**

MORE TRUMPETS AND THE FIRST WOE

The Fifth Trumpet and the First Woe (9:1): It was common for people or angels to be referred to as stars in Jewish imagery (Isaiah 14:12). Therefore, John is likely employing a common image for his day of an angel of some kind. The angel descends to the earth and receives a key to the opening of the abyss, which evidently has a narrow opening that then widens beyond the entrance (Revelation 9:2).

Demystifying Revelation

The pit, or abyss, is a place that is referenced nine times in the scriptures, seven of which are in the book of Revelation. The pit seems to be a place where God holds all of those who have died without faith. The glories of heaven are not fully open, and neither are the tortures of hell. The abyss is a place where people exist until the final judgment.

The smoke from the abyss is enough to block out the remaining light of the sun (8:12; 9:2). In addition, locusts poured from it. The locusts here represent the judgment of God just as they did in the plagues in Egypt and in the prophecy of Joel (Joel 2:25). In this case, though, the locusts are prohibited from plant life, which is their typical food source. These locusts were given power, presumably by God, to sting like scorpions. They could go after, but not kill, people without God's seal (Revelation 9:5). The effects would be torturous to the point that those affected would wish to die.

The five-month period of torment may correspond to the typical life span of the locust, or it may simply be a way to communicate that the torment would last a few months. This is the way the number five is used elsewhere in scripture (Acts 20:6; 24:1; Revelation 9:5).

Verses 7–11 describe the locusts. The description combines human and animal features, and reveals the locusts to be more akin to demons than insects. The importance of the comparison to horses is not that the demons looked like horses, but that they were prepared for battle like horses. This is to say that they were determined to accomplish the task.

In the same way, John's mention of crowns is not to say that the beings wear crowns, but that they resemble something wearing crowns. The crowns here may symbolize the authority to act and to get things done. The teeth like lion's teeth reveal more about the fierceness of the creatures than their physical description. And the breastplates reveal how well-protected the beings are. The loud noise made by their wings reveals their great number (9:7–9).

Critical Observation

Verse 11 is a difficult verse to understand because it is the only reference to this king—called the angel of the abyss. This is either referring to the fact that there is one who will control these creatures and they will be carrying out a mission on earth, or it is a cultural issue emerging that is contemporary to John's day.

At the time John was writing this letter, the emperor of Rome liked to think of himself as a reincarnated form of the god Apollo. Interestingly, Apollo was known as the god over the locusts. The locusts in this verse are from the underworld, and thus they are the power of evil being used by God, a message that would be relevant to John's readers. Both names listed in verse 11, *Abaddon* and *Apollyon*, can be translated as "destruction."

📄 9:12–21

THE LAST TRUMPET AND THE SECOND WOE

Since the appearance of the eagle announcing the three woes in 8:13, the trumpets have been identified as woes (9:12). What is identified as the second woe here is also the sixth trumpet.

The voice that follows the sixth trumpet comes from the horns on the golden altar before God (9:13). This is probably the same altar mentioned in 8:3, the place where the prayers of the saints have registered with God.

The four angels who are bound at the Euphrates River are the angels that God has set aside to pour out His wrath on the earth. They have not been able to perform their designed purpose until this moment in time (9:14–15).

Demystifying Revelation

The river Euphrates was the easternmost border of the Roman Empire. The army that occupied this part of the empire was the Parthian army, which was ready to attack at any moment. This army was feared by the people, and this description would have evoked fear in the minds of John's readers.

These angels are going to release an army on the earth to destroy a third of the population—millions of people.

When John claims there are two hundred million soldiers on horseback, this is probably an actual number (9:16). John is not estimating—he had been told the number.

John describes his vision in verses 17–19. It is not certain whether he is describing three different colors of breastplates or breastplates that are each three colors. However, the description of the horses—heads like lions, tails like snakes—expresses the ferocity and danger of this army. These are warriors bent on total destruction.

According to verses 18–19, it seems the riders do not play any active part in the destruction of the people; it is the horses who breathe the fire, smoke, and sulfur on the people. The fire, smoke, and sulfur represent three different, yet destructive, plagues.

Verse 20 transitions from the plight of the cavalry to a description of those who survived the plagues. Notice that John's description of the idols underscores the appalling reality that even in light of the destruction around them at the hand of God, these people failed to repent. His list of their sins in verse 21 doesn't seem to be in a specific order, and they don't correlate with another specific list in the scriptures—murders, magic, sexual immorality, and theft.

REVELATION 10:1–11

THE MESSENGER, THE MESSAGE, AND A MEAL

The Messenger	10:1–3
The Message	10:4–7
The Meal	10:8–11

Setting Up the Section

Just as there was a pause between the sixth and the seventh seal, there is now a pause between the sixth and seventh trumpet. This pause is composed of two main sections: First an angel and a little book, then two witnesses come to declare the glory and wrath of God.

The section provides a specific warning. God has judged people in general. Now He will judge the leaders of the world system that sets its agenda against God.

📖 **10:1–3**

THE MESSENGER

Verse 1 describes an angel descending from heaven (10:1). Clouds, like those he is dressed or wrapped in, sometimes symbolize those coming back to earth from heaven to carry out a task for God.

The rainbow appearing above his head signifies that he is going to bring judgment and salvation. In the Old Testament, the rainbow is a sign that God would never again flood the earth (Genesis 9:12–16). Yet this sign is meant to remind people of how God saved and judged people at the same moment.

The face of this angel is like the sun, which means that he is a source of power, and his legs are like pillars of fire, which means he has the power of judgment within him.

The angel holds a little scroll (10:2). This scroll is open, which means that what is on the scroll is about to be read and executed. The fact that the angel places one foot on the sea and the other foot on the land shows that he has authority over the entire earth. What he is about to announce is meant for everyone in the world.

The imagery of thunder speaking is also used in Psalm 29:3 to describe the voice of God. Many believe that the thunder in this passage is the Lord speaking, and He repeats Himself seven times, though that information is not given definitively in verse 3.

📄 **10:4–7**

THE MESSAGE

John understood the words spoken by the seven peals of thunder and intended to write them down, but he is instructed not to do so (10:4). While some seals used thus far in Revelation that functioned to claim someone, in verse 4, to *seal* means to hide what has been said.

Take It Home

One of the gifts of this passage is the realization that God has not given us all the information. There is always the temptation to take the information in Revelation and decide how God will act and when certain events will occur. But we are not given all that knowledge or understanding. God keeps mysteries for Himself, and He will reveal them in His own time.

The angel in verse 5 is identified as the same angel as in verse 2, who has authority over the land and the sea. He swears an oath by raising his right hand, a gesture common in both ancient and contemporary days. His oath is that when the seventh trumpet is blown—when all is done that needs to be done—there will be no delay before the fulfillment of the mystery of God (10:6).

The seventh trumpet mentioned in verse 7 is not actually blown until 11:15. What begins here is not a description of the chronological events in between the sixth and seventh trumpets, but is instead more like parenthetical information. John is not in control of his vision. Instead, he writes it down as he experiences it.

The "mystery of God" (10:7) is usually understood to refer to the gospel message, though it could have an even broader meaning than that. The prophets referenced here are not necessarily confined to the Old Testament prophets, but to those who have spoken God's truth, including the gospel message.

Critical Observation

While John eating the scroll is an unusual request by contemporary standards, it is not without precedent in the scriptures. In the book of Ezekiel, the prophet himself is asked to eat a scroll (Ezekiel 2:8–3:3). The idea is that eating the scroll is devouring the truth, or taking the words to heart.

📄 **10:8–11**

THE MEAL

When John is instructed to eat the scroll (10:9), he does as he is asked, and it changes him. The scroll tastes sweet but is bitter in his stomach. This is an apt image of God's commandments in the lives of His children. The picture here is that the commands of God are always good, and they are always something that the child of God can rejoice in. But at the same time, these words are powerful, and they will be difficult to grapple with because they tell of the wrath of God. This is the twofold nature of God's words.

This is the first time in these visions that John is a participant in the experience in heaven rather than simply an observer. As a participant, John has the opportunity to experience fully how God is going to work on and in this earth. Verse 11 explains why John has been asked to participate—he is to prophesy.

Also, up until this point, the judgment of God has not been directed toward anyone in particular, just humanity in general. Now God is using John to announce that specific judgments are on their way. The Word of God is to be in John's heart so that he can carry out the job God has called him to do.

REVELATION 11:1–19

TWO WITNESSES AND ONE LAST TRUMPET

Setting Up the Section

In this chapter we will see a measuring of the temple and two witnesses emerging to give testimony. As with much of Revelation, these events can be interpreted either literally or symbolically. If taken symbolically, many interpret the measuring of the temple to reflect a description of the emerging Christian church based on the familiar temple of Jerusalem. By the same token, a symbolic interpretation often sees the two witnesses as a reflection of the martyrs of the church who give testimony with their lives, rather than two specific men. Whichever interpretive path, this section continues the theme of God's judgment as He begins to hold the world outside of the church accountable.

📄 11:1–2

THE MEASURING

In the first century, as often today, a building was measured any time it was changing hands. It was a means of guaranteeing a fair exchange. In this vision, John is given some type of measuring stick and is asked to measure the temple as a sign that God will take the temple back (11:1). If this were a literal temple, it would most likely refer to the temple at Jerusalem. It can also be interpreted as a reference to the church, God's redeemed, but the language is written in terms of the temple.

John is instructed not to measure the court of the Gentiles (11:2). This refers to the outer area of the Jewish temple, a courtyard in which non-Jews were allowed. If John's image is meant as a picture of the church, then it may be that he is speaking of Christians to be the chosen nation. There would still be an outer court for those outside of the faith, which in this case would include all nonbelievers.

Regardless of the literal or symbolic path of interpretation, John delineates a forty-two-month period of time (three and one-half years) in which those outside of the Christian faith would trample God's city. A connection can be drawn to other scriptures in which a time period of forty-two months is delineated (Daniel 7:25, "time, times and a half a time" equals a year, two years, and one-half a year). This time frame comes into play in several places in Revelation as well. For John's readers, a time frame in itself is significant. It speaks to the fact that their suffering will not go on indefinitely. There will be an end to the persecution of God's people.

THE MESSENGERS

While the identities are not revealed, God will send two witnesses in the midst of the persecution. In verse 3, the time period is defined in terms of days but is the same amount of time as the forty-two months mentioned in verse 2.

The attitude of the witnesses is reflected in the clothes that they will wear—sackcloth, the clothes of mourning. This symbolizes the sorrow and grief that are about to come to the earth.

Some believe the witnesses are simply symbols that represent believers. Others believe that these two are Moses and Elijah. Still others think the witnesses are apostles, martyrs, or other prophets. The significance of the number of witnesses may relate the Old Testament command that two witnesses must confirm a story in order for it to be considered credible. The fact that there are two witnesses here reflects the fact that whoever these witnesses are, their testimony is enough to prove God's truth credible.

Verse 4 offers a description taken from Zechariah 4:3, 11–14. While there is only one lampstand in the Zechariah passage and two in John's description, the point remains that the lampstands are connected directly to olive trees. This means there will be an endless supply of oil and the lamps will never burn out. This could mean that the two witnesses bear testimony to an endless supply of life. While their identity is not known, it is evident they are special people who have been prophesied in the Old Testament as the ones to bring life to a dead Israel.

Because it is God's will that these men preach the Word of God, they will have the ability to protect themselves from any attack (Revelation 11:5–6). They can prevent rain and perform miracles if necessary, like turning water to blood and causing plagues. These references bring to mind Moses and Elijah who exhibited these types of miracles (Exodus 7:19–20; 1 Kings 17:1).

For the two witnesses, this ability to protect themselves is temporary. When their job is done, they are killed by what is referred to as "the beast" from the abyss (11:7–8). The beast is a figure that is prominent in the last half of Revelation. It is empowered by Satan and filled with evil.

For those who interpret Revelation in a more literal sense, the killing of the prophets will happen in Jerusalem, where the Lord was crucified. Jerusalem is also referred to as Sodom and Egypt, one a city famous for immorality and the other a country known for holding God's people in bondage. So those who interpret Revelation figuratively see this city as representative of the world's cities in general.

The fact that the corpses lay for three and a half days without being buried is an act of shame and triumph by those who were glad of their deaths (11:9). Due to the customs of the day, John's original readers would have felt the pain of this disgrace of no proper burial.

The general population rejoices that these two witnesses are dead (11:10). Because of the message they had and the power that was at their disposal, the forty-two months that they were on the earth were horrible for the unrepentant. Therefore, to those unrepentant, their deaths are almost like a holiday—people exchange gifts and celebrate. But this only happens for three and a half days.

Then the witnesses come back to life. First, God breathes life into them; then He calls them to heaven (11:11–12). All those watching are seized by fear. In a sense, this is a review of the gospel—new life and the conquering of death. While we can't be sure if everyone in the crowd watching hears God call out, or if just the two witnesses hear His voice, it is obvious to everyone that those who were dead have found new life.

Verses 13–14 draw this woe to an end. Those who had celebrated the death of the two witnesses have now experienced an earthquake that collapses part of the city and kills seven thousand. The unrepentant now honor God's power and authority. The third woe associated with the seventh and final trumpet is on the way.

📄 **11:15–19**

THE SEVENTH TRUMPET

The seventh trumpet is not just one short event; it actually comprises the rest of the judgment of God and then the final end of the age with the new heaven and the new earth. It also serves as a prompt for the next series of visions recorded by John.

The seventh angel blows the seventh trumpet, and instead of immediate destruction, there is loud praise from voices in heaven (11:15). The reference to loud voices implies a group, but we are not told the specific identity of the group. Perhaps it is everyone who is in heaven. The focus of this praise is this: The kingdom of this world has become Jesus' kingdom.

The twenty-four elders, not mentioned since the last of the seals (7:11), worship God and give thanks because:

1) He has begun to reign on earth.
2) His wrath has punished the rebellious nations. All of the kings that try to rule the world challenge God, and therefore God defends His honor by judging the nations.
3) He has judged the living and the dead. God gives each person the reward he or she deserves (11:17–18).

The people in heaven are seeing God bring about the final day of reckoning. For this they worship the Lord.

Verse 19 contains meaningful Old Testament Jewish imagery. The temple of heaven opens up and the ark of the covenant appears. In the Old Testament, the ark was the symbol of God's presence and God's covenant with humankind. In the Old Testament tabernacle, the temple of that day, the ark resided in the innermost chamber, the Holy of Holies, sealed off from everyone except the high priest. Here God is allowing people into the real Holy of Holies and is, in essence, saying that His covenant is complete.

The thunder, lightning, and hail are reminiscent of the power of God that was present the first time He revealed His covenant with the children of Israel, unveiling the Ten Commandments on Mount Sinai (Exodus 19–20).

⌂

Take It Home

When the trumpet blows, the people praise God because they know that He is now bringing all things to their appointed end and the kingdom of heaven to its appointed beginning. This is great news and worth praising God over. At this point there is a shift in John's visions from heaven to the kingdom of the earth and the fate of Satan.

For John's original readers, the idea of God establishing a place where He alone rules and justice is complete is a reason to hope. It is the same for contemporary culture. Amid the imagery and symbolism of Revelation is the message that God is moving toward a specific end and that His children are cared for within that plan, even though temporary suffering is a reality.

REVELATION 12:1–17

THE SEVEN SIGNS

Setting Up the Section

Chapter 12 begins a series of seven visions that will extend into chapter 14. These visions do not have a repeating symbol, like the seven seals or seven trumpets. But they are similar in that they flesh out the conflict between God and His church and the forces of evil that would seek to destroy both.

▤ **12:1–6**

THE WOMAN AND THE DRAGON

In the first of the seven signs, a woman is described as a picture of Israel (12:1–2). She has been called by God and is clothed with the sun, which means she is reflecting the power of God. The moon is under her feet, which indicates that she is the nation God has marked as special, and she has twelve crowns that correspond to the twelve tribes of Israel. She is with child, which is the picture of the Messiah. Her labor pains represent the struggles that were a part of the life of Israel.

Demystifying Revelation

For John there is always a connection between Old Testament Israel and the New Testament church. In his theology, the church has become God's chosen nation. Here in chapter 12, the image of the woman represents Israel, but later in Revelation a woman will represent the church. Understanding John's visions requires that his readers stay sensitive to the fact that images can sometimes maintain their meanings between visions, but at other times the same image can carry a different message.

The next sign John sees is that of a dragon, not an uncommon concept in ancient literature (12:3). This dragon is red, the symbol of blood. This fits the image of Satan—he is a murderer. He seeks to kill and devour.

The dragon has seven heads. *Seven* is a number that symbolizes perfection or completion. This many heads may imply that the evil one is all over the world. In other words, his evil is everywhere. On each head are seven diadems, or crowns. These crowns are not merely the wreaths worn by the victor of a contest; they are the crowns of royalty and symbolize the dragon's ability to rule. Whatever authority the dragon has, though, is limited and delegated. God has allowed it.

In addition to the seven heads, there are also ten horns, which in the most basic sense imply great strength. Some interpreters understand the ten horns to represent the ten nations that will rule under the Antichrist during the final days. Others believe the ten horns represent the leaders or rulers that have been a tool of Satan to attempt to oppose the Messiah.

The dragon's tail sweeps away one-third of the stars (12:4). Some see this as a reference to Satan taking one-third of the angels with him when he fell from heaven. Others simply think it represents a show of power by the dragon. He has only one goal in mind in this particular vision, and that is to destroy the child, an image of the Messiah.

In verse 5, the Messiah arrives on the earth in order to rule with an iron rod. This is not a picture of a tyrannical rule as much as it is a firm hand in the power of a king. The child is immediately caught up into heaven, or He ascends into heaven. This ascension means that the Son is waiting for the day when He will rule.

Critical Observation

Some question the fact that John's vision includes this obvious reference to Jesus' birth, cutting directly to the ascension without any reference to His ministry or death and resurrection. But there is no explanation given here. It is important to remember, though, that the purpose of this section is to give hope to the church by highlighting God's power over Satan rather than to give a review of Jesus' life.

In verse 6, the 1,260 days, or three and one half years, show up again (11:1–3). In this case, the woman, a picture of Israel, hides for three and a half years. She hides in a place that has been prepared by God in order for her to be cared for. Satan has power, but he cannot oppose the plan of God.

🏠

Take It Home

What do we see in this text? We see that God is finally going to bring an end to the delegated and defeated power of Satan on this earth.

What do we learn from this? We learn that Satan has some limited power, and we must be careful dealing with him. Also we see that his goal is to attack Jesus, but he cannot win, because God still has control over him.

📖 **12:7–17**

A BATTLE WITH THE ENEMY

Verses 7–8 describe the battle between Satan, the dragon, and Michael. Michael is the angel who was given to Israel to protect her as a nation and as a people (Daniel 12:1). Thus, this battle can be understood as a direct attack by Satan on Israel.

Both Michael's and the dragon's armies are referred to as angels, a designation that simply means "messenger" (Revelation 12:7).

The reality is that Satan is not strong enough to overtake Michael. The original readers of this letter would find great hope in this description. Without this kind of encouragement, their suffering could push them into thinking that Satan was finally going to do away with not only Israel, but all of the people of God.

According to verse 9, at the end of the war Satan is thrown out along with all of his army. The idea here is that God stops Satan from ever attacking again. In verse 9, John uses several of Satan's designated names:

- *Serpent*—the first term used to describe Satan (Genesis 3:1)
- *Satan*—accuser, adversary (Job 1:6)
- *Devil*—deceiver, slanderer (Matthew 4:1)

After this final expulsion from heaven, there is an announcement: Salvation—the power and the kingdom of God, as well as the authority of Jesus Christ—has come. Satan is finally prevented from ever entering heaven for the purpose of interrupting the plan of God. This final expulsion provides a great outburst of praise in heaven (12:10–12).

Notice that this announcement is spoken in first person plural—the accuser of *our* brothers and sisters. It is probably proclaimed by a group of angels, but any of the heavenly members in the vision could be the source.

According to verse 11, the people's power to overcome Satan is found in three things:

1) *The blood of Jesus.* It was the death of Jesus that took the power of death away from all those who place their faith in Jesus alone.

2) *The word of their testimony.* The people continued to proclaim Jesus no matter the consequences. The proclamation of the gospel is the power that will see Satan defeated.

3) *Not loving this life over the next.* Satan uses death as a means to intimidate people into denying Jesus. Nevertheless, the saints who deal with the complete onslaught of Satan realize that their only hope is to proclaim Christ, no matter the cost.

Verse 12 contains a woe to the people of earth, warning them that Satan is now truly a being with nothing to lose. He knows his final defeat is simply a matter of time (12:12). The heavens are rejoicing because Satan is cast out forever, and the believers know how to handle him. The rest of the world, however, will have to endure his wrath for a short while. This will be a bad time on earth. But these days will not go unpunished.

As the vision continues in verse 13, when Satan realizes that he can't reach the child, he goes after the woman. In other words, Satan sets out to persecute Israel. He surely knows that he will not defeat her, but he can inflict pain and suffering.

In verse 14 God provides divine protection for Israel. The protection is found in the symbolic picture of an eagle. The eagle has large wings and is strong enough to carry the people of God. This image is reminiscent of Exodus 19:4, a description of Israel's deliverance from Egypt.

So not all of Israel is destroyed. Some are protected for the three and one-half years ("time, times and half a time"). This would be the second part of the three and a half years when Satan is allowed to unleash his fury.

At the end of verse 14, Satan is referred to as the serpent rather than the dragon. He has been referred to as the serpent in verse 9, so there is little doubt that the serpent and the dragon are one and the same.

Two more attempts are made by Satan, the dragon. First, he spits floodwaters to sweep the woman away from her wilderness safe house, but the earth swallows the floodwaters (12:15–16). Then, when he is unable to attack, he goes after her children. In other words, he turns on the church (12:17).

REVELATION 13:1–18
THE ANTICHRIST AND THE FALSE PROPHET

Setting Up the Section

At this point in Revelation, we have seen the judgment of God on the earth in a general sense. This judgment has been carried out toward the earth and the people of the earth.

In chapter 10, God begins to deal directly with Satan and all those who have intentionally and directly supported his efforts to oppose Jesus. This final judgment on Satan is the reason worship breaks out at the end of chapter 11.

Chapter 12 describes the plight of Israel (the woman), Jesus (the child of the woman), Satan (the dragon), and the church (the other offspring of the woman). Satan, as revealed in this chapter, has one goal—to destroy the Messiah. Because he cannot destroy the Messiah, he seeks to do away with Israel. Because he cannot do away with Israel, he goes after the church.

In chapter 13, the story line continues with a final move of Satan in trying to oppose the Messiah through a false messiah—otherwise referred to by the contemporary church as the Antichrist. (Chapter 14 will show that this attempt will not be successful.) Also in chapter 13, we will see the description of the man whom the Antichrist will possess, referred to as the false prophet.

📖 13:1–4

THE BEAST'S ANCESTRY, AUTHORITY, AND ADORATION

It is already established that the dragon is Satan, and he has in mind to do away with the Messiah. If he can't accomplish that, then he will do away with Israel and the church. The way in which Satan will try to do away with all three of these is found here in Revelation 13.

At the end of chapter 12, Satan is standing on the sand of the seashore. This represents Satan standing at the edge of the abyss.

In essence, he is summoning the beast, the one who has been called the Antichrist. This is the offense that will cause Satan, and all who directly follow him, to be judged in a direct and painful way by God. The offense of Satan is that he offers a false messiah to the world in order to deceive and destroy.

The beast is described in verse 1 as having ten horns and seven heads (as does Satan, the dragon, in 12:3), with crowns on its horns. Typically, the horns on an animal represent the strength of that animal to attack and defend. There are also diadems or ruling crowns, but they are on the horns of the beast rather than the heads. Some believe each of these crowns represents nations or kingdoms that will make up his ruling empire.

On each of the beast's multiple heads is written a blasphemous name. This may mean seven different names or the same name on each head. This beast is a culmination of all that is evil in this world.

In verse 2, we find a description of the power and authority that is given to the beast. He is described in terms of a leopard, a bear, and a lion. Each of these animals was used by governments to describe their power. The leopard describes swiftness in battle, the bear is the strength and stability that comes with enough power, and the lion describes the fighting power of a nation.

Critical Observation

While the beast is described as having seven heads, he has only one mouth ("like that of a lion," NIV). This is a reminder that John is describing a vision. His interest is not in making all the visual pieces fit, but rather in describing them and allowing them to flesh out the truth.

Some interpret the beast in John's writing to represent the Roman leadership in the first century. They would see the multiple heads as the Roman emperors, citing the myth that Nero was too evil to die and would therefore be resurrected. They connect this myth with the wounded head described in verse 3.

This beast will have a consuming power that could be used to overrun the world—and all the power is given to him by Satan. The territory Satan has been allowed (the earth) will be given to the beast so he will be able to rule the entire world without much restraint. The wickedness that is on the earth will rule all at once.

The man the beast represents—often referred to as the Antichrist—will have absolute authority over the entire world. It is delegated authority in the sense that God could stop it at any point, but nevertheless, it is a moment in time when evil will rule. God is centralizing all of the wickedness into one place to deal with it completely.

According to verse 3, one of the beast's heads has been fatally wounded, then healed, or brought back to life. This adds to his popularity. He is seen as supernatural, and this causes people to be deceived into following him. In the remainder of John's description of the beast, this head that has been restored becomes his calling card.

The people will begin to ascribe to him and to Satan the worship due to God. This is the ultimate in blasphemy. The question, "Who is like the beast?" may be a satiric reference to Psalm 35:10, "Who is like you, O LORD?" (NIV), highlighting this blasphemous worship.

THE BEAST'S ARROGANCE

The beast has been given everything he has. In other words, he is still bound to the ultimate sovereign control of God. There is nothing in this man that God has not allowed and that God cannot take away.

He is allowed to rule for forty-two months, the now familiar amount of time for several significant events in Revelation—three and one-half years (11:2; 13:5).

The pride of this man goes beyond the pride that most powerful leaders struggle with from time to time. This man considers himself to be God (13:5). He believes he possesses all the authority of God, and he acts on that belief by blaspheming God and all who dwell in heaven with Him (13:6).

Critical Observation

Keep in mind that one of the struggles for John's readers in their political climate was the pressure to worship the emperor as deity. This emperor worship was seen as blasphemy. This passage would likely have touched on that hot-button issue in their minds.

THE BEAST'S ACTIVITIES AND ADMIRERS

This man, depicted by the image of the beast, is more than talk; he also acts in a deadly and powerful manner. At the focus of his attack are believers in the one true God. All of the saints present on earth will be in his radar, and if he finds them, he will kill them. The situation John describes in verse 7 is such that, if it continues, there will be no believers left on the earth.

According to verse 8, this beast rules the world. The beast is the fulfillment of evil, the ultimate fulfillment of every evil power that has existed. The focus in verse 8 is that those who are not believers will worship the beast. Those who are true believers will not, for they will see that he is not the Messiah. The beast is the ultimate moment of separation; he will be the dividing rod of humanity. The true believers will not submit, and the world will.

Verse 9 contains a common New Testament warning: "He who has an ear, let him hear." It is used fifteen times in the New Testament. It means that if anyone understands the real meaning, he or she must respond. Some will read this and not get the message. Others will understand the message, and it will change them.

Verse 10 contains instructions. In essence, if you are marked out to be arrested, then go. Do not resist. If you are to be killed, do not fight back. Submit to what happens. There is a day of reckoning coming, and you are to wait for that day. The idea is to leave the fighting to God. By trusting in the faithfulness of God to bring about retribution, you will persevere.

THE FALSE PROPHET'S PRESENCE AND PURPOSE

At the time the beast comes to power, another beast will rise to power with him. He will be called his prophet. This prophet's purpose is to make sure that everyone worships the beast and to ensure that all humans are sealed with the mark of the beast. This prophet is a critical part of the attack of Satan.

Some believe that this second beast will be a nation or a government. But that theory is difficult to accept because the Greek says *another* beast (13:11). The way it is constructed denotes another of the same kind. Therefore, the most natural way to read this is that another man is on the scene performing critical works.

The first beast came out of the sea, which denotes the abyss or the mysterious place of Satan. This second beast comes out of the earth, which denotes he is satanic in his power (13:11). To the first-century readers, the earth was a little less foreboding than the sea. It was a picture of an evil place but not the place of hell. This would suggest that this will be an evil man but not as evil as the first.

The second beast has two horns (13:11). Horns symbolize power and sometimes nations. Interpreted the latter way, this man will have the authority of two nations under him. It also may simply parallel the two witnesses who were killed and then resurrected (chapter 11). The horns on this man are the horns of a lamb, which may be a parallel of Jesus, the Lamb. This suggests that he appears gentle and meek, but that appearance is deceptive. The reason for the guise is that his role is to get people to worship the beast, and he therefore has to be a salesman. He must make all of the evil of the beast look good to humanity. Even though he will have two horns like a lamb, he will speak like a dragon—he will speak the words of Satan. He will appear harmless, but in reality his words will be deadly.

This second beast exercises the delegated authority of the first (13:12). In application, the second beast is indwelt with the same evil power as the first, and therefore he will be given some of the responsibilities to carry out the first beast's will on the earth. All of this power is centered on one goal—to get every living being to worship the Antichrist rather than Jesus Christ.

Verse 13 offers their strategy for accomplishing this. The second beast, the false prophet, will perform miracles. These miracles will draw attention to the first beast, and particularly to the fact that the beast was wounded yet survived. In this way, the healing of the one damaged head becomes a point of tribute and worship. The main tactic is this: The prophet gets everyone's attention with his own powers, and when he has their attention, he speaks as front man. The spin of his message? The fact that the first beast was restored to life shows his ultimate power in the world, and therefore everyone should worship him. Note that both verse 12 and verse 14 identify the first beast as having a fatal wound that was healed.

The second beast, the false prophet, will also be able to mimic the prophets of the past by calling down fire from heaven (13:13). Because of these powers, he will be able to convince people that he preaches the truth, and everyone who is not a true believer will be fooled (11:14). He will encourage people to make an image of the beast so that all can worship him in their homes. In this way, he will have the entire world consumed with the first beast, the one with the restored head, the Antichrist. He will be a household word, even a way of life.

📄 **13:15–18**

THE FALSE PROPHET'S PLAN

The prophet's plan for carrying out these tasks has two parts. The first part is supernatural, and the second part is economic.

According to verse 14, the prophet instructs people to make an image of the first beast and to put it in their homes. Then, according to verse 15, the prophet gives the image, or idol, the power to speak. The word *speak* is often translated "spirit." This seems to mean that not only can the image speak, but it has a spirit within it that will be watching everyone in his or her home. If anyone strays from total allegiance, that person will somehow be killed, apparently by the idol itself.

The second part of the plan—the economic part—is found in verses 16–17. The prophet will control access to the food supply of the world so that all people, no matter who they are, will look to him to gain access to food. The way to participate in the global economy will be through taking his mark. This mark is a mimic of the mark given to protect the 144,000 in Revelation 14:1. This mark will be placed on the right hand or forehead and will allow people to participate in the global economy. Without it there can be no participation, and people will starve to death.

The mark is either a name or a number. Verse 18, which reveals the number 666, opens with a call for wisdom. Wisdom is the application of the knowledge of God into real life. If Christians are wise, they are living for God and should be discerning as to who the beast really is. They must not be fooled into thinking that this is Christ reigning or that it is the advent of the kingdom of God. Instead, they must see that all of this is merely the power of a person. That is why the mark given to the people does not reflect the glory of God but instead the glory of humanity.

For centuries, people have searched for the meaning behind the numbers 666. Since numerical values were often applied to letters in the ancient world, many have looked for a name that, when converted to numbers, would equal 666. No solutions to that equation have been widely accepted. And in truth, this number may represent some symbolism that has thus far not been taken into account.

REVELATION 14:1–20

THE PROTECTION AND POWER OF GOD

Setting Up the Section

In chapter 14, we see God's response to the attack of the two beasts described in chapter 13. The beast's goal has been to stop the Messiah, destroy the Jews, and persecute the church. Here God claims His own and begins the final harvest.

📖 **14:1–5**

THE PROTECTION

God prevents the plan of the beast from coming to completion by sealing 144,000 people to keep them from being killed by the beast. He will seal them with a sign on their foreheads (14:1).

Demystifying Revelation

The idea around the sign on the forehead is that God is marking these individuals as being His and His alone. The marking of the forehead is an Eastern practice, both in the first century and today. A person places the mark of the god he or she serves on his or her forehead. When God marks His name on these people, He is declaring them His exclusive property.

In verses 2–3, John hears the singing of a song that resembles rushing waters, thunder, and harps. The song is powerful and beautiful. It is sung before the throne of God, and the only people able to sing it are the 144,000 whom God purchased from the earth (7:4–8).

There are two notable things in this passage. The first is that this song is exclusive to this particular group of people. The second is that these people have been purchased from the earth—God has redeemed them.

Critical Observation

Many believe the 144,000 represent a remnant of Jews brought to faith to represent the restoration of Israel. Others see this number as a symbol of completion. They see the 144,000 as a representation of all the redeemed who are now the spiritual children of Abraham—in other words, the church.

Verses 4 and 5 offer five characteristics of these worshipers:
- **Sexually Pure.** The first description is that these individuals are not married and have not allowed themselves to indulge in immoral relationships.

Critical Observation

The New Testament does not represent sex within marriage as anything sinful, though certain vows included abstaining from sex. This description of sexual purity raises some questions about how to interpret John's comments. For those who interpret this passage symbolically, this description simply implies that this group has been spiritually faithful to God—spiritual virgins. For those who interpret it as a literal group of 144,000 Jews, this description implies that the group is all male and that they have never married.

- **Devoted to Jesus.** These individuals not only believe that Jesus is the Messiah, but they are also completely devoted to obeying Him and doing His will.
- **Purchased as Firstfruits.** Firstfruits were the first of the harvest offered to God as an act of worship. Offering the firstfruits indicates that the worshiper understands that all things belong first to God. Here, these people were the firstfruits offered to God and to the Lamb, Jesus.
- **Righteous.** When the text states that no lie is found in their mouths (14:5), it means that because their hearts are righteous, their words and actions are righteous as well. To say a person speaks no lie is to say that his or her heart is governed by truth.
- **Blameless.** The final characteristic is that these Jews are blameless. This means that people live lives that are beyond reproach. To be righteous is to have a heart that is pure before God, and to be blameless means that your life is pure before the world.

14:6–13

THE PROCLAMATIONS

In verses 6–12, John witnesses three angels each making a proclamation.

First proclamation: The Gospel (14:6–7). John sees an angel that appears in mid-air, or midheaven. This is the place in the sky where the sun is at high noon, the highest point in the sky. The image is that this angel will be in the center point of the sky preaching the gospel to the whole world. There are three parts to the angel's message:

1) Fear God. The fear of the Lord means to treat the Lord with awe and reverence. The call is to acknowledge God's control and power over the earth. At this time, the beast is ruling and the world is giving its respect and reverence to him. Yet the angel has stated that fear must be given to God and not to the beast.
2) Give God glory. To give glory to God is to announce the marvelous wonders that He has done. The glory of God is the manifestation of His attributes. To give God

glory is to announce His attributes to the world.

3) Worship God. The beast may be manipulating the earth, but God is the *maker* of the earth. To worship God is to acknowledge who He is. In this case, He is to be acknowledged as the maker of the universe.

At this point there is another announcement; this one about the destruction that is to come.

Second Proclamation: The Destruction (14:8). This proclamation states that Babylon has fallen. The angel is letting everyone know that God is going to do away with the beast's empire. It will fall. Notice the terminology: This nation makes people drink the wine of her immorality. Every thought and every desire of this nation is so wicked and evil that its heart is bent on destroying God.

Demystifying Revelation

This is the first of several times in Revelation that Babylon is mentioned (16:19; 17:5; 18:1–24). The actual city of Babylon began after the flood with the story of the tower of Babel (Genesis 10:10; 11:9). Throughout the history of the Bible, Babylon represented pride, power, and wickedness. Some say that John was using Babylon here to represent Rome. Certainly his original readers would have seen Rome as the oppressive power they were experiencing. But there is a much broader interpretation as well. Babylon can represent the pride and wickedness of humanity that opposes God.

Third Proclamation: The Punishment (14:9–12). Punishment is awaiting those who take the mark of the beast and worship him. Keep in mind that the mark of the beast represents humanity. It is not just a number—it is a religion and a life philosophy. Those who receive the mark of the beast will experience the following punishments:

1) Drink of the wine of God's wrath. This refers to both His power to punish and the totality of all of His anger.

2) Be eternally tormented with fire and brimstone. This refers to the burning of hell. This hell is a place the angels and Jesus will be able to view.

3. Be tormented continually. Their lives will be tormented, both day and night, without rest.

The ones who keep their eyes on the way of God and the work of Jesus will avoid this torment. Those who want to stay true to the Lord during this time risk almost certain death, and for that reason John is told that those who die for the Lord are blessed.

⌂

Take It Home

Verse 13 serves as a reminder (and encouragement) to John's readers that while they may face trials even to the point of death, what they have done with their lives will continue on beyond the grave. This theme is woven throughout Revelation and serves to remind all readers of this letter that God's economy exists outside of this life. That which we do for Him is not destroyed or discredited even if it is rejected by the surrounding culture.

📄 **14:14–20**

THE HARVEST

Some interpret John's vision in verse 14 to be a picture of Jesus bringing judgment to the earth. Others view it as an angel using his sickle to do God's bidding by bringing in a harvest.

The first interpretation is based on the use of the name *Son of Man*, which often describes Jesus in the Gospels. The second interpretation focuses on the fact that this being is described as *like* a son of man (meaning like a human being), which is more similar to the description of an angel. Then verse 15 begins by referring to another angel, as if an angel had just been mentioned.

In the vision, someone like a son of man sits on a white cloud (Daniel 7:13–14; Revelation 14:14). He is wearing a crown and holding a sickle. Another angel then appears to announce that it is the right time for the harvest. For John's original readers, this idea of it being the right time would have been meaningful. Since they are facing persecution, they would surely be eager to know when God is going to intervene on their behalf.

In verse 16, the one who is sitting on a cloud swings his sickle over the earth and reaps a harvest in one swing. Because there is no mention of wrath, those who interpret the person on the cloud as Jesus hold that this reaping is the time when the followers of God are being brought to heaven. For those who hold that the one doing the reaping is an angel, this harvest is undefined.

Verses 17–20 describe a grape harvest. Another angel appears with a sickle, this one coming out of the temple. Then another angel, this one from the altar, joins him and offers the instruction to gather the grapes because they are ripe. When the angel gathers the grapes, he tosses them into God's winepress. This is most likely a picture of judgment, since it is a winepress of wrath. We aren't told who presses the grapes, but the huge amount of blood that pours from the winepress reveals a devastating judgment.

John describes the amount of blood as deep enough to reach the height of horses' bridles stretching for nearly two hundred miles. The Greek reads 1,600 *stadia* (see NIV). A stade was about 607 feet, so the distance was about 180 miles. The greatest concern here is not the exact distance; it is the immeasurable extent of God's judgment falling on those who refuse to believe.

REVELATION 15:1-8

PRELUDE TO DESTRUCTION

Setting Up the Section

Chapters 15–16 include another sevenfold image. In this instance, the image is of seven angels pouring out the contents of bowls. The contents contain God's wrath—His final judgment.

📄 **15:1–4**

THE AGENTS OF WRATH

This is the third time in Revelation that John introduces a sign. The first was the image of a woman that represented Israel (12:1). The second immediately followed: Satan in the form of a red dragon (12:3). This third sign is the angels of destruction with seven final plagues (15:1). These angels hold the wrath of God, which will be used to destroy Satan—it will settle the issue of sin once and for all. After this, the judgment of God will be complete.

An area that resembles a sea of glass appears in Revelation 4:6 and now here in 15:2. This time, though, it is mixed with fire. Some have speculated that this "sea" represents the evil in the world, with those who have overcome that evil standing beside it. Others have supposed that this "sea" is the same one mentioned in Revelation 4:6—a glasslike platform that surrounds the throne of God offering an image of His purity—with the added feature here of God's anger (fire).

The victorious ones described in verse 2 had endured three things:

1) The beast—the evil of the man himself
2) The beast's image—the power of the image that would draw attention to the beast
3) The number of his name—the identification with his teaching and worldview

In John's vision, these conquerors are standing before the throne of God holding harps. They are prepared to worship God. The song that they sing is referred to as the song of Moses and the song of the Lamb (15:3–4). While the words to this song are not the same as the song attributed to Moses in Exodus 15, it is a similar theme—deliverance and justice. Through their song, those who have avoided the wrath of God are worshiping Him because He will make Himself known in the world. The next section in this prelude to final destruction is the description of the angels who will do the destroying.

📄 **15:5–6**

THE ATTIRE OF WRATH

In verse 5, John includes what is actually an Old Testament reference to the presence of God. The tabernacle was the portable temple the Israelites used for their worship as they were traveling. The innermost part of the tabernacle, a shrine to the one true God was the place where His Spirit resided. This innermost chamber was called the Holy of Holies, and it was a room off-limits to everyone but the high priest, and he could enter only once a year on the Day of Atonement. Understanding this reveals the significance of the fact that this room was now opened.

Critical Observation

In Exodus 38:21, this inner room is referred to as the "tabernacle [tent] of the Testimony" because it held within it the ark of the covenant, which contained the Ten Commandants. When this room is opened, as described here, it not only reveals God's presence but also His moral code. It is out of this moral code that people will be judged—it won't be an irrational or emotional moment, but a moment based on basic moral standards.

The seven angels with the seven plagues enter the main stage (15:6). Everything about the description of this scene implies that these angels and these plagues are sanctioned by God Himself. The angels are dressed in clean linen cloths that reflect purity. (The cleanliness of linen often refers to the holiness of the person.) The golden sashes allude to the sashes worn either by priests or warriors. Both would have meaning within this context of exercising God's judgment.

📄 **15:7–8**

THE ATTITUDE OF WRATH

In verse 7, the four living creatures that exist close to the throne of God give the seven angels bowls filled with judgment. The word translated *bowls* is the same word used for the bowl that contained the prayers of the saints in Revelation 5:8.

Demystifying Revelation

Understanding the temple is a key to understanding many of the terms John uses to describe his visions in Revelation. For instance, there were bowls in the temple that served a significant role in worship. In the sin offering (Leviticus 4), blood was put in a bowl and then sprinkled and poured out during the ceremony. The bowls are used similarly here in the vision of the seven angels with seven plagues. In this case, the angels do not receive bowls with blood; instead, they receive bowls with anger and judgment. The eternal God who cannot be in the presence of sin will fill these bowls with His wrath, and they will be poured out on the earth.

Verse 8 describes the temple as filled with smoke. In the scriptures, smoke has often accompanied majesty and power. It was one of the signs of the presence of God (Exodus 40:34–35) and one of the signs of the awesome wrath of God. In this closing verse of chapter 15, God's glory, all the attributes of His character, and His power fill the temple, and there is no room for anything else until the plagues are poured out by the angels. All must stop and watch the mighty power of God on display.

REVELATION 16:1–21

THE SIX BOWLS

Setting Up the Section

In the judgments up to this point, there has been partial destruction. A portion of the stars, a portion of the earth, or a portion of the sea was destroyed, but not the whole of anything. In this case, total destruction will begin. All of the people who worship the beast are affected, all of nature is affected, and the end is destruction.

Seven bowls of judgment are described in the upcoming chapters, and they symbolize the final events of God's punishment of those who reject Him.

📄 16:1–12

THE FIRST SIX BOWLS

In verse 1, John describes a loud voice from the temple. This means that the actions that are about to take place are being driven and controlled by God directly. In the same way, the judgments that are about to fall are falling upon those who have directly scorned God. For these people, following the beast is a conscious attack against God.

Critical Observation

Isaiah 66:1–6 has a warning for Israel. The warning is to any of the Jews who refuse to accept the message of the Lord and instead serve the sin of the world. That message is simply that the Lord will call out from heaven and kill the rebels. Isaiah 66:6 describes the sound of the Lord destroying people.

This points out that God the Father is the One who will avenge His honor and name. Thus, in the following verses in Revelation, we see Him shouting from heaven about the coming wrath. God made a promise that He would destroy the dragon/serpent and its power over the earth in Genesis 3:14–15. At the cross, the power of sin had been broken in the lives of those who call out to God by faith. But still, God plans on removing the power of evil from the earth altogether.

The First Bowl (16:2): The first bowl is a physical attack against all of the people who worship the beast. This wrath is not just anger; it is actual punishment in the form of pain—ugly and painful sores. This attack will render those who worship the beast useless. Then, once those who are opposed to God are out of commission and the beast is unable to help them, they are available to watch the judgment of God fall upon the earth.

The Second Bowl (16:3). Not only do the people get sores, but the water is turned to blood, much as it had been in the famous plagues of Egypt (Exodus 7:17–21). Earlier in Revelation, during the second trumpet (8:8–9) the water was turned to blood, but this is a little different. In this case, *all* of the water of the world is turned to blood, which means that life can no longer be sustained. Also, this is the blood of a dead man, meaning the blood has already coagulated. It is thick and stale and useless. As a result, all of the creatures of the sea die. Not only has the water supply ended, but also a major source of food.

God has rendered the people useless and in agonizing pain. Now the water supply is corrupted and so, too, all of the life that depended upon it. Any hope of survival is diminishing.

The Third Bowl (16:4–7). When the third bowl is poured out by the angel, the rest of the water supply is affected—the rivers and the streams. There is nothing to drink. When this happens, an angel offers up a word of praise, but it is praise for the retribution. As this angel expresses it, God's retribution has been justly poured out on those who shed the blood of God's followers and even opposed God Himself.

The "angel of the waters" (NET) mentioned in verse 5, the one who spoke the praise, is not mentioned anywhere else in the Bible. We can't know details of his identity other than this designation.

Notice in verse 7 that it is the altar that speaks. Earlier in Revelation, a voice came from the horns of the altar (9:13), but in this case, it's the actual altar offering praise.

🔍

Critical Observation

The third trumpet also dealt with the water supply (8:10–11), but in that case, only a part of the water became toxic. In this case, all the waters were ruined.

The Fourth Bowl (16:8–9). In some of the past judgments described in Revelation, the sun has been diminished (6:12; 8:12; 9:2). But in this judgment, the intensity of the sun increases so much that it is scorching people.

Unfortunately, rather than crying out to God, the hearts of the people are unchangeable. They blaspheme the name of God. This means they degrade His character and call Him evil.

While the first four plagues poured out by angels affected the natural world, the next plague is more political in nature.

The Fifth Bowl (16:10–11). The fifth angel turns his attention upon the beast. In fact, he pours his bowl on the beast's throne and darkness takes control. John doesn't give a specific explanation for what caused the people's pain. Their sores are still present

ccording to verse 11. Also, there could be many who were burned from the scorching
un but were not killed by it. While all the details are not known, it is obvious that
eople are miserable, in pain. Yet they curse God rather than acknowledge Him as the
ne who could ease their suffering and the One who has the power to control the
lagues.

The Sixth Bowl (16:12). The sixth plague removes the water from the Euphrates. This
might not seem like such a bad thing given the fact that the river is filled with blood.
ut it is important because the next judgment is the great war of Armageddon that will
estroy the armies of the beast once and for all. Drying up the riverbed removes an
mportant obstacle for attacking armies.

John mentions that the kings from the East are the threat that will come across the
ry riverbed left behind in the path of the Euphrates, but this is the only time these kings
re mentioned. The Euphrates River did serve as the boundary of the Roman Empire, so
n the minds of John's readers, assaulting enemies could easily lay beyond the river. And
vithout the river to block them, the empire was much more open to attack. Still, as for
hese kings from the East, no more explanation is given than is mentioned in verse 12.

📄 **16:13–16**

PREPARATIONS FOR WAR

As with the previous sets of seven events in Revelation, there is a pause between the
ixth bowl and the seventh bowl. (There is a pause between the sixth and seventh seals
nd the sixth and seventh trumpets as well.) In this case, the pause allows the armies of
he world to gather in one place.

Out of the mouths of the dragon, beast, and second beast, come demons that go to
ll of the kings of the world (16:13–14). These demons are spirits that perform remark-
ble miracles to entice the enemies of God to gather. Why would these armies need to
e enticed to wage war against God? Because they are infested with sores, their water
upply has dried up, and the sun is scorching people to death. The only way these people
re going to move is by some form of deception. The deception is that the beast is
tronger than the One doing this to them, and if they unite they will be victorious.

Critical Observation

he fact that the three demons are compared to frogs (16:13) is an interesting element in
evelation. Some have supposed that this is actually a form of mockery aimed toward Satan
nd his armies.

Before the seventh seal and the seventh trumpet an announcement is made. The series
f bowl visions contain the same kind of element. In the case of the seals and trumpets,
n announcement of salvation was made to the world. In this case, an announcement
s made that the coming of the Day of the Lord is like a thief in the night (16:15). The
eality is that no one will know the day when the fury will strike. Therefore, those who

are ready and know that this day will come are the ones who walk through life prepared. Those who do not account for this day are the ones who walk around the world vulnerable and naked—which means that at the very least they will be ashamed when they are caught unprepared. This announcement is the final act of judgment upon these people.

The froglike spirits are successful, according to verse 16, and the armies of the beast gather in one place—Armageddon. The name probably stands for Har Mageddon, which means "the mountain of Megiddo." There is no known mountain with this name, so some have considered it to be merely an element of John's vision—a symbol of God's judgment. Others, however, identify it as the plain that lies beside the ancient city of Meggido.

Demystifying Revelation

Megiddo was a much desired spot because it was a junction for roads running north and south as well as east and west—with control of these trade routes the location was a boon to merchants of all kinds. Because it was such an advantageous location, many battles were fought in the vicinity.

📖 16:17–21

THE SEVENTH BOWL

When the seventh angel pours his bowl of wrath upon the earth, a loud voice comes from the throne in the temple shouting, "It is done" (16:17). While the speaker is not identified, it is likely that it is God, even if simply based on the fact that the voice came from the throne. This is similar to the announcement of Jesus at His death—"It is finished" (John 19:30). When Jesus uttered those words, He was saying the payment for sin was paid in full. When God expresses these words, He is saying there will be no more judgment—the serpent and all evil are being punished on the earth.

God uses two things to destroy the earth. The first is a severe earthquake (16:18). Notice the precision with which John describes just how severe this earthquake is. There has never been an earthquake like it. The earthquake does several things: It kills people and rearranges the landscape of the earth, islands disappear, and mountains fall into the opening where the ground split into three parts (6:19–20).

The great city that the earthquake destroys may refer to humanity in general. The fact that it breaks in three parts (as opposed to simply dividing into two parts) implies complete destruction. The whole picture here, including the second reference John makes to Babylon (which serves as an excellent picture of human arrogance, see Genesis 10:10; 11:9), builds a picture of more than specific cities, but of the destruction of the part of civilization that demands to remain godless (Revelation 16:19).

Next come hailstones that weigh up to one hundred pounds according to some translations. They fall from the sky, crushing the people beneath. And while these people are receiving their judgment, they are cursing God (16:21).

🏠

Take It Home

Two things about this passage are important to understand. First is the destruction of sin. Sin is rebellion that disconnects us from our Creator.

The second is how quickly and simply God can destroy those who follow after sin. He requires no nuclear holocaust, no human-made weapons. The Creator of the universe can use His creation to destroy those who have rejected Him. He has the power to rearrange the earth, which reveals His true sovereignty.

We fear or worry about many things in life—things that can't hurt us. When we truly acknowledge God's power, it should give us pause. We should respect the power that could crush us yet offers us the opportunity over and over again to change our ways and be treated as beloved children.

REVELATION 17:1–18

THE DESTRUCTION OF BABYLON

Setting Up the Section

Thus far in Revelation, John's message has carried the theme of God's sovereignty. No matter what powers *seem* to exist, God is the One with the ultimate power and with the choice to decide when to display that power.

With chapter 17, the theme of the remainder of the book becomes the final judgment of God. He has chosen to display His power against evil, and the final throw-down is in sight.

Chapter 17 is built upon the vision of a woman, a prostitute, who seems to symbolize the same thing that Babylon symbolizes in 16:19—civilization convinced it doesn't need God.

📄 17:1–7

THE VISION OF THE PROSTITUTE

This prostitute, revealed to John in verses 1–2, is the leader of the immorality of the world. She leads the kings to commit acts of immorality and causes the people of the world to be led astray. The description "sits on many waters" is the same used by the prophet Jeremiah for the Old Testament city of Babylon (Jeremiah 51:13). As Revelation 17 and 18 play out, the image of this woman is identified with Babylon in many ways.

Critical Observation

The fact that the woman in Revelation 17 is referred to as a prostitute rather than an adulteress is telling. Throughout the Old Testament, when the nation of God strays into sin, it is often described as an adulteress. This, of course, is because these people were considered God's bride.

But here the people who are living outside of God's law are simply referred to as a prostitute. They were never in a relationship with God, so they were not forsaking that relationship.

In verse 3, after having the prostitute described to him, John sees her for himself. After being carried away, he sees the woman on a scarlet beast. This is presumably the same beast described in 13:1, with seven heads, ten horns, and labeled with blasphemous names.

The woman is dressed in purple and scarlet, the colors of royalty (17:4). She is glittering with her accessories of gold, pearls, and precious stones. Many interpret this description, particularly the royal colors, to mean that the prostitute symbolizes a kingdom. She holds a golden cup, but inside the cup are immoral, disgusting things.

There is a title written on her forehead (17:5). This is one of several times in Revelation that people are identified by their mark, or seal, on their foreheads (7:3; 9:4; 14:1). Rather than understanding her name as being *Mystery*, her name *was* a mystery. More explanation is given later in this chapter, when an angel explains some of the symbolism to John (17:15–18).

The next thing written on her forehead is *Babylon*, a city that has already been mentioned several times in Revelation. In this case, the name Babylon is not used to identify a place but more to identify a godless culture.

It is clear, though, that not only is this woman (or whom she represents) evil herself, but she births evil. Identified as the mother of all prostitutes, she represents the source of all of the immorality in the world. In addition, she is the source of all of the evil that seeks to desecrate God. And as verse 6 states, she clearly opposes the children of God as well.

Verse 6 draws an even more vivid description. The woman is drunk with the blood of the saints, which implies she is responsible for their deaths. The language here is not that of something done long ago, but rather something that is still continuing. She enjoys the destruction of that which she has partaken. And John is amazed at what he sees.

17:7–14

THE ANGEL'S EXPLANATION

The angel offers some explanation of the scene that has astonished John (17:7). While John has described the woman prominently in the vision, the angel reveals that it is the beast—identified by his heads and horns—that seems more prominent.

Several times in the angel's explanation, the beast is described, with some variations, as the one who "was, now is not, and will come" (17:8). This is a way of saying that he has been resurrected, but it is a false resurrection. It is probably meant to stand in contrast to the description of Jesus in Revelation 1:4, "Grace and peace to you from him who is, and who was, and who is to come" (NIV). This beast lived, died, and is going to come back to life—a sign of false divinity. But in the end, this coming back serves the purpose of his final destruction.

Demystifying Revelation

Much of John's visions in Revelation would have had political implications in the ears of his original readers. There was a myth that the evil Nero would be resurrected. Many saw this resurrection coming true in the cruel rein of Emperor Domitian. It was probably during this reign that John was writing.

Just as in 13:18, when the number for the beast is cited, the angel states that the mind that grasps the explanation of this vision requires wisdom (13:18; 17:9). Lest we think these should be simple concepts, they are not. They are truths that require a lot of understanding.

According to the angel, the seven heads on the beast are seven mountains on which the woman sits—as well as seven kings (17:9-10). For some contemporary interpreters, this means that the heads on the beast represent seven nations or emperors that this woman controls. To others, this is an obvious reference to Rome, which was often described as a city of seven hills. Certainly, in the days of John, Rome would have fit much of the description of Babylon given in this book.

Verse 10 mentions the seven kings, five of which have fallen. Those who see the heads of the beast as nations interpret this verse as a reference to five kingdoms who have stood against Israel but are no longer in control. For those who see the heads of the beast as rulers, this verse references emperors or perhaps empires. Others offer the option that the number 7 may, as it has before, represent completion. Rather than a specific nation, ruler, or kingdom, it could denote all that has stood against God.

In verse 11, we read that there will actually be one more to rule. Whether interpreted as a ruler, a nation, or a symbol of evil, this eighth king refers to the beast himself. Somehow, he belongs to the seven yet rules again. The angel's interest in this explanation, though, doesn't seem to be identifying the beast in a definite way or explaining the symbolism without question. The focus seems to be that this beast is on his way to destruction at the hand of God.

Next, the angel begins to explain the horns (17:12-14). The ten horns represent ten kingdoms as a confederacy that will rule with the beast for a definite time—a quite short period of time. They will be completely united with the beast in opposition to the Lamb, but they will be defeated.

Jesus is described as Lord of lords and King of kings, a name similar to that which describes God in Deuteronomy 10:17. He will be accompanied by His chosen and faithful followers. This is not to be understood as His army; the Lamb needs no army to defeat evil. Rather, it is the family of those He has redeemed.

🖹 17:15–18

THE RELATIONSHIP BETWEEN
THE BEAST AND THE PROSTITUTE

In the explanation, the angel reveals that the waters on which the prostitute sits represent the influence she has over the entire world. Many believe this is a description of a world religion. For the first time, the entire world will share a common belief system. Others see it as a description of an immeasurably large empire (17:15).

In either interpretation, the main players turn on each other. The beast, with his army, first shames the prostitute, then destroys her (17:16). This is a picture of the nature of evil and of the sovereignty of God. Evil's nature is to turn even on its own. God's sovereignty is such that His will is done even by those who defy Him. God uses the hatred of the beast to do away with the spirit of evil that rules the world.

In verse 18, the angel who is making this explanation offers John some clues to the identity of the prostitute. The angel says that she is a great city who rules over the kings on the earth. In John's culture, this certainly would have been taken as a reference to Rome. In regard to the end times, it can be seen as an organized, but false, world religion or simply as a reference to organized humanity, yet outside of the law of God.

REVELATION 18:1–24
THE FUNERAL OF HUMANITY

Setting Up the Section

Chapter 18 records the destruction of Babylon. There are similarities here with the Old Testament accounts of the destruction of Tyre (Ezekiel 26–28) and with the destruction of the actual city of Babylon (Jeremiah 50–51).

When Babylon is destroyed, the entire infrastructure of humanity will be destroyed. This will create an undoing of the world that will leave humans hopeless. For John's original readers, this prophecy would have held some significance regarding the Roman Empire, but it is also the picture of all human civilizations that focus on earthly accomplishments rather than the power of the Creator.

🖹 18:1–8

THE WARNING

Chapter 18 opens with an angel coming from heaven with authority, splendor, and an announcement that Babylon has been destroyed (18:1–2). This opening part of the nnouncement is in the past tense, as if the event is completed. The angel describes abylon four ways:

1) It is the home for demons and unclean birds. The unclean birds were probably scavenger birds, like buzzards, that preyed on dead things. This was despicable to the Jews. It was also an apt image of a deserted place (18:2).

2) It is a source for all of the evil in the world. This is pictured by the nations drinking the wine of Babylon's immorality (18:3).

3) It is a source for all of the wicked leadership in the world, thus the image of the kings committing adultery with her (18:3).

4) It is a source for all of the ill-gotten gain in the world. This can be seen by the mention of the merchants making their profits from Babylon's lavish wickedness (18:3).

At verse 4, there is a shift in the tense of the passage. Chapter 18 opens with the proclamation of Babylon's destruction as a completed event. With verse 4, the voice from heaven sends out an address while Babylon is still in the process of being destroyed. The warning is to stay away from the city because it is already condemned.

While verses 4–5 are addressed to the people of God, verses 6–8 seem to be addressing those who can inflict justice. They are a request for punishment, not simply according to the amount that Babylon has inflicted pain, but double that. In fact, the punishment this voice is calling for is not according to Babylon's cruelties, but according to her demand for luxury. As extravagantly as she has lived, so let her punishment be (18:7).

Critical Observation

Babylon's claim not to be a widow and not to have to mourn may reflect the nation's arrogance and demand for profitable times (18:7). She seems to believe that no power can take away the extravagance with which she lives. Babylon is a diva of a nation, looking down on all others.

According to verse 8, her due punishment will come all at one time through four plagues: death, mourning, famine, and fire.

📖 18:9–19

THE WEEPING

While no one runs to Babylon's rescue, according to verses 9–11, there are some who mourn her passing—those who profited from her trade. The kings who traded with her stand at a distance and verbalize their lament over her quick (one hour) demise (18:10).

In verse 11, the merchants join the lamentation for the simple reason that Babylon is not there to buy their cargoes any longer. Verses 12–13 list the kinds of merchandise that made up that cargo. Most are easily recognizable still today. The precious stones could denote stones such as granite, as well as what we consider precious stones today. The colors of the cloth—scarlet and purple—are both colors the scriptures associate with splendor, even royalty, and also with sin. Citron wood is a hardwood well-known for its deep grain. The mention of bodies denotes slaves and what we would refer to today as human trafficking.

Verse 14 caps off this list of cargo with a parenthetical announcement addressing the destroyed city directly and adding a general description of the splendor lost.

The section closes with more mourning of the merchants but includes more specifically the sea merchants who lost their overseas business (18:15-19). Their lament echoes the previous laments in the description of the city as lavish and in their sorrow for the loss of profits. The economic foundation of their existence has been destroyed.

📄 18:20–24

THE WRATH

Verse 20 is another parenthetical address, in this case perhaps by John himself (see also verse 14). This statement addresses the saints, apostles, and prophets attributing this great act of judgment to God. It is a call to rejoice.

John's vision in verse 21 involves an angel who picks up a millstone and throws it into the sea. This image is reminiscent of the Old Testament prophet Jeremiah's actions in Jeremiah 51:63, which are also a picture of the destruction of Babylon.

Demystifying Revelation

The typical millstone in that day was four to five feet in diameter and a couple of feet in thickness. It would have been quite heavy and would have sunk instantly when thrown into the water. In other words, it would seem to disappear. That is an apt description of the sudden destruction of Babylon. The entire system of the world will be done away with in an instant.

When the millstone is thrown down, it is done with violence. The judgment comes in an intense and destructive moment that changes the foundation of life forever (18:21). Verses 22-23 list the things that will never happen again in light of Babylon's destruction: Musicians won't play, craftsmen won't practice, and everyday life—like grinding grain into flour, marrying, and even lamps lighting homes—will cease.

While the previous verses were addressing Babylon, verse 24 is a statement *about* Babylon (much like verse 20). The deaths of prophets and saints and all those killed on earth have been attributed to her. In light of such a broad scope of destruction being credited to Babylon, many believe that the destruction represents not just the destruction of one city or power, but a representation of all the world's cities that have chosen to operate outside of God's laws.

REVELATION 19:1–21

WORSHIP AND WRATH

Setting Up the Section

Chapter 19 includes the great marriage ceremony of the Lamb and the return of Jesus. It is a chapter of both worship and victory, including the final destruction of the beast and his prophet.

📄 **19:1–6**

PRAISE FOR THE JUDGMENT OF BABYLON

Chapter 19 opens with a great multitude singing God's praise. These are probably angels, but John doesn't specify. In this song, God is worshiped for His twofold work of judgment and of salvation:

1) Salvation and glory and power belong to God.
2) God's judgments are true and righteous.
3) He has judged the great prostitute who corrupted the earth with her immorality.
4) He has avenged the blood of His servants on her, blood that was on the great prostitute's hands (19:1–2).

Critical Observation

The song opens with the word *Hallelujah*, such a familiar word of praise in contemporary culture, yet this is the first time it is used in the New Testament. It does appear in the Psalms, and in that case is often related to the destruction of the wicked and the salvation of the children of God.

When the multitude sings out a second time, a picture of smoke rising from the battle is a sign of the permanence of the destruction (19:3). Then, for the final time in Revelation, the twenty-four elders and four living creatures, those who have been described as the ones closest to God's throne, take part in the worship. They offer their agreement. *Amen* means "so let it be." It is a statement of finality. And they offer their own praise (4:10; 19:4).

Take It Home

Yet another unidentified voice calls out in verse 5 for all God's servants to praise Him. The attitude of the worshipers indicates that they fear the Lord. Their praise is simple—the acknowledgment of the reign of God. Today we can still answer this call to worship, acknowledging God's present and evolving reign as His established kingdom (19:6). When we worship as the servants of God, we join this multitude.

📖 **19:7–10**

THE WEDDING CELEBRATION

Throughout the scriptures, the picture of a bride has often represented God's faithful people. In the Old Testament, the prophet Isaiah spoke of Israel as God's bride (Isaiah 54:6). Here, in Revelation 19:7, the bride is a picture of the church, and the Lamb is a picture of Jesus. Redeemed believers are welcomed into heaven, and they have the privilege of having union with Christ forever.

The bride of the Lamb is dressed in clean, fine linen, which represents the good works of the faithful. This kind of imagery is common for those who are spiritually clean (Zechariah 3; Revelation 19:8).

In verse 9, the angel instructs John to write. Several times John is instructed to create a written record of what is happening, and only once is he forbidden from doing so (10:4).

Critical Observation

Those who are invited to take part in the great wedding banquet are called *blessed*. This would have had particular meaning to John's original readers. Facing persecution and even death, they had to wonder if blessings would indeed be theirs. The words of the angels, attributed to God, would have been a good reminder to these believers (and to believers through the ages) that in His kingdom there is a different timetable and a different measure of blessing not determined by the particular circumstances of the moment.

The angel also tells John that these are the words of God, and this declaration prompts John to worship the angel himself (19:10). The angel's response makes several things clear:

1) Angels are not to be worshiped.
2) Angels are fellow servants with Christians, all bearing witness to Jesus.
3) The testimony about Jesus is the spirit of prophecy.

The entire prophetic message of God from the beginning of the world has pointed to Jesus. He is central to everything for this life and the next.

THE RETURN OF THE MESSIAH

The portrayal of Christ's coming takes the form of a series of symbolic pictures that highlight aspects of an event too great to comprehend in advance. When heaven is opened, the first thing John sees is a white horse, with Faithful and True riding it (19:11). This is a representation of Jesus, the almighty Conqueror, the Word of God (John 1:1–3), coming to subdue the rebellious of earth, which are led by the powers of hell.

His blazing eyes relate to judgment (Revelation 19:12); His many crowns to His position as King of kings and Lord of lords (19:12, 16). He has a name that only He knows, yet His names are given in verses 11, 13, and 16.

His blood-dipped robe is that attributed to God by the Old Testament prophet Isaiah (Isaiah 63:1–6; Revelation 19:13). First-century rabbis claimed God would wear this kind of robe on the day of His vengeance on Rome.

Verse 14 mentions the armies that follow Jesus, also on white horses. These armies are the angels that surround Him. While the description of their white clothes does resemble the description of the redeemed in verse 8, the church is just described as the bride (19:14). For them to appear as an army here would be too quick of a switch.

Verse 15 employs several descriptions that have already appeared in John's visions. The sword extending from Jesus' mouth is His true weapon, rather than His armies (1:16). The iron rod of His rule depicts His absolute authority (12:5). Finally, the winepress of God's wrath is an image of judgment also used in chapter 14 (14:19–20).

Some translations are unclear as to whether Jesus' name appears both on His thigh and on His clothing (19:16). The name probably does appear twice, but there is some question as to how it appears on His thigh. There is no question, though, that He is coming to earth to enforce the reign of the Word of God.

THE REIGN OF THE MESSIAH

Verses 17–21 paint a picture of final disaster. An angel appears midair and calls to the birds to come and feast on the flesh of everyone—from those in highest power to the slaves who serve (19:18). This represents everyone who took the mark of the beast, including the beast himself and his false prophet (described in chapter 13 as a secondary beast).

This is a judgment scene that exhibits the power of the Word of God. The picture holds one dominant reality: Christ's victory over those who oppose Him is total. The Antichrist and the false prophet are thrown into the fiery lake of burning sulfur—this is complete destruction.

Demystifying Revelation

This fiery lake is a picture of hell, which in the New Testament is commonly called *Gehenna* (Matthew 5:22; 29, 30; 10:28; et al.). The Greek word is a transliteration of a Hebrew phrase meaning "the valley of Hinnom," a valley on the south side of Jerusalem where the Jews of Jeremiah's time offered human sacrifices by fire (Jeremiah 7:31). This was an appalling act that brought God's judgment upon them. The valley later came to be used as the city's garbage heap, where fires burned constantly. Such a place of constant stench and burning became an appropriate symbol for the place of eternal judgment.

REVELATION 20:1–15
THE COMPLETION OF THE PROMISES OF GOD

Satan Bound — 20:1–3
Saints Ruling — 20:4–6
The Completion of the Promise to the Serpent — 20:7–10
The Completion of the Promise to Humanity — 20:11–15

Setting Up the Section

To this point in Revelation, we have seen all those who stood on the side of the beast destroyed, except one. That is Satan himself. In this section, Satan receives his judgment.

There are many interpretations of the events John describes here, as well as a variety of timetables proposed for those events. The underlying truth remains, though, that John's visions reinforce God's ability and decision to deal with sin once and for all.

📄 **20:1–3**

SATAN BOUND

Chapter 20 opens with an unnamed angel descending from heaven holding a key and a chain. The obvious picture here is that the angel has authority over the abyss. It is interesting to note that, while we might expect John's vision to include the most famous of angels to deal with Satan himself, in this case it is simply an unnamed angel who is given the task.

The abyss mentioned here is a kind of spiritual holding cell. It is not the final place of judgment.

In verse 2, Satan is identified by several terms that have already been used in Revelation—*dragon*, *serpent*, *devil*, and *Satan*. He is thrown into the abyss for one thousand years (20:3).

Critical Observation

As with much of Revelation, this passage has been interpreted in many ways, much depending on whether the details are viewed symbolically or literally. Some see the binding as a future event that will take place literally after the return of Christ to earth. Others see it as a symbolic binding that occurred at Christ's death and resurrection when he achieved victory over Satan. The length of time is also debated. Many believe the thousand years denotes the actual number of years that Satan will be bound. For others, it is simply a good round number, one that communicates that God will bind Satan's power and influence for the right amount of time that He will determine.

📄 20:4–6

SAINTS RULING

The next part of John's vision includes those who have been martyred for their faith. The typical form of execution in first-century Rome was a beheading with an ax or sword, as the wording in verse 4 mentions. In this case, though, the language probably implies more generally those who were martyred for their faith, whatever the method.

John further describes the restraint of these sufferers: They had not worshiped the beast nor received his mark. Because of this, they were mistreated by the authorities of their world and thus will be given authority by God. They are resurrected to rule with Jesus.

John calls this the first resurrection. He mentions that the rest of the dead will come to life after the thousand years is complete, but he does not refer to that as the second resurrection. Instead, he only speaks of a second death, from which these martyrs are saved (20:5–6).

📄 20:7–10

THE COMPLETION OF THE PROMISE TO THE SERPENT

At the end of the one thousand years, Satan is released from the abyss and begins to gather his army. Gog and Magog are hostile leaders included in a prophecy of the Old Testament prophet Ezekiel (Ezekiel 38–39). Their names are used here to represent the world's evil. The picture in verse 7 is that of an innumerable army gathered from all over the earth (Revelation 20:7–8).

The fact that this kind of army can be gathered seems to imply that even though Jesus has ruled the earth for a thousand years, not everyone has followed wholeheartedly.

According to verse 9, the armies of Satan are able to gather in an advantageous position. They encircle the saints and the "beloved city" (20:9 NET). This beloved city stands in stark contrast to the description of wicked Babylon as the "great city" (17:18; 18:10). Many interpret this beloved city to be Jerusalem. Others interpret it to represent the actual body of believers who now embody God's presence as the temple once did.

Notice the understated description of the victory in verse 9. It is no problem for

God to defeat Satan when the time is right to do so—fire comes down and the army is destroyed.

Consequently, the devil is thrown into the lake of fire and sulfur to accompany the beast and false prophet who are already there. Their torment will be continuous. God had promised Eve that the serpent would be dealt with eventually, and that promise is fulfilled here (Genesis 3:15; Revelation 20:10).

📃 20:11–15

THE COMPLETION OF THE PROMISE TO HUMANITY

The throne in verse 11 is distinguished from the other thrones mentioned in Revelation in that it is large and white. It is such a powerful place of righteousness that nothing will be able to stand before it. While John does not identify who sits on the throne, most likely it is God the Father.

Demystifying Revelation

Some have noted that things seem out of order in these verses. Verse 11 has heaven and earth fleeing, yet in verse 13 the sea gives up its dead. There have been several solutions offered for this perceived problem. The mention of heaven and earth fleeing could be simply a metaphor explaining the power of the One who sits on the throne. Others suggest that these events could be happening simultaneously. A final solution is to recognize that John is not arguing for a strict chronology but is writing for emphasis. This is a vision meant to enlighten, not a history lesson with a strict timeline. Verse 11 provides a picture of the power of God's presence, while verse 13 gives the picture that none of those who have died will be overlooked in this resurrection to judgment. Even those lost or buried at sea will be held accountable.

Verse 12 states that this judgment is going to be for everyone who ever lived. John declares that he saw the dead, the great and the small, standing before the throne.

The books mentioned here are apparently records of all the deeds by which these lives will be judged. The book of life, separate from the other books, represents the names of those who have been redeemed and will find their home in heaven.

Verse 13 reinforces the idea that no one will be overlooked in this judgment. All those who have died, no matter their fate, will be called up.

The power that held physical bodies in bondage (death) and the place where all the wicked went until the Day of Judgment (Hades) will both be destroyed in the lake of fire (20:14). There is no reason for these two things to exist, because sin is finally being removed from the earth.

Verse 15 paints the picture of two distinct fates. The book of life is the determining factor.

REVELATION 21:1–27

ALL THINGS BRIGHT AND BEAUTIFUL

Setting Up the Section

Having described the fate of evil in the previous chapters, the remaining two chapters of Revelation describe visions of a new world established and ruled by God. This is the fate of the faithful, a spiritual destiny described here in earthly terms.

📄 **21:1–8**

THE NEW HEAVEN AND EARTH

John's vision opens with not only a new earth, but a new heaven. He is describing a whole new existence in the presence of God. The fact that the sea no longer exists is a mysterious image. It may relate to the fact that the dragon came from the sea (21:1). The sea was also viewed by ancient peoples as a place of danger and death, where evil spiritual forces lived. In the new heaven and earth there will be no danger or death.

The New Jerusalem is described as a bride coming down from heaven (21:2). The bride is completely prepared, at her best for her husband.

The great pronouncement in verse 3 is that God is now living among His people. Any separation is gone. Heaven and earth have joined together to make one place; there will be no more pain, sin, tears, or death. All of the misery that the children of God had to endure on their way to heaven will be wiped away. God will restore every believer (21:3–4).

In verse 5, God speaks directly, one of the few times in Revelation. John has to be reminded to write down the proclamation that God is making all things new. Then God continues with a confirmation that what needed to be accomplished is complete. He also identifies Himself as the One with the authority to make this claim—the Alpha and Omega. *Alpha* is the first letter of the Greek alphabet, and *omega* is the last letter. This imagery shows God's nature to be eternal.

Finally, this eternal God says He will forever be a source for the water of life—free of charge (21:6). His eternal nature provides people with the new life necessary for participating in this new world.

According to verses 7–8, those who do not succumb to evil and remain true to God are the ones who will engage in this complete relationship with God. There are those who will not, however, and their fate is the second death in the lake of fire as described in the previous chapter. The list given in verse 8 opens with cowards, the opposite of those who persevered and conquered.

📄 **21:9–21**

THE CITY OF GOD

In verse 9, there is a reference not only to the bride of the Lamb, but to the *wife* of the Lamb. This parallels the idea of God's work being complete. The wedding has taken place, and the relationship is solidified.

Jerusalem is called the bride because the children of God are now all one, and all in the city are married to God. In the past, it was called the bride because of its splendor; now it is called the bride because the redeemed inhabit it.

John again sees Jerusalem descending from heaven (21:10). The city is described as a clear jewel. The stone that is now known as jasper is not transparent, so the name *jasper* may have been applied to a different stone in John's day (21:11). Nevertheless, the description here of the city of God is that of a beautiful, costly jewel.

A more physical description of the city is given in verses 12–14. The walls, though unnecessary in a world without enemies and natural disasters, still denote a protected and safe place.

The twelve gates, guarded by angels and labeled with the twelve tribes of Israel, can easily be seen as a fulfillment of God's promises to His chosen people throughout history (21:13). The gates are positioned to reflect the way the twelve tribes encamped around the tabernacle in Numbers 2.

The inclusion of the names of the twelve apostles is an inclusion of the Christian church, the redeemed of God (Revelation 21:14).

The angel measures the city, and while it is described as square, it is actually an even cube, given that the height is also the same as the length and width—about fourteen hundred miles each (21:15–16).

🔍

Critical Observation

The next number given is related to the wall of the city. Verse 17 describes it as 144 cubits, or about 200 feet. The angel doesn't state whether the measurement is of the height or the depth of the wall, but either of these is difficult to reconcile with the measurements given of the city in verses 15–16. This is a good reminder that John's visions point to the underlying truth rather than the specific details.

New Jerusalem's walls are made of jasper (21:18). In Revelation 4:3, God is described as jasper, so there may be an allusion here to God as the city's protector.

Demystifying Revelation

It's puzzling, by contemporary standards, that the city is described as pure gold yet transparent (21:18). Gold, as we know it, is opaque. This may be more of a reference to something very shiny and completely pure. Glass was not crystal clear in the first century, and mirrors were dark and inconsistent in comparison with their modern counterparts. This description may reflect John's attempt to describe something so fine that it would have been unimaginable to his own cultural background.

The stones described in verses 19–20 seem to correlate with the stones in the Jewish high priest's breastplate as described in Exodus 28:17–20. It would be difficult to define each of the stones since not only has the study of stones become much more specific through the centuries, but even in the first century, stones were identified differently in the Hebrew language than in the Greek. It is certain, though, that these stones are of great value, which is the reason they are used as the foundation of the city. The New Jerusalem is not a place built on simple brick, but even the foundation is made of precious jewels.

The gates into the city are not only made of pearl, but each is one giant pearl. And again, as in verse 18, the main street is pure gold, clear and perfect (21:21).

Take It Home

John's vision of the world God creates for His people is one of perfection from the bottom to the top. To the original readers of this letter, this would have spoken to a hope that the imperfect and even cruel world that they endured was not a reflection of God's vision for them, nor the only thing they had to look forward to.

For modern believers, also, this perfect city reminds us to keep looking up to God's standards for life. We cannot imagine the way God actually intended our world to be, but we can participate in that kingdom with our obedience and with our eager anticipation of God's ultimate justice and reign.

📖 21:22–27

THE TEMPLE, SUN, AND MOON

Verses 22–27 reveal three things missing from the New Jerusalem: the temple, the sun and moon, and the presence of sin.

There is no temple because the Lord dwells in this place (21:22). God is the temple. There is no sun or moon because God's glory and the light of the Lamb provide all the light needed. There is no night or any need for locked gates for protection (21:23–26).

Verse 24 reveals the wide breadth of redemption. The nations of the earth and the kings of the earth add grandeur to this place, but because of redemption, they bring none of their sin.

Finally, there is no sin (21:27). The description of sin here may apply specifically to idolatry. Also, there is no untruth. The expectation is that those who are included in the Lamb's book of life bring no sin to this place.

REVELATION 22:1–21

EDEN RESTORED

Setting Up the Section

Chapter 22 continues John's vision of the new heaven and earth begun in chapter 21. Then the chapter closes with an epilogue of observations about the collection of visions that make up the book of Revelation and the promise that Jesus is coming again.

📄 **22:1–5**

THE TREE OF LIFE

In verses 1–2, an angel shows John a vision of a river made up of the water of life. The water sparkles brilliantly, is clear as crystal. It originates with God's throne and flows down the center of the main street (22:1–2). The scriptures offer allusions to the water of life in other places. The Old Testament prophecies of Ezekiel and Zechariah include mention of such (Ezekiel 47; Zechariah 14:8), as well as Jesus' teaching in the Gospels (John 4:7–14; 7:37–38).

The tree that is on this river is the tree of life. The Genesis creation account includes the description of two trees—the tree of the knowledge of good and evil and the tree of life. Many see this tree John describes by the river as the latter tree from the Garden of Eden. Somehow, in John's vision, this tree grows on both sides of the river (22:2). Also, it produces a different fruit each month (rather than twelve different fruits all year long).

The leaves of this tree are described as bringing healing to the nations. After the description in chapter 21 of the idyllic surroundings with no tears, sickness, or sin, one can wonder what these leaves will actually heal. Neither John nor the angel answers this question, so we can only appreciate the fact that these leaves are health-giving in some way.

Verse 3 says there will be no more curse, which some see as a fulfillment of Zechariah's prophecy in Zechariah 14:11. God and the Lamb are there with their people who both offer worship and bear God's name on their foreheads (Revelation 14:1; 22:4).

🔍

Critical Observation

The Old Testament prophet Ezekiel described the name of the eternal city of God as, "The Lord is there." Certainly John's vision in chapter 22 bears out that name.

Because God will be the center of this city, there will never be any darkness. No lamps are necessary; no sun is needed to light the way. God is the light for this eternal place. The idea that the inhabitants will reign with God is not to indicate that there will be multitudes to reign over, for everyone there will be a child of God. But it is an indication that everyone there will be considered royalty, children of the King (22:5).

📄 **22:6–21**

EPILOGUE

In verse 6, the angel confirms the credibility of what has been revealed to John. While his claim that the words are reliable and trustworthy could simply apply to the immediately preceding verses, it is likely that they can be understood as a claim for this whole book of visions. This prophecy is of God.

The quote in verse 7 can be attributed to Jesus. The word *soon* is used here as in the verse above. In this case, *soon* means not so much that these events will happen sooner rather than later, but that they are the next event on God's schedule.

With verse 8, it is clear that John is speaking rather than the angel, offering his own testimony to the credibility of this prophecy. Then he again shows reverence to the angel, who reminds him that only God should be worshiped (19:10; 22:9).

John is told not to seal up the words of this book (22:10). They are to be shared and understood. Keeping a book unsealed means the words will be proclaimed, and God will give understanding to the people who hear it. According to the angel, though, some who hear the words of this book will continue on in their sin (22:11). In essence, the angel says, let each person respond as he or she will respond, for God will be the One who will judge people by their deeds.

Verses 12–13, just like verse 7, are the words of Jesus. He repeats His promise to come soon and to reward each person according to the life he or she has lived. He also states the same claim that was attributed to God in Revelation 1:8. In this case, Jesus adds two additional descriptive phrases, but all three mean the same thing—He is the beginning and the end.

Verses 14–15 are probably spoken by John, but this is not completely clear. These two verses first claim blessings on the ones who keep their clothes clean—keep their lives righteous—and thus have access to the tree of life and city in which it dwells. Then verse 15 draws a comparison with those who choose to live outside of the city, which in this case implies they are living outside of God's laws. The sins listed here have appeared elsewhere in the descriptions of those who followed the beast (9:21; 21:8).

Demystifying Revelation

It seems odd that there would be talk of all this sinfulness, when just verses ago John includes such a beautiful description of the new heaven and earth after sin is removed. The information in this closing section, though, is outside of the vision. It is a movement back toward the reality faced by John's readers who are attempting to live according to the kingdom of God in a world that resembles this description of those outside the new city gates.

Verses 16–17 again offer an invitation to come to Jesus and drink of the water of life. Jesus describes Himself as both the root of David (that from which David's bloodline sprang) and a descendant of David (that which sprang from David's bloodline). He is the One who came before David and before the great political empire of Israel. He is also the One who is the human descendant of David. He is the center of everything.

Jesus' claim to be the bright morning star may be a reference to Numbers 24:17, a prophecy stated by a prophet Balaam, who claimed a star would come out of the family of Jacob, father of the twelve tribes of Israel.

The warning in Revelation 22:18–19 covers both those who would add to John's prophecy and those who would diminish it. Neither will be tolerated.

John closes this prophecy with both a promise from Jesus that He is coming and a prayer from John that Jesus will come (22:20–21). Notice that in verse 20 Jesus is described as the One who testifies to these prophecies and confirms His intent to return. This must have resonated greatly with those first-century Christians enduring persecution, wondering about God's timetable, praying that their good deeds would not be forgotten by God, even if they were disdained by their own culture and government.

⌂

Take It Home

Verse 21 is a typical close to a letter of this era but an unusual close to such a dramatic writing. These closing words are a good reminder to all that no matter the situation—whether facing persecution or any of the situations described in the churches at the beginning of Revelation—we all are in need of the grace of the Lord Jesus.

The point of this book is not to show us who the beast is, but to show us how Jesus is going to overcome the beast. It is not to offer us a mysterious timetable over which we can quarrel, but to unite us in our eager anticipation of God's kingdom. It is not an apocalypse meant to scare us into obedience, but a promise of God's character no matter what the circumstances of the moment might present to the contrary.

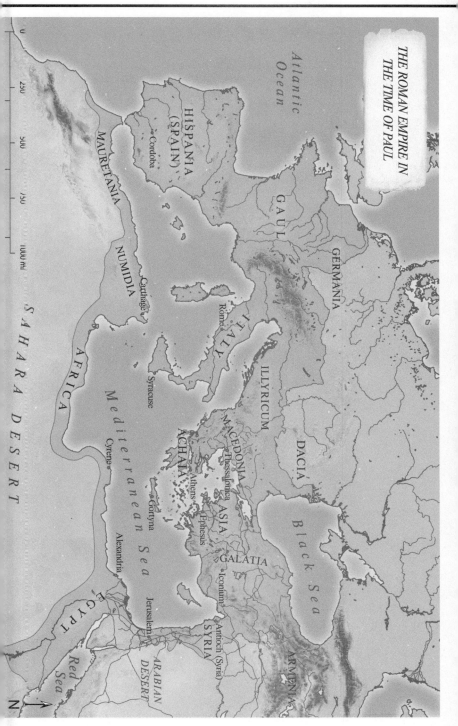

THE ROMAN EMPIRE IN
THE TIME OF PAUL

*Atlantic
Ocean*

HISPANIA
(SPAIN)

Cordoba

GAUL

GERMANIA

MAURETANIA

NUMIDIA

Carthage

ITALY

Rome

ILLYRICUM

DACIA

*Black
Sea*

S A H A R A   D E S E R T

AFRICA

Syracuse

M e d i t e r r a n e a n   S e a

MACEDONIA

Thessalonica

ACHAIA

Athens

Cyrene

Gortyna

Ephesus

ASIA

GALATIA

Iconium

Alexandria

EGYPT

Jerusalem

Antioch (Syria)

SYRIA

*Red
Sea*

*ARABIAN
DESERT*

ARMENIA

N →

0   250   500   750   1000 mi

THE CHURCHES
OF REVELATION

✚ one of the seven
churches addressed
in Revelation

THRACE

Byzantium Chalcedon

Nicomed

Sea of Marmara

Nicea

Sangan

Cyzicus

BITHYNI

Abydos

Ilium (Troy)

Troas

Assos

Adramyttium

MYSIA

Tembris River

LESBOS

Mytilene

Pergamum ✚

Selinus River

Thyatira ✚

ASIA

Hermus River

CHIOS

Smyrna ✚

LYDIA

Sardis ✚

Philadelphia ✚

Apamea

Cayster River

Ephesus ✚

Magnesia

Tralles

Meander River

Hierapolis

Laodicea ✚

Lycus River

SAMOS

Priene

Colosse

IKARIA

Miletus

CARIA

PATMOS →

John is exiled to the island of Patmos,
where he writes the book of Revelation.

COS

Halicarnassus

Cnidus

LYCIA

Indus River

Xanthus River

RHODES

Rhodes

Xanthus

Myra

Patara

N

Copyright © 2007 by Barbour Publishing,

CONTRIBUTING EDITORS:

Robert L. Deffinbaugh, Th.M., graduated from Dallas Theological Seminary with his Th.M in 1971. Bob is a teacher and elder at Community Bible Chapel in Richardson, Texas, and a regular contributor to the online studies found at Bible.org.

Dr. Hall Harris W. III is professor of New Testament Studies at Dallas Theological Seminary and is also the project director and general editor for the NET Bible (New English Translation). For over twenty-five years, Hall has taught courses in intermediate-level Greek grammar and syntax, exegetical method, and various courses in the Gospel and Epistles of John. He received a Th.M. from Dallas Seminary and a Ph.D. from the University of Sheffield, England.

Dr. Stephen Leston is pastor of Kishwaukee Bible Church in DeKalb, Illinois. He is passicnate about training people for ministry and has served as a pastor at Grace Church of DuPage (Warrenville, Illinois) and Petersburg Bible Church (Petersburg, Alaska).

Jeff Miller holds a Th.M. degree from Dallas Theological Seminary and has been in ministry for nearly ten years. Jeff is coauthor of the *Zondervan Dictionary of the Bible and Theology Words*. He enjoys writing articles for magazines and journals and has written *Hazards of Being a Man* (Baker Books). He is currently working on a Greek-English dictionary (forthcoming from Kregal Publications). Jeff lives in Texas with his wife, Jenny, and two daughters.

Dr. Robert Rayburn holds a Master of Divinity degree from Covenant Theological Seminary and a doctorate in New Testament from the University of Aberdeen, Scotland. His commentary on Hebrews was published in the *Evangelical Commentary of the Bible*.

CONSULTING EDITOR:

Dr. Mark Strauss is a professor at Bethel Seminary's San Diego campus. He is the author of *Distorting Scripture? The Challenge of Bible Translation and Gender Accuracy; The Essential Bible Companion; and Four Portraits, One Jesus: An Introduction to Jesus and the Gospels*. He is presently revising the commentary on Mark's gospel for the Expositor's Bible Commentary series.

WITH SPECIAL THANKS TO BIBLE.ORG

Bible.org is a nonprofit (501c3) Christian ministry headquartered in Dallas, Texas. In the last decade, bible.org has grown to serve millions of individuals around the world and to provide thousands of trustworthy resources for Bible study including the new NET BIBLE® translation.

Bible.org offers thousands of free resources for:
- Spiritual formation and discipleship
- Men's ministry
- Women's ministry
- Pastoral helps
- Small group curriculum and much more

Bible.org can be accessed through www.bible.org.